N♦GALES

A MEMOIR OF COURAGE, SURVIVAL, AND ESCAPE

Stephen H. Wilson

iUniverse, Inc.
New York Lincoln Shanghai

NOGALES
A MEMOIR OF COURAGE, SURVIVAL, AND ESCAPE

iUniverse books may be ordered through booksellers or by contacting:

iUniverse
2021 Pine Lake Road, Suite 100
Lincoln, NE 68512
www.iuniverse.com
1-800-Authors (1-800-288-4677)

ISBN: 978-0-595-44453-3 (pbk)
ISBN: 978-0-595-68804-3 (cloth)
ISBN: 978-0-595-88780-4 (ebk)

Printed in the United States of America

Chapter One

The overloaded VW van edged its way up the steep incline, spewing exhaust into the Mexican night. Rocks and potholes were haphazardly strewn about the worn mountain path. I pulled the van to the side of the makeshift road and brought it to a halt.

We had been wandering in the jungle mountains for more than three days, as often lost as not. The harsh and relentless terrain was taking its toll on the van, causing it to burn oil. Each time the wheel found a pothole, I was afraid the vehicle would collapse into a pile of rubble, leaving us on foot in the middle of God-knew-where. Time and time again, I wondered why we had not stuck to the main road on the map—the adventure, I supposed, of traveling in the wilds of Mexico, away from the tourist traps, seeing the reality of the people and their country. Only now, I could not see beyond the headlights in the immense jungle darkness.

"I think we ought to put more oil in this thing, just in case," I said to Bob as he strained his eyes to pierce the night.

"Okay, Steve, I'll get it this time." He reached behind the seat and removed a car headlamp we had rigged to a large DC battery. Bob slid the rear door open and hopped out of the van. While he added the oil, I got out to stretch my limbs.

I had known Bob Smith for a little more than five months. We were both from the same university town in North Carolina. Bob was a 21 year old biology student who loved to surf. I was 24 and worked as a therapist and substance abuse counselor at a mental health center. We both had shoulder length hair and moustaches, but Bob was built like a runner and I was built like a football player. Even so, we could have been mistaken for brothers. I had grown to like and respect this quiet, sincere man rather quickly. Ordinarily, being in close quarters with people for extended periods of time made me uncomfortable, but so far everything had been going well. I felt a peace of mind that had not come in many years. This hobo trip was a success. I was glad Bob had convinced me to go.

I moved to the rear of the van, pulling on my thick mustache as I always did when I was thinking. I helped Bob aim the beam of light onto the engine block.

He squatted behind the van, a trickle of sweat running down his neck under the long hair that clung to him in the jungle humidity.

"Damn!" Bob muttered. "It sure is quiet here. It's making me feel a little eerie. How 'bout some music to put the oil in by?"

I made my way back from the illumination thrown by the headlamp and pressed a tape into the cassette player. Rock music escaped from the six speakers and broke through the night. The music didn't seem to ease Bob's nervousness as he punched a hole into the oil can. He kept looking over his shoulder into the darkness. Something was wrong. It was too dark and too quiet, even with the music. We were intruders in an imaginary world of ghosts and beasts. I pressed my back up against the van, trying to calm my imagination.

"Hey, man, you ever get the feeling we're being watched?" Bob drawled out the words as he twisted his head to look once more into the blackness.

"It *is* quiet: no crickets or bugs or anything! Let me see the flashlight for a sec, so I can have a glance around this place." I picked up the light and aimed it to the right of the van, not expecting to see anything unusual.

They squatted almost forty yards from the van, twenty or more of them. A few had machetes stretched across their knees; the rest had long pointed poles. They wore the straw hats of the Mexican peasants, and a few had ponchos. Most wore only white shorts or loincloths. Nobody moved.

"Holy shit. Circle the wagons!" Bob whispered as he fumbled to his feet, spilling the remaining oil on the ground. I stood transfixed, holding our observers in the beam of light while trying to make a decision. Should we wave and smile or run like we hadn't in years? It sure was a rotten time to have legs of lead, as I was certain I did.

The observers shifted with Bob's movement. They stood up silently but quickly and began to spread out along the embankment. My legs decided to lighten up and take control.

"Bandits!" I yelled at Bob as I tossed the light into the van and leapt for the driver's seat. I felt Bob grab for my belt in an attempt to clamber in behind me, pulling me backward as he did. "Hey, we are supposed to be on the same side!" I fell into the seat and switched the ignition key simultaneously. The engine hesitated and then began to turn over.

"Please, please, you piece of tin. Come on, *come on, baby!*" I coaxed the van as giddiness enveloped me. Bob slammed and locked the doors from the inside. The windows were still down. The music blared on.

I punched the headlights on as the van attempted to accelerate up the sloping road. We could see the bandits. They were heading towards us from the right, at full speed, screaming obscenities into the night and hurling projectiles at us. One of the sharpened poles rattled across the top of the van as the vehicle sluggishly made its way up the grade. We rocked back and forth, trying to coerce the van into picking up more speed as we bounced into and attempted to avoid the potholes and rocks. We both whispered nervous encouragement as the bandits closed the gap and more objects dented the van.

"Get the hell out of here!" Bob yelped.

"I'm trying."

"Pump the gas."

"I'm pumping it!"

The van engine only rattled.

"Step on the gas!"

"I'm flooring it!"

A hand reached through my window and grabbed me by the neck. I tried to break the grip with one hand while hanging onto the steering wheel with the other.

Bob leaned over to help me as a machete thrust through his window, its blade narrowly missing him and connecting with the top of his seat. He leaned back, grabbing a gallon water jug as he did, and smashed his assailant in the face with it. The bandit fell backward.

I was now gasping for air and pounding my assailant in the face with my right hand and clawing at his grip with my left, leaving the steering wheel on its own.

Bob grabbed a steak knife from underneath his seat and rammed it into the arm of the guy choking me. Bob quickly withdrew the knife as blood splattered on my shirt. The man screamed. He was no longer on the van.

I grabbed the steering wheel with both hands, pumping the gas pedal and urging the van to move faster.

Two bandits jumped onto the back of the van. Another one sprawled onto the hood.

"Do something!" Bob screamed.

Panicking, I turned on the windshield wipers.

"One's on the roof! One's on the roof!"

The van suddenly accelerated and lurched forward. The front end slammed into a pothole, and the men on the windshield and roof went flying through the air.

"How's that?" I said to Bob, grinning nervously.

The rear window shattered. One of the bandits was still on the back of the van, breaking out the remaining glass with the butt-end of a machete.

"Now you do something!" I yelled to Bob. But he was already moving. He grabbed his surfboard and charged the broken window. The tip of the surfboard rammed through the window and punched the bandit in the chest. He flailed off the back of the van into the darkness.

Bob flopped into the front seat.

"You okay?" he asked.

"Yeah, but that is the last time we are taking the scenic route." My voice was shaking.

We were coming to the crest of the hill. I turned the van sharply to the right in order to follow the road. My hands squeezed the steering wheel in a death grip as my mind raced over what had happened.

Suddenly, I saw movement on the side of the road a short distance ahead. More bandits? I strained my eyes to see as I prodded Bob on the arm.

"Over there."

"What's that?"

A man dressed totally in white was frantically waving his hands and yelling for the van to halt. This stranger certainly did not resemble any of the bandits we had seen. He wore glasses and had on a three-piece suit, complete with white hat. Standing slightly behind him was a young woman dressed in a plain skirt and blouse.

"Who in the hell?" Bob questioned. "What are they doing out here?"

"He could be the leader. It might be a trap!" I responded. I was looking for logic in a situation where logic had seemed to vanish.

"They look real worried, and he does have a girl with him," Bob yelled back.

"Yeah, maybe the bandits were after them, too. But we can't be too careful. Should I stop?"

"I don't know, I don't know," Bob stammered. "They both look desperate. Hell, the girl looks scared to death."

"Okay, I'll slow down, but won't come to a full stop. You slide the back door open and check everything out the best you can when we get alongside. If it looks safe, pull them in. Any sign of trouble, kick them out."

The headlights illuminated the couple as the man in white continued to try to flag us down. Bob scrambled to the back of the van. He hit the handle, and the momentum of the vehicle sprung the door open. The man grabbed the girl and hurried her toward the open door.

"Wait!" Bob put out an arm to keep her from getting in. "Who are you? What's going on?" he almost screamed.

The girl fell back, confusion and fear in her expression. She stumbled as the man grabbed her arm and righted her.

He shouted in English as they both trotted to keep up. "Help us! My car broke down. It's very dangerous for the girl. Help us!"

Bob was trying to decide what to do. "He speaks English," he said, almost to himself.

I glanced once more at the girl, who appeared genuinely terrified and ready to burst into tears.

"Pull 'em in!" I yelled.

Bob reached for the girl and yanked her into the safety of the van. She scrambled onto the back seat to make room for the man, who was now huffing and puffing. With considerable effort, Bob managed to pull him inside. The man lay on the floor of the van, trying to catch his breath.

"I wasn't sure if you were going to stop or not." He began to giggle.

"Bob, see if they're armed."

"You should have asked me that before I pulled them in."

"A very good point." The man grinned as he lifted his jacket to reveal a revolver stuck in the waistband of his pants. I could tell by Bob's expression that he felt almost as stupid as me. Bob and I were relatively defenseless and in no position to bargain with a gun. I started to feel sick to my stomach.

The man lightly fingered the handle of the pistol as he began to ramble in a continuous flow of English.

"I am armed, but not dangerous. Not to you, anyway." He seemed very pleased with himself.

"It will be so good to talk English again. My name is Frank. This is my niece, Pati."

The girl smiled nervously, and he patted her knee.

"I wasn't sure if you were going to stop or not. It's dangerous to travel at night around here, you know? Did they steal anything from you?"

We stared incredulously at the two of them. He resembled a Peter Lorre character from an old movie. He lay there, talking incessantly, while trying to catch his breath. He looked to be around forty years old and had a compact build and the beginnings of a pouch around the middle. He had on light tan leather boots and dusty white pants, with matching shirt, vest, jacket, and hat. He wore glasses as thick as the bottoms of Coke bottles. Although the pistol alarmed me, his mannerisms and appearance were not threatening.

She, on the other hand, was a direct contrast to the cartoon caricature of the uncle.

She wore an off-white blouse, a dark blue skirt, and plain sandals. She appeared to be nineteen or twenty. She was taller than Frank, with long legs. She was thin but not skinny. Her dark hair was unadorned and fell below her shoulders. Her nose was prominent but not unattractive on her narrow face. Even in the dark, her beautiful eyes were her most striking feature. She sat stiffly on the back seat, somewhat tense, apprehensive, and absolutely gorgeous.

I kept glancing in the mirror and over my shoulder to stare at her.

"Did you see what happened to us?" Bob finally asked.

"Of course we did. Why else do you think I'd risk my niece by jumping into a van with two strangers? These hills are unpredictable. *You* might have been killed. We all were in danger. You are armed, aren't you?"

"Yes!" Bob answered too quickly.

Frank broke out laughing. "No you aren't. If you were, we'd have heard gunfire."

"What happened to your car or truck?" I asked, trying to change the subject.

"Alternator. We pushed it into the brush. Not that the truck won't be picked clean by morning. I seem to lose more trucks lately … Are you from California?" He went on, "I used to live in California, but haven't been back to the States for years."

"No, we're from North Carolina," I replied, glancing into the mirror to catch another glimpse of the girl. "You are from the States?"

"Well, I am and I'm not. I live about one or two hours from here. If you're going our way, we'd sure appreciate the ride."

The girl, Pati, seemed to regain some of her composure. "Thank you for stopping." Her voice was thickly Mexican accented and melodic.

"Can we get gas where you live?"

"Sure, sure! It's perfect. I own an avocado and banana plantation, and you're welcome to be our guests in the village for a while. I'll tell everyone you're my cousins from the United States. They don't trust strangers in the village, so it will be best if they think you are relatives. You can sleep in your van until we make better arrangements.

Bob gave me a "where else do we have to go?" look, and I nodded my head in agreement.

In the mirror, Pati closed her eyes and seemed to sleep immediately. Frank glanced up at her affectionately as he lifted himself from the floor and sat beside her.

"Okay, we'll take you there, but first, answer a question. Who were those guys that attacked us? Did they want to rob us or kill us or what?" I wanted to know.

"Well, I imagine you were lost and not too smart. Why else would you be out here?" Frank kept his voice low so as not to disturb Pati.

"What do you mean, not too smart?" Bob sounded defensive.

"We could hear your American music from a good distance, and your lights showed everyone exactly where you were and what you were doing. Dangerous. In these hills, there are both bandits and crazies—Locos, the mountain people who live in the area. It is very isolated. The Locos are worse than the bandits because they are so unpredictable. They may come down upon you, cut you to pieces, and leave all your possessions to the animals, or they may let you pass. They're crazy. You were like a target out there, asking for it! I think you found the Locos."

The van lurched into a pothole, jostling all of us.

The truck I was driving broke down in the early afternoon. Pati and I made it as far as we could on foot until nightfall. At dusk we found a dark, comfortable place to hide. It's much too dangerous to stay on the roads or high ground at night—and I'm armed. Pati and I were still hiding when all the commotion erupted over you. I figured you might be our only ride for days, and here we are. Not much traffic along this way, you know?"

"Yeah, we noticed. I'm Steve Wilson and this is Bob Smith. Now, if you'll just point us in the right direction, we'll get the two of you home."

"Oh, you're going in the right direction," Frank responded as he changed seats with Bob. "This is the only road to the village from this side of the mountains."

Bob sat next to Pati, who remained asleep. I was sorry it was not me sitting next to her as the van moved towards a tiny village somewhere ahead in the velvet darkness.

Chapter Two

Sunlight drenched my face. I had been trying to sleep in the front seat of the van after we took our passengers to their home. My muscles ached and my neck was stiff. The sleeping area in the van was trashed from the attack, and shards of glass were everywhere. Bob slept in the seat opposite mine, chin on his chest, looking quite uncomfortable. He also had a bit of drool escaping from his mouth. I briefly thought of taking a picture of him for posterity.

I looked into the back of the van. The rear window was all but gone. Broken glass and our supplies were intermixed. The interior was in shambles. Bob's seat had a large gash in it.

I groaned and decided to get out of the van to inventory the body damage.

I walked around, shaking my head in disgust. A door side-panel was bent. The rear window was gone. There were numerous dents and dings, and the roof was slightly caved in.

"Fuck, it's not even paid for!" I kicked a tire.

It was not until then that I noticed my surroundings. The village had been covered in darkness when we arrived; I was seeing it for the first time. The streets sloped off to the left and right. Brightly painted adobe buildings lined those streets. The village was surrounded by mountain peaks. Smoke from a live volcano could be seen drifting skyward on the horizon. Banana trees grew in a small park where the streets intersected. To my right, peasants worked in a distant field. The air was filled with the sound of a waterfall I could not yet see.

"Will you look at this place? It's actually cute." Bob was awake and trying to stretch out his neck.

"A lot cuter than my van. Did you check out this mess?"

Bob whistled. "They did a job."

"Yeah, and you've got drool on your shirt."

Bob started to dab at his shirt when an open-bed truck at the intersection caught our attention. It was filled to capacity with young men who looked to be on their way to work in the fields, with one exception: every one of them had a rifle slung over his shoulder or cradled in his arms.

A few stared in our direction, but most seemed to ignore us. The truck rumbled on.

"Duck hunting?" Bob asked sheepishly.

"Who knows? All I know is we've gone from one weird situation into another. Let's see what we can do to put the van in shape and get us out of here."

A group of five or six men turned a corner and halted abruptly when they saw us. Only one carried a rifle slung over his back. The rest carried brooms and rakes. They gave us suspicious looks as they chattered amongst themselves. The one with the rifle took several steps forward and pointed his finger at Bob and me. "*Quien es? Por que esta aqui?*" he shouted.

"What did he say?"

"How should I know?" I knew even less Spanish than Bob. "We aren't having much luck with crowds, are we?"

"Quien es!? Por que esta aqui?" The man with the gun took several steps closer, followed by his pals. He sounded angry.

"Uh, Frank … we're friends of Frank."

"*No hablo espanol!*" Bob chimed in.

The group of men looked at each other, confirming they understood some association between Frank and us.

"Smile at my men. They are cautious because they don't often see strangers in the village." Frank's voice startled us. He stood behind us, dressed in a fresh white suit. Pati was at his side. Today she looked rested and, if possible, prettier than last night.

Frank spoke to the men in rapid Spanish. They immediately broke into smiles and rushed to us. They slapped us on our backs and pumped our hands as they chattered happily in Spanish.

Pati was smiling too. I took the opportunity to speak to her.

"What did he say to them?"

"You don't speak Spanish very well, do you?"

"Not at all. Bob knows a few more words than me, but not enough to get by."

"He said you were his long lost cousins visiting from the United States. Now you are part of the family." When she talked, she blushed.

One of the men patted me on the shoulder as Frank pulled me out of the crowd by the arm.

"Your van is a mess. What do you plan to do?"

"I don't know. I figured we'd clean it up best we could and try to make it to the nearest city."

"You helped Pati and me last night, so let us offer to help you. My men do a little bodywork and maintenance on our trucks. We'll have to search out a rear window, and it may take a while, but let us try; let my men fix your van. We'll make arrangements for you to camp nearby, and you'll have the freedom of the village."

"Well," I hesitated, "how long do you think it will take?"

"Maybe a week, maybe less."

I glanced at Pati. She nodded encouragement.

"Bob, they want a chance to fix the van. What do you think?" He was still surrounded by his new "relatives."

"Sounds okay to me. I think they're trying to tell me they want to buy me a beer."

"Fine. It's settled. Now let me take you up to the cantina for a classic Mexican breakfast." Frank ordered the other men to go about their business.

The four of us strolled the quaint main street of the village. Frank and Bob walked ahead as I positioned myself next to Pati.

"My uncle is glad you are staying."

"What about you?" I teased.

Pati averted her eyes and blushed; splotches appeared on her cheeks and neck.

The cantina was primitive and too dark, but clean. The breakfast consisted of fried eggs and a variety of fresh fruits: small sweet bananas, mangos, watermelon, and cantaloupe.

Other patrons looked at us curiously as Frank rambled on about the village, the plantation, and the surrounding area. The land belonged to Frank's grandfather. When the grandfather died, Frank took over as the *jefe*—chief. Frank, Pati, and most of the villagers were of indigenous descent, but Frank had been born in the United States. His mother and father immigrated to the United States a few weeks prior to his birth. He spent his early years in Arizona, but moved back to Mexico to be raised by his grandfather after his parents were killed in an auto accident.

The village, which was located in the State of Michoacan, had only two access roads and less than one hundred inhabitants. The land and orchards, under Frank's guidance, made an adequate living for the villagers.

Frank seemed genuinely glad for our company. He talked for hours. I sat, content to listen and watch Pati, while Bob wolfed down a third helping of breakfast.

The rest of the day was spent exploring the village and its surroundings. Despite the altitude, Frank was like a mountain goat. He took long strides and moved quickly on paths and up embankments, rarely getting winded. Bob and I had to push ourselves hard to keep up with Frank, and we were drenched in sweat. When we returned from climbing an adjacent hillside, Pati sincerely asked if Bob and I had been swimming. Frank thought that hilarious.

In the evening, Frank and Pati walked us to one of the banana orchards. We carried our sleeping bags and a few supplies.

"It won't rain. It's not the season. It will be cooler here than in the village, and you can always pluck a few bananas if you get hungry." Frank was piling dried banana husks in an area upon which we could place our sleeping bags. Pati cleared an area to set our lantern.

I was exhausted and looking forward to sleep. Pati wished us *dulces suenos*—sweet dreams—as Frank shook our hands. "Tomorrow you start Spanish lessons!" Frank yelled before they disappeared in the receding sunlight.

Bob peeled a banana. "It really is beautiful here, you know? Food, fresh water, friendly people … Pati." He gave me a knowing grin.

"It's that obvious, is it?"

"Yeah, you could say that. Of course, who wouldn't be attracted to her? I was, until I noticed you stumbling all over yourself. I decided to give you a break."

"Don't do me any favors," I quipped. "I can do fine on my own."

"Should I remind you why I was able to convince you to come on this trip? Could it be a woman broke your heart and you needed to get away from the 'entire species' for a while?"

"Okay, point made. But I'm over that now."

"Sure you are," Bob laughed. "Here we go again, except this time I approve. Pati's English is great, and I love the way she pronounces her Ys."

"Yeah, I noticed. She pronounced her Y like a J. I melted every time she said *jes* for *yes*."

"Dulces suenos," Bob mocked.

"Good night to you." I rolled over in my sleeping bag.

"Bob?"

"Yeah."

"One thing that has been bothering me …"

"What's that?"

"The guns. These people are armed to the teeth. There are guns everywhere."

"Uh huh. I couldn't help but notice. Maybe to protect themselves from the Locos?"

"Maybe, but any time I tried to bring it up to Frank or Pati, they avoided the subject."

"They seem peaceful enough. Ask again tomorrow. Now, go dream about Pati."

"Yeah, we'll find out tomorrow."

Chapter Three

Next morning, I lay on my side as the sun sparkled on the early dew. The air was slightly damp, so I stayed in the sleeping bag. Bob was sitting on top of his bag, legs crossed, eating a banana.

"Want breakfast?" Bob pointed a banana at me.

"I'll pass. You been up long?"

"Long enough to heat up some water for instant coffee. Want some?"

"For coffee, I'll get up."

We drank our coffee, enjoying the solitude of the orchard.

"Steve, what did you do before you became a therapist?"

"I was a fifth grade school teacher for a couple of years."

"No kidding. You're a teacher? What'd you do, say, 'Learn to read or I'll strangle you little bastards'?"

"Not such a bad idea."

We were interrupted when someone approached. It was Frank, strutting like a peacock, dressed in his obligatory white. I was sorry to see Pati was not with him. "Well, gentlemen, I hope you've had a good night's rest. Today I have a special treat."

"You're not going to walk us to death again, are you?" Bob interrupted.

"No, not yet, anyway. Since you obviously know so little of our language, and you certainly need to know more to get by, I've arranged for you to have lessons. I think you will find your teacher quite interesting. Lessons begin this morning."

Bob pointed his finger at me. "Your disgruntled fifth graders paid the man to do this just to torture you, and I'm being dragged along. I'm innocent, I tell you. I've never strangled anyone!"

"What's he talking about?" Frank looked puzzled.

"Never mind. He goes off on these tirades every now and then." I stood up, brushed some leaves from my pants, and reached for my Nikromat camera with its 70 mm portrait lens.

Frank led me, camera slung over my shoulder, and Bob along a path we had not taken before. Again, it was an upward climb, and Frank bounded from one rock to another, skirting the trees and underbrush.

"See, I told you he was going to walk us to death," Bob puffed.

We continued into a lush jungle, where I discovered numerous flowers and plants that were new to me. One type of flower resembled a lily with massive blooms in vivid red, orange and a hint of purple. I would occasionally halt our procession to photograph one of the more overwhelming varieties. It was during one of these stops that Bob and I thought we heard someone calling in Spanish.

"*Culero! Culero!*"

"Did you hear that?" Bob was scanning the shrubs and trees to see where the voice came from.

"Culero! Culero!"

"There it is again."

"I heard it too. It sounds like it's coming from up in the trees." I looked to Frank for confirmation.

Frank first appeared amused. Then he couldn't control himself and burst out laughing. Tears rolled down his cheeks, he was laughing so hard.

"What's so funny?"

Frank attempted to point towards a tree branch but was having difficulty because he was laughing so hard.

I followed the direction of his arm and spotted a bright contrast of color in the trees. The color made a slight movement and a sound emitted from it.

"Culero! Culero!"

"Shit," I said, fascinated. "Look, it's a parrot!"

"What's it saying?" Bob asked Frank.

"Asshole! Asshole!" Frank answered between fits of laughter. "They hang out around the village and pick up words now and then. It seems he knows one of you."

"Oh yeah, what's a stupid bird know anyway? Damn talking chicken is all you are." Bob waved his fist in the bird's direction as we continued down the path.

I began to hear water cascading over rocks. Occasionally, the trees would open up and I could see women at a stream far below, beating clothes on flat rocks. The jungle, flowers, parrots ... it was strangely alien to me, yet wondrously different.

"Be careful now; we have to make quite a leap up here. Then we have to edge down along the rocks to get to a waterfall and your lessons." Frank leaped across two vine-covered boulders as he talked.

I followed, much less assured, along the precarious path. Bob was next. We were about to lower ourselves into paradise.

A sparkling waterfall dropped approximately twenty feet into a crystal-clear pool. The pleasant odor of freshly cut bananas permeated the air. The pond area would be completely invisible from an uninformed observer's point of view. Frank plopped himself down on a rock. I let some of the cool water splash through my fingers.

"Is this where we're going to meet our teacher?"

"Yes, I figured there would be less distraction here. This is one of my favorite places. I come here when I need to organize my thoughts."

Pati stepped out from behind some bushes. She obviously had been swimming. She patted herself dry with a towel as she walked to Frank. She stood before us, her dark, expressive eyes half-lowered to the ground and her long hair braided in the back. She wore only a two-piece flowered bathing suit. She was innocently gorgeous and, seeing the expression on my face, I think she knew it. She blushed splotches again. She combined the appearance of a little girl who was caught doing something naughty with the lithe body of a woman. Shyly, she lifted her eyes and smiled a hello.

Bob and I stood up immediately, trying not to gape at her. She made me feel awkward and clumsy in her presence.

Frank smirked. "Pati decided she wanted to be your teacher. She has enjoyed practicing her English with you, so now it is your turn to learn. Besides, this is one teacher from whom you will not be easily diverted!"

Pati wrapped herself in the towel and sat on a nearby rock.

"Well don't just stand there and gawk! Get busy. I've got business to finish." Frank turned to leave, as Bob and I sat down across from Pati. She giggled. "You both have much to learn, jes?"

Bob and I smiled in agreement. "Jes!"

We began our lessons on the rocks in the early morning sun, accompanied by the sounds of the waterfall and the jungle.

Pati proved delightful. She balanced the lesson between Spanish vocabulary and numerous questions about North Carolina and our personal lives. When I told her I was a therapist she seemed confused. I explained further and she looked worried and a little embarrassed.

"Does that mean you know what I am thinking?" She asked wide-eyed.

"No", I laughed, "but I wish I could. Do you have a boyfriend?"

"Not now. Are you married or have a girlfriend, jes?"

"No to both questions." I smiled at her. What do you do when you're not teaching Spanish?"

"I attend the university to be a secretary." She smiled back.

She had an inquisitiveness about her that charmed. She exhibited patience over our bizarre mispronunciations and a welcome sense of humor when she teased us.

Frank returned in the early afternoon, and I was surprised how much time had passed. "Enough school for today. Tomorrow morning you can start again."

Pati slipped back into the pond. Bob and I were wearing cut-offs so we took off our shoes and T-shirts and joined her. The cold water, in contrast to the heat of the day, took my breath away. Pati immediately climbed onto my back in an attempt to dunk me. "You will learn Spanish or I drown you."

Bob playfully pushed her off. "Oh yeah! Get the teacher!"

We frolicked in the water as Frank stretched out in the sun, dozing, swatting flies, and grinning to himself as if he knew of some wonderful, private joke nobody knew but him.

That's how it was for the next few days. We would have our Spanish lessons with Pati in the mornings, swim or go exploring with Frank in the afternoons, drink beer and swap stories at the cantina in the early evenings, and retire to our orchard at night. It was an idyllic, wonderful time. However, I still had unanswered questions about the weapons. I even heard volleys of gunshots one afternoon, but that didn't seem to matter as much now. It was as if I was meant to meet the squat dry-humored man with the stunning girl on the road that night. Frank and Pati were making a permanent impact on my life. I liked him immensely and found myself drawn to her more each moment we spent together.

About a week after our first lesson, I was lying on my side in the orchard, mentally practicing my Spanish, awake, but not enough to get up, when my eyes focused on two perfectly rounded calves a few feet from my head.

"*Buenos dias*, Esteban," Pati's voice whispered. "Did you sleep well?"

"Yeah, sure," I said, rubbing my eyes as I sat up.

"Shhh. Don't wake your friend. Would you like to have breakfast with me?"

I didn't bother to answer as I leapt from my sleeping bag. Our eyes met as we smiled. I wanted to pull her to me, but held myself in check. I decided it was better to practice my Spanish than be impulsive.

"*Buenos dias, senorita. Como esta?*"

Pati giggled. "I am fine, but you are *flojo*—lazy—to sleep late, jes?"

"Jes." I smiled as we walked in the direction of the cantina. I left Bob asleep in the orchard, enjoying my first time alone with her.

There were no other customers in the cantina. "Hey, you accused me of being flojo or whatever, but no one else is up yet. It must be dawn."

"I could not sleep. I was hungry and did not want to eat alone. You can go back to sleep if you want."

"No. No. If you can't sleep, I'll suffer with you." I reached over and touched her hand. She didn't pull away. My heart pounded when she applied gentle pressure to squeeze my hand and smiled at me with her eyes.

We ordered breakfast and talked, holding hands, through the early morning, as other customers began wandering in. Too soon, Frank made his entrance, gesturing toward and greeting everyone in the cantina. He fell into a chair at our table. Pati didn't let go of my hand, which Frank noticed immediately.

"Well, well! Early Spanish lessons?" He nudged me with his elbow and winked.

This time, I blushed as I took a bite of my now cold eggs.

Frank pushed a bowel of small round peppers that was sitting on the table towards me. They were red and the size of peas. "If you like those eggs you might want to try this spice with them. You bite down on one of them and follow it with a forkful of eggs. Delicious!"

Pati was squeezing my hand hard. I did not notice the customers in the cantina staring in our direction. "Sure, sounds great." I said as I picked up one and placed it in my mouth. I bit down. It was crunchy. Immediately my tongue seared with pain; my eyes bulged; my face turned red; beads of sweat appeared on my forehead. I gasped and choked as I let go of Pati's hand to grab a glass of water. I took a gulp and shoved a piece of bread in my mouth. I began sneezing. I had never tasted anything so hot.

Frank was laughing so hard he was crying. He fell out of his chair. Pati was not laughing. She was wide-eyed and covered her mouth with her hand. The cantina's customers were pointing and laughing out loud. I was today's floor show.

Frank, still laughing and crying, pushed himself off the floor and back into the chair. "That's the funniest thing I've seen in ages." He slapped his leg. My tongue felt blistered and I was still sweating, but the bread had helped calm the fire. Pati reached over and took my hand again as she rolled her beautiful eyes. "Sorry", she said softly, "that's Frank's favorite trick to play on new visitors."

Eventually Bob stumbled in. He also noticed the handholding. I started to take my hand from Pati's, but she squeezed and gave me a determined look. Bob rolled his eyes and pretended to whistle towards the ceiling.

He ordered eggs and fruit. "If you like eggs, then you're gonna love this spice." Frank said with a straight face." He pushed a bowl towards Bob.

After Bob's pain entertained Frank and the cantina customers, myself included, Frank asked, "How would you guys like to go armadillo hunting tonight?"

"Armadillo hunting? How do you do that?" Bob asked, still red-faced.

"Well, you take a pistol and a flashlight. When you hear the armadillo coming, you shine the flashlight on it and shoot."

Bob was skeptical. "Sounds more like snipe hunting to me. I think I'll pass. I'm not much of a gun person."

"What's a snipe?" Frank looked at me.

"I think it may be like a North Carolina armadillo." I felt like I was being set up, but decided to play along. "I'd like to try that with you, if you could loan me a gun."

"No problem. We'll go tonight, after dark. Sure you don't want to come, Bob?"

"Naw, I'll hang out and keep Pati company." Bob smiled at my dirty look.

We left the cantina and walked towards our Spanish lessons. Pati and I held hands the entire way.

Later that night Bob and I sat by the light of our lantern in the orchard. A flashlight beam appeared through the trees, bouncing in our direction. Frank strutted into the light. He carried a large flashlight in one hand and a canvas bag in the other. "Ah, what a good night for a hunt!" He plopped the bag onto the ground and unzipped it. He handed me the flashlight as he rummaged through the bag. He pulled out two revolvers, two penlight flashlights, a box of .38-caliber ammunition, and a roll of duct tape.

"This one's yours." He handed me a nickel plated .38 Smith and Wesson revolver with a six-inch barrel. He placed one of the small flashlights on top of the barrel of his gun and taped it in place. "Do yours the same way. You want to let the end of the flashlight stick a bit over the end of the barrel so you can tape it on." I secured the flashlight to my pistol as Frank shoved the box of ammo at me. "Load up, and we'll be ready to go." I loaded and followed Frank's example of sticking the pistol with the flashlight in the waistband of my pants.

Frank led the way into the night with the large flashlight.

"Gee, I bet armadillos everywhere are quaking in their boots. I certainly feel much safer!" Bob called after us.

We moved through the jungle until Frank came to an area of thick, tall grass. He waded in, with me close behind. When it seemed we would be swallowed up by the grass, he stopped. "This looks good. We'll set up here." He cleared a small area, flattening the grass, and sat down. I followed, still suspicious of a trick.

"Now, we just sit here and wait. Armadillos move at night. We'll easily be able to hear one crashing through the grass. When you do, turn on the light that's taped to your gun. Point it in the direction of the sound and start shooting!"

"What? Start shooting? What if it's not an armadillo? How do we know it's not one of your people?"

"Well, for one thing, armadillos don't shoot back."

"Oh, just great." I resigned myself to a long night. I hoped the grass wouldn't move.

I sat, straining my ears, listening, my pistol in my lap.

"What do you do in North Carolina, Steve?" Frank interrupted the silence.

"I'm a therapist at a state mental health program. I do a lot of work with kids."

"Are you successful?"

"If you mean do I make a lot of money, no. I guess I have been successful in other ways. Prior to this trip, I was given an award for developing the best children's program in the state."

"And Bob?"

"Bob's still at the university. He wants to be a biologist." We lulled back into silence.

"Frank?"

"Yes?"

"Why all the guns? Except for the soldiers and Federales, I hadn't seen any guns in Mexico until we came here. What's going on? Are the Locos that bad?"

Frank remained silent for a long time. "I had a daughter, Pati's cousin. Her name was Maria, and I loved her very much. She looked so much like her mother, who died when Maria was young. Maria was smart, smarter than me. I was so proud of her when she was accepted to the University of Mexico as a student. She left me. She left the village, but I sent my hopes with her. Five years ago, before the International Olympics in Mexico City, she joined a protest. You know how idealistic children can be. She was upset that hundreds of thousands of people were living in poverty within sight of the Olympic stadium. Billions of pesos were spent on preparations for the Olympics and nothing for the poor. She wrote me about it. Her passion was obvious. She was always stubborn, like her mother. It would have done no good to try and change her mind. It was the last letter she ever wrote me. She joined thousands of students who marched on the stadium. Something went wrong. Things got out of hand, and the soldiers opened fire on the children. Some say as many as 350 were killed. I got a telegram. When I went to claim my little girl's body, she was already buried in a mass grave." Frank's voice broke. He spoke through clenched teeth. "I guess I went sort of crazy. I swore I would get even. I came back to the village and have been acquiring weapons at every opportunity."

"Frank, I'm sorry. I had no idea." I could sense his pain. "But what can you do?"

"It gets worse. I think that at first I collected the guns for my peace of mind. I wanted to make a fortress of the village and protect my children from the outside world. Now the outside world comes here. A few months ago, a government expedition found silver ore and opal deposits on this land. We know what will happen. The government is corrupt and will confiscate whatever it pleases. They will tell us to move, and they will take our crops and our land, which are our life. We are armed, not for protection against Locos, but for protection against soldiers and police. It is only a matter of time before they come. The villagers and I had a meeting. We will fight. We watch the two access roads, and we practice shooting every couple of days. We know we will not win, but we must try … for Maria and the other children."

"Is there anything that can be done? There's got to be someone in the government who will listen. Someone to plead your case."

"No. No one will listen. No matter what political party is in power, it is corrupt. It is the nature of Mexico."

"Frank, what is the name of the village?"

"Zirosto," he replied with a sadness that overwhelmed me. The rhythmic sounds of nocturnal animals and insects continued, yet we did not see or hear from an armadillo that night.

At daybreak, I returned to the orchard and explained the events of the previous night to Bob. He, too, expressed disbelief, then concern, for the village and its people. "How are a couple hundred people going to stop an army?"

With this knowledge, the atmosphere in the village seemed to change for us. The villagers no longer seemed as carefree as I had thought. There was concern in their eyes. I was afraid for them. They were afraid for themselves.

Chapter Four

A few days after my armadillo hunt with Frank, Pati asked Bob and me if we would be willing to drive to the other side of the village to visit with her friends. Of course, we agreed and hopped into the van. Pati sat in the passenger seat opposite of me. We drove up the mountain road into the village and maneuvered through the narrow streets. Pati guided us through the streets until we came to a row of whitewashed houses. Children played outside and men carted large bottles of sterilized water to various locations. The street was dusty, but well kept. Pati told us to stop in front of a house where a group of girls were gathered. We got out of the van and Pati excitedly ran up to the girls.

As Bob and I walked toward the group, I felt like I was on exhibit. Children peaked into our van while curious parents stared at Bob and me from their windows and doorsteps. Pati introduced us to five girls, all about her age and all chatting and giggling.

Bob whispered out of the side of his mouth, "Is my fly open or something?"

"Sure is," I said as he shot a glance toward his crotch. He looked relieved when he realized I had been joking.

"Made you look." I smiled.

When Pati's friends calmed down, we were invited into a house by one of the girls and offered fruit and sweet candies. The home had a small enclosed garden in its center, with a variety of beautiful plants. Perched in a cage in one corner of the garden was a large parrot that squawked loudly.

"If this one calls us assholes like the one in the jungle, we may have to cook it," Bob growled as he eyed the bird.

I wanted to reciprocate the hospitality of Pati's friends and offer something in return. "Bob, do we have any canned goods left in the van?"

"I'm not sure, but I'll go check." Bob returned with a half-dozen cans. "The only thing we had left were pinto beans." We offered them to the girl who lived in the house and her mother. The mother accepted them graciously.

Pati watched with a big smile and then slipped to my side. She squeezed my hand as her eyes sparkled playfully. "You two are the only people who would travel thousands of miles to deliver beans to a family of Mexicans," she joked.

After a while, Pati suggested we walk to the market, so we all headed up the street, including the five girlfriends. The market was small but sold everything from dried dates to sandals. Pati expertly bargained for groceries as Bob and I investigated the other vender's stalls.

"Esteban!" Pati waved me back towards a stall that had lightweight straw cowboy hats. The vender of this stall plopped one of the hats on my head. It was much too small, so he continued to switch hats until he and Pati could agree on one that fit.

"Am I buying a hat?" I said, reaching into my pocket to pull out some pesos. Pati affirmed that I was indeed buying the hat. "I am going to make you into a classic Mexican. It is a traditional hat."

"What do you think?" Bob interrupted. He stood amongst the five giggling girlfriends, wearing a giant Mexican sombrero of sequined gray. "It weighs a ton and hurts my head, but it's only sixteen U.S. dollars. A bargain by any means."

I tilted my new hat towards Pati, who was politely trying not to laugh at Bob. "Now *that's* a classic Mexican!"

We returned to the home of her friend and had dinner: chicken, spicy rice, and pinto beans. During dinner Pati asked, "How would you like to go to a party?" Her five friends, who spoke no English, nodded encouragement.

"I don't think we have a choice." Bob smiled and nodded back at the girls.

After dinner, all eight of us piled into the van. Pati directed us through the streets until she asked me to stop in front of a nondescript brick building with shuttered windows. We paid a young man a small cover charge and walked into the village version of a hard-rock club. Rather than mariachi music, as I had expected, I was surprised by psychedelic lights and the sounds of Led Zeppelin. Several people crowded up to greet Pati and her friends. The dance floor was packed, and the building was hot and very stuffy.

Pati tapped me from behind and asked me to dance, "*Quires bailar conmigo?*"

"Pati, I really don't dance too well." Out of the corner of my eye, I saw Bob being pulled onto the dance floor by all five girls.

Pati looked at me with her large brown eyes, and I marveled at how her off-white dress with lace short sleeves complimented her tanned skin.

"Oh, ok! But I'm not very good," I said as she yanked me onto the dance floor.

"Ha!" Bob gave me an exaggerated laugh as we squeezed beside him. Pati's friends surrounded him.

Eventually the disc jockey in the club switched from hard rock to a slow song. "*Bailar?*" I mispronounced as I held out my hands to her. She smiled and moved into my arms. She placed her head on my shoulder as I squeezed her to me. She smelled wonderful.

There were too few slow songs for me that evening, and too soon it was time to go. We drove the girls back to their homes, bid farewell amongst hugs and giggles, and headed back to our familiar banana orchard.

Bob hopped out of the van and slid the rear door shut. "Good night, you two." Pati and I were left in the van, illuminated only by the moonlight. I leaned over and kissed her. She shyly kissed me back. "You are beautiful," I whispered as our lips parted.

She tilted her chin down. "Frank says I am not too pretty. He says I am too skinny, my ears stick out, and my feet are too big. He says I didn't grow up; I grew out. My feet and ears grew out."

I couldn't help but laugh. "What's he know? His glasses are so thick, he probably can't see you anyhow." I leaned over and kissed her again. This was a long, deep kiss. This was not an awkward kiss; it was a kiss of two people who seemed to fit together.

I took her by the hand and led her between the front seats of the van to the back, where there were blankets. I lay down and pulled her next to me. I kissed her on her shoulders, her neck, her ear. "Do you have any idea how happy I am when I'm around you? How wonderful you make me feel?" I whispered the words that stuck in my throat. I kissed her again as I moved my hand to her right breast. She stiffened, but then relaxed and let out a soft moan. My heart was pounding.

Pati hesitated and then whispered, "Steve, maybe we should just be friends, no?" There was a short silence as my heart went up into my throat. "Like you and Bob?"

"Like me and Bob? I don't think so! Pati, it's too late for me to just be friends." I couldn't hide my disappointment.

"Okay! Good!" she laughed as she leaned forward for another kiss, sliding her fingers into the back of my hair.

She hesitated again. "Are you sure you don't have a wife back in Carolina del Norte?" she asked, teasing.

I shook my head "Yes! Now shut up before you scare me to death. Friends??"

She giggled and moved back into my arms. I unbuttoned her dress and kissed her on the belly, the breast, the thigh. I trembled at the touch of her beautiful skin. She let me explore.

Later, I walked Pati back to her house. She could not spend the night with me. The stars filled the sky. The moon gave off an exceptional glow. It was a beautiful night, but I barely noticed. I was so glad Pati and I were no longer just friends. She would come to me every evening after this night and we would make love in my van. I hadn't yet admitted it to her or myself, but I was falling in love.

The days melted by until it was June 25, 1973. Almost a month had passed since we first entered the village. Pati was playfully chasing a lizard across the banana orchard near where our van was parked. Bob was making coffee. It was 11:00 AM. I walked to the van, pulled out my camera, and started shooting pictures of Pati running after the lizard. She was laughing. The sun was bright. It was a beautiful day.

I heard gunshots, but that was not unusual. I had become accustomed to the intermittent cracks and ignored them. Yet today the gunfire seemed more intense. Suddenly, there was a loud explosion off to my left, back towards the village. Bob jumped to his feet. Pati stood still, hair lightly blowing in the wind, approximately one hundred yards from us. Another explosion! It was closer to us this time, and debris from a smashed tree rained down upon Bob and me.

We could not yet see them, but soldiers were coming up the mountain toward the village, and they had brought a tank. The gunfire became more frequent and seemed to be coming from all sides. A villager ran through the orchard, yelling something to us. He appeared to trip and fell to the ground. My van was sitting on the edge of the orchard, not twenty yards from me. Something slammed into it, tearing a piece of the sheet metal. I felt immobilized. I was standing upright in shock and confusion. Bob, on the other hand, grabbed the steak knife, still our only weapon, and was holding it in front of himself, like it might do some good. I pulled myself out of my initial inability to react and turned toward Pati. "Run! Get out of here! Run!" I screamed. She stood there, looking puzzled for a second, then began running in our direction. "No," I screamed at her as I waved in the other direction. She was the last thing I saw as something slammed into the side of my head. A roar burst in my ears, and my neck was violently jerked to the right. Everything went black.

I had no idea how long I was out. As I started to come to, my head throbbed and I couldn't focus my vision. I could sense activity and movement around me. My eyes eventually began to focus, but my head continued to throb. I touched my left temple and pain seared through my brain. I attempted to sit up.

Soldiers and men in fancy *guayabera* shirts were moving about. Some were roughly leading villagers toward a staging area, hands tied in front of them. Many of the villagers appeared wounded or were splattered with blood. The villagers moved passively, eyes focused on the ground.

I tried to sit up some more, and a soldier noticed my movement. He whirled around, pointing his rifle at my head. He was yelling at me in Spanish. He was very young and looked very frightened. He continued to point the rifle and yell. An older man, in a guayabera shirt, grabbed me by my belt and yanked me to my feet. There was instant pain in my head. I staggered, felt nausea flow over me, and almost blacked out. I could feel blood trickling down the side of my head, and my left eye was starting to close. He said nothing as he wrapped my wrists in front of me with cord. I attempted to glance around for Pati and Bob, but the soldier with the rifle began yelling again and the man in the guayabera shirt pushed the back of my head so I'd be looking at the ground. More pain and nausea.

Chapter Five

A soldier pushed me along, poking me in the back with the rifle barrel. We moved out of the banana orchard until we came to an open area where a group of the villagers had been herded. Some of the wounded were lying or sitting on the ground. The rest were forced to stand. Soldiers surrounded the group, rifles aimed directly at them. The thought that they might kill us slammed into my mind. I was pushed hard into the circle of villagers; I stumbled and almost fell.

I saw Bob several prisoners to my left, and was overwhelmed with relief. He looked roughed-up and frightened, but with no visible damage. He was nervously looking in my direction. He had watched me being moved to the group. Slowly, attempting not to be noticed, we started shifting our positions to get closer. Our group of prisoners seemed to number twenty-five or so, and a few of the wounded were moaning or crying out, distracting some of the soldiers.

We finally made our way next to each other. I whispered, barely moving my lips, "Have you seen Pati and Frank?"

On a breath, Bob responded, "Rumor has it that Frank and most of the villagers escaped into the jungle. That's why the soldiers are so nervous and those other guys so angry."

"Pati?" I breathed.

Bob was silent. His eyes started to well up in tears, and he was trembling. "She's dead, Steve. She was shot while trying to get back to us." His lips quivered and tears streaked his cheeks.

My mind went numb. I didn't want to believe it. I felt like a large hand was trying to crush my heart. I couldn't even cry. My legs weakened, and I dropped to my knees in grief. My ears were ringing, and somewhere, almost in a dream, I could hear a soldier telling me to stand up or he would shoot—but I didn't care. I just didn't care. In a few moments, my world had changed forever.

Much later, Bob would tell me that either shrapnel or bullets riddled my van. A piece of the sheet metal must have ripped off and slammed me in the left temple, leaving a huge bruise, swelling, and bleeding, but no entry wound. Bob moved to my prone body to guard me with the steak knife. Pati apparently saw me go down and continued running in our direction. A soldier emerged from the trees and shouted a warning for her to stop, but she kept on running. He fired a single shot into her back. It was the same soldier that demanded Bob drop the knife and took him prisoner. "He couldn't have been more than sixteen years old," Bob said with tired sadness and no small amount of anger.

There was an argument between several of the guayabera shirts. There was a lot of fist waving and stomping of feet. The villagers began to shift about and glance nervously at each other. The argument was over us. Some of the guayabera shirts wanted to execute the prisoners immediately. One particular large man seemed to have other ideas. The soldiers appeared frightened, in general. All were very young.

Hours went by in the heat of the midday. The arguments continued. Finally, a line of pickup trucks arrived, and one guayabera shirt threw his hat on the ground and crushed it with his foot. Our fate was sealed.

The loss of Pati and the head injury had left me in a daze. My heart actually ached to the point that my head was only an afterthought. Yet, I wasn't given time to grieve. Our group of prisoners was divided up and herded to the back of the pickup trucks. The wounded were placed in two of the trucks while the rest of us were put in the remaining four.

Two armed guards were placed at the tailgate to ride in the back with us, and two were in the cab. Bob managed to maneuver me into the same truck with him.

Our caravan headed north. Six pickup trucks with a cargo of peasant Indian farmers and two unlikely Americans were leaving Pati and Zirosto behind forever.

I stayed in a fog most of this trip, which, for us, lasted days. Our shoes, watches, wallets, and money were confiscated. Occasionally they would stop for gas, and civilians would stare or point at our group. We would stop and rest at night and occasionally be given a corn tortilla. The guards spoke very little to the captives, and other than relieving ourselves by the side of the road, we spent the time in the back of the truck. On the way, we separated from the trucks with the other prisoners. They turned off to other destinations until there were just two trucks left heading steadily north toward the town of San Luis Del Rio Colorado.

The two trucks entered the outskirts of the Sonora, Mexico, town, driving along dirt streets, until they eventually stopped in front of a cement building with a large plate-glass window. The guards, still holding their guns on Bob, me, and the villagers crammed in the truck, jumped off the back and waved to someone standing inside the building. A large Mexican ran out and motioned for all of us to get out of the truck. Awkwardly, with our hands still bound, we got out of the truck and were led into the building.

Inside the building, typewriters busily clicked. Two large desks were against the left wall, and chairs were lined along the right wall. A secretary was seated at a third desk at the far end of the room. There were three doors: one on the left, one on the right, and also one at the far end of the room. Men dressed in the loose-fitting guayabera shirts of the Federales shuffled about the office. We were left standing in the middle of the office, each held by the back of our belts by our Federale guards.

The door on the far left opened, and a stubby, wiry-haired man stepped out. He looked directly at the two of us.

"Well, what do we have here? Two Americans with these Pinchi Indios?" he said in accented but good English. He stared at my bruised and blood encrusted head and smiled. "I am Malpica, special investigator for the Federal Police."

"What are you going to do with us? Why were we brought here?" Bob asked shakily. Bob attempted to explain our circumstances that led up to our capture, but Malpica interrupted him.

"Oh, it's probably all a mistake," Malpica replied pleasantly. "But we have to have an investigation. You're being held for ... investigation." He sniffed deeply and rubbed at his nose. "Why were you in that village, and how long were you there?"

Bob and I tried to respond when Malpica asked, "Where is Lucio Cabanas?"

"Who?" Bob asked, puzzled.

"Lucio Cabanas. You may also know him as Frank Soto Munoz." Malpica's pleasantness was beginning to fade.

"So he did get away," I said more to myself than to Malpica.

Malpica gave me an irritated stare. "You are in big trouble. You cooperate and cause no trouble, and things will be easier for you. Remember, you have no rights in Mexico. You are guilty of whatever I want until I prove you innocent."

"We haven't done anything. Let us explain ..." Bob started to say as the Federale holding him jerked hard on his belt.

"That is for me to decide. Yes, yes, it's probably all a big mistake." Malpica pulled a wallet out of one of the large pockets of his shirt and began flipping through its contents. The wallet appeared to be Bob's. "Is this all the money you have?" he asked rather disgustedly.

Bob and I nodded in affirmation.

"Now *that* is a problem! Which one is Wilson and which is Smith?" he asked.

"I'm Wilson and he's Smith," I said slowly.

"Good, good. That's a start. You'll be held briefly for", there was a long pause, "investigation."

"Rapido." Malpica waved his arm at the Federales holding us.

The Federales shoved us toward the front door and led us to an old car parked in front of the building.

"Where are we going now?" Bob asked me, but I could tell he wasn't expecting an answer.

We were shoved into the back seat of the car, hands still tied. The Federales got into the front. The one in the passenger seat twisted in our direction, holding a pistol in his right hand.

The car made its way across town and eventually came to a stop in front of a large adobe-walled building. Bob and I still didn't have shoes. Our socks were filthy. My body wouldn't stop trembling. I hoped Bob was holding up better.

Think ... think! I tried to order my mind, but it remained in a state of confusion. This was all too unreal.

We were pulled out of the car and shoved through an arched gateway to a large, barred gate.

Several men in police uniforms stood in a wide, dirt-floored courtyard on the other side of the bars. One of the policemen unlocked the gate, and we were taken inside the courtyard on the other side of the bars. The police untied our hands and motioned for us to stand facing the wall, hands up in the air, as we were searched. Both of our belts were pulled from our pants and thrown on the ground. Bob was standing incorrectly, so a policeman kicked him hard on the ankle to teach him the proper stance. The Federales who brought us stood smiling for several moments, then left. The gate slammed and locked behind them. An elderly policeman grunted something in Spanish and motioned for us to move to a barred door on the left side of the courtyard. On a walkway above, I could see a policeman looking down on me with a lever-action rifle. There was a large, barred door further to the right. Bob and I stood miserably before the smaller of the two doors as it was unbolted. We smelled the stench of vomit, feces, and urine emitting from the dark corridor. The corridor was approximately fifty feet long and five feet wide.

As my eyes adjusted to the poor lighting, I could make out cell doors on the left and a lime-covered wall on the right. About thirty feet overhead, there was a wooden catwalk for the guard to move about and observe the corridor below. I could make out figures hunched together in the first cell that we passed, and heard groans. The stench became worse as I moved, zombie-like, further down the corridor. Arms reached out to grab at us, arms that belonged to filth-ridden, sweaty, malnourished bodies … bony fingers and hands …

The policeman stopped in front of the second dark cell. Voices of protest rose from within, but the policeman banged on the bars angrily with a rounded stick he carried in his belt. He unlocked the cell door and motioned for Bob and me to go in. We stood, blinking at him.

"*Andale!*" the policeman yelled angrily. "*Andale, rapido pinchi, gabachos!*" He struck Bob between the neck and shoulder with the stick. I raised an arm to protect myself, and the next blow caught me on the elbow. Both of us were shoved into the cell, fear taking a toll as I moved on wobbly legs. My head swam as I tried to keep from vomiting. Bob looked at me, trembling and wide-eyed. The door slammed shut and was locked.

Chapter Six

The most prominent feature of the cell was the stench. The odor was so strong it could almost be tasted. The cell was about eight feet by twelve feet. The ceiling rose about twenty-five feet in the air, with only one small window, maybe a foot square, next to the ceiling. The heat made the cell feel like a brick oven. In the far left corner was a hole in the cement floor. The hole was smeared with feces and urine, the major source of the stench. It appeared to be an indoor toilet.

There were bodies—standing, squatting—strewn everywhere in the cell. All eyes were upon Bob and me, the new residents. In my daze, I tried to count: ten … fifteen … twenty … twenty-four men already in the cell! I tried to push back the fear but couldn't stop my inner trembling.

It's a nightmare, I thought. *It's all a nightmare* … Bob attempted to say something, but the words caught in his throat. He had tears in his eyes.

The other prisoners in the cell continued to stare at us with hate-filled eyes. There was no room to move. The only space left for a man to squat was located directly next to the hole. Bob tried to step between two men. They yelled at him and pushed, causing Bob to lose his balance and step on another man's fingers.

"Fuckin' gringo pig!"

"Sit down, you jerk-off motherfucker," a voice called. "*Pinchi putos!*"

The Mexicans in the cell began pushing and shoving—first Bob, then me. We would fall over someone else and be shoved again.

We finally gained some footing and stood back-to-back, fists ready for an attack. A few Mexicans laughed. The majority settled back into their selected space and ignored us. I breathed a little easier, but refused to drop my fist. The heat weighed upon us. I glanced around the small room once more, than made my way with Bob to the only open space in the entire cell—directly next to the dark hole used for a toilet. The rancid odor gagged me but there was nowhere else to go. We were in no condition to fight twenty-odd men for a space of concrete. Humiliated, Bob squatted closest to the hole. Wild-eyed, I squeezed next to him and a sleeping Mexican. The sour sweat from our bodies stuck us together like glue. The weight of what was happening to us crushed down upon our thoughts.

Occasionally a Mexican would rise and make his way to the hole to urinate, and the urine would splatter on Bob and anyone else nearby. I could feel Bob shiver in revulsion. My thinking became clouded. I sat, grieving over Pati. A guard walked by, and Bob started yelling.

"Hey, we want the American consulate! American Consulate!" A few Mexicans grumbled; a few jeered.

"*Consul Americana, consul Americana, chingada …*" The guard ignored our shouts. Bob started to get hysterical.

"They can't do this to us! We have our rights. We must talk to the American consulate!" Bob tried to shake me out of stupor. I stared blankly at him.

A young Mexican with long greased-black hair made his way over to us.

"You gottee money?" he sneered at Bob. "For ten dolares, I get you outta here. Gimme you money!"

"We don't have any money. They took it," Bob answered.

"Aw, fuck you, gringo! What you here for?" the Mexican asked curiously.

"I'm not sure," Bob answered. "Do any others speak English in here?"

"I speakee good English, no? Maybe one, maybe two speakee here. I from Los Angeles, until they catch. Polica get you?"

"No, Federales," Bob admitted unhappily.

"Federales! Ay chihuahua! Federales mighty bad. You in big trouble, gringo!" The young Mexican turned toward the others in the cell and said something about Federales. The others shook their heads or moved their hands in a fanning motion and rolled their eyes.

"Will you help us ask the guard to let us talk to the American Consulate? We don't speak enough Spanish," Bob pleaded with the young Mexican. The boy narrowed his eyes and grinned.

"Yeah, guy, sure. Okay, the *la guardia* name is Pendejo. You call him by name. He like it. Say 'pen-de-jo.'" Bob repeated the name carefully, trying to remember the pronunciation. "My name Phillipe," the Mexican added. "You?"

"Steve and Robert," Bob answered.

"Okay, gringos," Phillipe said. He stood up and relieved himself, splattering more urine on Bob.

The cell was dark. It was impossible to tell how much time had elapsed. I glanced down at my dirty, sweat-soaked pants. I saw several large cockroaches move confidently across the floor, towards my stained socks. Sweat poured down my forehead, burning as it rolled into my eyes. Everyone in the cell was still, as if in a semi-conscious state. Bob was staring at the cell door where the guard, Pendejo, might pass. I tried to mentally block out my horrible surroundings and endure the filth. I thought of the wind, of cool air, of home and green trees, of Zirosto. I tried not to think of Pati, but failed.

The time crawled. Flies settled and buzzed everywhere. The cell door rattled. It was the fat guard with the large moustache, the one Phillipe called Pendejo. He had a plastic container with two spoons protruding from the top. He was attempting to squeeze this through the bars to a prisoner as a gray liquid splashed out. Bob leaped to his feet.

"Senor, Senor Pendejo, the Consulate! Please!" The guard looked up angrily as the Mexican prisoners howled with laughter. I glanced at Phillipe, who was grinning and nudging someone awake with his elbow. Bob called out again, "Senor Pendejo!" The guard jammed his hand into the container, shoveled out a handful of soggy pinto beans, and flung them in Bob's direction.

"*Pendejo* means jerk," Phillipe called out, almost choking on his laughter.

"Senor Jerk, Senor Jerk," he bellowed mockingly.

"You fucking bastard!" Bob screamed. Everything fell deadly quiet. Phillipe started to stand up. The guard snarled and made a threatening hand gesture. He pointed to the food, to Bob, and then to Phillipe. Phillipe glowered, but sat back down. Humiliated, Bob settled back also. The guard shoved a plastic milk container full of water through the cell, made one last hand gesture, and left.

The prisoners passed the container from person to person.

Two men, eating out of the container at the same time, gobbled down spoonfuls of beans. By the time it got to Bob and me, there was not much left. The spoons had been passed from mouth to mouth and still dripped with saliva. I glanced into the bottom of the container and swore I saw a piece of feces floating along with the beans. I gagged. Bob took the container from me.

"You've got to eat," Bob murmured. "No matter how bad it looks, you got to eat. You've got to keep your strength up or they'll stomp us for sure." He carefully spooned out the feces-like object. He put some of the beans in his mouth and chewed half-heartedly. "You've got to eat," he pleaded again. I looked at him vacantly. The water was passed, but I had made up my mind that I would not eat or drink anything in this cell. Everyone has heard about the bad water and dysentery of Mexico, and this water certainly must be infected. Bob shoved the water container at me several times, but passed it on when I did not respond.

Night came slowly. The cell got darker, and it cooled off a few degrees. The prisoners began to stretch and shift positions. A Mexican, not in a guard uniform, squatted down in front of the cell door and whispered to one of the prisoners. He pulled a crinkled money note from an oversized pocket and stuck his arm eagerly through the bars.

"*Chiva, chiva* ..." the whisper ran through the cell. Almost all the prisoners lined up at the cell door to pay their money or trade a belt so they could stick their pockmarked arms through the cell door. The man on the outside routinely stuck the arms with a needle.

Bob and I took this opportunity to move further from the stinking hole. The first Mexican who had thrust his arm through the bars swayed to his feet and staggered for the hole. He gagged a few times, than spewed forth vomit all over the corner of the hole. He hung his head momentarily and then moved back to his original spot. Another Mexican followed suit, then another and another, until the stench of vomit was so powerful as to weaken the strongest of stomachs.

"What the fuck is going on?" Bob asked as he slid further out of the splattering range, away from the hole.

"Heroin," I mumbled. "Probably too strong."

"Oh, Christ, what next?" Bob moaned. The Mexicans stumbled around or fell in heaps about the cell. A few didn't seem to mind occupying the "choice" place next to the hole—it was easier for them to puke. Bob and I huddled together as the drugged, sweaty prisoners settled into a restless sleep.

The sound of rattling keys woke me.

Please call us, I thought desperately. *Get us out of here*. My mind begged to hear our names called. I shook Bob awake. There were three guards standing in the shadows in the hallway. One of them was reading from a list.

"Rodrigues Bustante Cordoza."

A short, stout Mexican stood and moved hesitantly toward the door. He whimpered, cowering in fear, as grimy hands pushed him forward. The cell door swung open and the three guards grabbed him. A chant spread up and down the hall as the chosen prisoner was dragged down the narrow corridor. The Mexicans in our cell and the adjoining cells of the wing began to wail and holler, banging and pounding on the walls. It was interrogation time. The Mexicans chanted and wailed to drown the screams that would come from their comrades. The vocal barrage also served to hide their own fears. More names were called by the three guards. Sometimes the prisoner named would stand and walk out proudly; others screamed or begged to remain. The guards would call several names, haul the prisoners off, and return to call more names. This went on for hours as did the chants. A few men were taken from one cell, a few from another. The names seemed to be called at random. Eventually, most of the men or young boys were brought back, torn, bruised, or blood-stained. A few never came back, creating more terror for those who awaited their own fate.

The wailing and chants continued. We strained our eyes in the dark, now praying our names would not be called, yet sadly hoping they would, just to get the waiting over with. Eventually the guards quit coming and the chanting stopped as quickly as it had begun. My ears buzzed in the silence. Bob breathed a sigh of relief. We both worried; when would our names be called?

I wanted to sleep and wake up to find myself out of this dungeon; but I resisted this time because I didn't want to put my head down in the filth and awake again to the sound of rattling keys. As each person grew tired and tried to lie down, the floor space shrunk and the prisoners had to lay crisscrossed over each other. Already a set of legs stretched across my feet and another set across my chest. Their weight and body heat made me want to scream. My throat was swollen and parched. I ached for water, yet I was glad I did not drink.

Oh, God, I thought, *get us out of here ... please ...* and my head nodded towards the slimy floor.

My dreams were uneasy, fever-ridden nightmares of a crushing weight on my chest. Someone was holding me down!

"Aggghhh, let me up, let me up!" I would wake, yelling, realize where I was, and, with shuddering repulsion, try to block it out and sleep again.

I heard the cell door open and slam shut, but my mind did not want to register what it was. A rustling fluttered through the cell. People were getting up, moving around. Voices stabbed into my sleep.

"*Sus ropas ... dame mi su ropas.*" Yet I was only vaguely aware of the activity.

A shrill scream echoed against the walls, then another. It jolted me from my sleep, and I leaped to my feet, fists ready to strike. I reached down to grab Bob in the inky blackness, but Bob was already up and ready.

"This is really getting nuts," Bob whispered through clenched teeth. We stood side-by-side, straining to see through the darkness, ready for an onslaught. In the center of the room, someone was surrounded by a group of nine or ten prisoners. The prisoners had belts either wrapped around their fists or held loose to be used as whips. The man in the center screamed out again, high and shrill.

"*No, nooooooooooo ... mi madre de dios, no!*" A few of the prisoners lunged forward and connected with the belts, causing their victim to twist and scream in pain. They pushed him from one prisoner to another, yelling at him, lashing out with belts, while the pleading man tried to cover his head with his arms.

"What the fuck is all this about?" Bob stammered.

"I'm not sure I want to find out," I answered, half expecting the other prisoners to turn on us next. Not all the prisoners were taking part in the beating. Phillipe bounced by, giggling, a belt wrapped around his fist. I reached out and grabbed him.

"What's going on?"

Phillipe tore his arm from my grasp. "Not your fuckin' business, man." He hesitated, then in a confidential tone, said, "A rich kid. You know? He's trippin', freaking out on acid. He brought here. We tell him give clothes or bad things happen." Phillipe giggled again. "So we teach him a lesson. Fuckin' rich bastard. You stay out. Not your business." Phillipe hurried back to the circle.

The kid tried to break out, but was beaten unmercifully. I wondered where the guards were. The kid slammed himself up against the wall, trying to claw his way up out of their reach. The other prisoners rushed him. He screamed again as he fell to his knees. Even in the dark, I could see the blood oozing from the kid's body. There was one final scream that ended in a gurgle. The kid fell to the floor, silent. The prisoners returned to their spots.

We did not lie down for quite a while. We squatted, wide-eyed, in the cell for a long time, bodies trembling. We were still awake hours later when two guards made their way into the cell to drag away the broken body. It was over, but the screams were burned into our memories.

The cell changed slowly from dark to a gray twilight.

It must be morning, I thought, dazed, as I tried to restore circulation in my legs. *Maybe today. Maybe today we will be taken out of here. How long can we survive like this? How long have the others been here?* I stared at Bob. He had been resting with his back against the wall, with his arms and head perched on his knees. He looked up; dirt and sweat streaked down his face. I smiled weakly. I felt like Bob looked.

"Maybe today they'll let us talk to the American consulate," I said, trying to convince Bob and myself.

"Yeah, maybe today," Bob mumbled. We saw the dried blood on the wall, left from the night before.

The temperature climbed as the morning passed. The Mexican prisoners shot up more heroin and puked as before. A few argued among themselves, but we were generally ignored. Occasionally a new prisoner was brought in, making the cell space even smaller.

Around noon, the guards threw an exceptionally filthy old man into the cell. One guard said something about the old man to the other prisoners. The prisoners hooted and jeered the old man, who was shoved to a space nearest the hole. He grinned and made mule sounds at the men. The Mexicans yelled back disgustedly and shook their fists in his face, but the old man continued to grin and flopped his penis out of his ragged pants. He began masturbating, screaming obscenely and hee-hawing like a mule.

This action made several Mexicans punch and spit on the old man. Phillipe told Bob and me that the old man had "fucked a stinking burro" and had been arrested for a crime against nature.

"I wonder what we ever did to get put in jail with an old mule fucker?" Bob asked sarcastically. I was amazed Bob still had his sense of humor. I was glad he was with me.

The beans and water were brought in the late afternoon, and the prisoners finally left the old man alone. The thick heat, along with yet another afternoon shot of heroin, quieted the prisoners. I would not eat, although my stomach ached. I swished water on my cracked lips and dry mouth and then spit it out, afraid of swallowing it. I was feeling weak and dizzy.

"You gotta eat," Bob implored as he gagged on the slimy beans. I still couldn't make myself put the beans in my mouth, much less swallow them. My fear of dysentery and food poisoning was still stronger than my fear of starvation.

We struggled to pass the time with sleep, but sleep was impossible in the day's heat. The old man, meanwhile, slept in the urine and appeared comfortable. He stunk as bad as the hole itself.

I watched the old man twitch in his sleep as two young prisoners crept to his side. They stealthily wrapped pieces of a plastic bread bag around the calf of the old man's leg and tied the bag in such a way as to hang like a fuse. One of the two prisoners lit the plastic, backed off to a corner of the cell, and watched. The fuse quickly burned and the plastic sizzled into flames. The old man lay still for a moment, then screamed awake, ripping at the burning plastic. The plastic would not come off. It was melting into his leg. The skin bubbled and blistered as he kept screaming while flailing his arms and legs. The plastic relentlessly melted into the bone.

He was a madman, screaming and contorting in the light of his burning flesh. We stared, helpless, at the grotesque sight. The flame flickered and died. The old man continued to scream until there was no more than a whimper from his throat. No guard came … no one helped. It was over except for a few moans and cries from the old man. The Mexican prisoners gradually relaxed and settled into their corners. Occasionally a nervous giggle was heard.

Bob and I did not look at each other, nor did we speak. Repulsion and shame held us trance-like as we stared into the darkness at the spot where the flame had been; the smell of burned flesh and plastic gagged us.

"Oh God," Bob sobbed. "What's happening to us? What's happening to us?"

Tears trickled down my cheeks.

I did not sleep that night. I stared into the darkness, oblivious of my surroundings, letting hate and fear take me nearer to insanity.

Chapter Seven

Morning light crept slowly into the cell. No prisoners had been called for interrogation overnight. The old man lay in a heap, deathly pale and mumbling incoherently to himself. The other prisoners began to stir. Bob was still asleep.

How many days have we been in here? I tried to remember. *Is this the third day? I feel like I was born here.* I tried to stretch the stiffness out of my body.

"You okay?" Bob asked me as he woke up.

"Good as can be expected. Maybe we'll be taken out of here today."

"I hope it's soon." Bob glanced in the old man's direction and shuddered. "Please, dear God, let it be soon."

The day passed uneventfully. None of the prisoners were called. We tried to sleep through the hottest part of the day and avoid the vomit of the junkies. I finally drank water, but still would not eat. The guards ignored the old man's wound and his pleas for medical help. It was just like any other day ... in hell.

Darkness came again and the cell cooled. My stomach was cramped from lack of food. The stale air was suffocating. Bob and I tried to talk just to pass time. Now we were beginning to understand what the term *doing time* really meant.

"Where are your parents from?" I asked.

"Uh, New Jersey. My mom and grandmother live in New Jersey. My dad lives in Georgia somewhere."

"Got any sisters?"

"Um, one. Never really got along with her ... or my parents. My grandmother raised me. You'd like her; she's one good lady."

Bob had been speaking in a monotone, answering my questions automatically, when he burst into tears. "I sure hope grandma never finds out about this. It would kill her." He sobbed himself into silence.

A while later the guards appeared at the door. They rattled their keys and grinned ominously into the cell. Interrogations were to start again.

It is a horrible sensation, wanting to be called in order to get out but fearing what would happen to you once you were out. Bob fidgeted nervously as the guards began calling prisoners and pulling them from the cell.

"This is worse than going to the dentist." Bob smiled and wiped his tears.

Like before, the prisoners wailed and chanted to drown out the screams from the interrogations. The clamor of the chants and the high pitched wails produced an eerie effect.

For each prisoner that was pulled from the cell, new prisoners were thrown into the cell. The guards brought three new prisoners, then five, then two.

"What the fuck do those bastards think they're doing? There's no room left in here," I rambled. "They can't put any more people in here. There's hardly any room to even squat as it is. There must be thirty people in here now."

Throughout the night, even after the interrogations ended, the guards kept throwing in new prisoners. Soon there was no room to squat, and barely room to stand. The prisoners quarreled and screamed at the guards each time another prisoner was brought in. The guards laughed and kept shoving more people into the glutted cell.

Prisoners started arguing and fighting. If a person was knocked down or fell, he was stepped on and kicked. Phillipe shoved a larger Mexican, and the man elbowed Phillipe in the nose. He threw Phillipe to the floor. Phillipe grabbed at his foot, but several other prisoners screamed at Phillipe and kicked him in the head and face until he was bleeding.

"Good, good," muttered Bob. "I hope they kill the bastard!"

As long as it's not us, I thought. I felt weak. "I can hardly breathe in here. It's too crowded. Let's see if we can make our way over to the cell door. I'm feeling real dizzy and I'm afraid I'll pass out." We squeezed and edged our way carefully to the door. Everyone seemed equally miserable regardless of where they were in the cell, so we were allowed to squeeze through without incident.

"There must be forty-two people in this rat hole," I mumbled. When we finally reached the door, Bob found a place to lean his shoulder against the wall. I crushed my face against the bars on the door and tried to breathe the air in the corridor, which felt just as stale. I began feeling weaker and sicker. Someone leaned against my back, pushing me tighter against the bars. My knees began to buckle, and I began sliding to the floor. Bob grabbed me by the arm.

"Hey, Steve, you gotta stay on your feet. Stay awake, man!"

"I can't any longer. I keep getting dizzy and I'm gonna pass out."

"Take off your shirt and tie your arm to the bars," he said. "That will at least keep you off the floor." I took off the remnants of my shirt, slid my arm through the bars, and Bob helped tie my arms to the cell door. As I started to drift into semi-consciousness, I remembered how cool the breeze felt against my skin in Zirosto. I remembered Frank, and tried to talk with him, knowing he was thousands of miles away. I thought of Pati, and I thought of myself hanging by the arm in a stinking Mexican jail.

Several times during the night a guard threw a foul smelling bucket of liquid on me, possibly urine or stagnant water. I would be shocked awake, but the shirt held, and I did not fall to the floor. The smell of my body and clothes reeked—even for this stinking jail.

The next morning I was weaker. It was difficult to stand. The arm that was tied burned and ached from lack of circulation. Bob was pale, his eyes sunken with dark rings under them. I managed a smile.

"You stay awake all night?"

"Yeah. Sure am glad to see morning. Maybe today ..."

The cell started to empty out. The guards began taking prisoners away. A Mexican prisoner walked up to Bob and made a motion with his hands saying that he wanted Bob's shirt. Bob indicated he didn't want to surrender the shirt. The Mexican swung at Bob, hitting him on the shoulder. Bob shoved him, and the prisoner moved in on us.

Oh, fuck, I thought. *This is it.* We were both too weak to fight. I numbly untied my shirt and moved next to Bob. I could feel my legs tremble slightly, and I prayed I didn't look as frightened and weak as I felt. I remembered the kid they had beaten to death only nights before ...

The Mexicans stared, cursed, but eventually backed down. Maybe it was because there were two of us or maybe they were as exhausted as we were. We breathed a joint sigh of relief.

Chapter Eight

"Smith, *el otro*," a voice ordered. "Smith!" It was two guards and a Mexican in plain clothes. "*Rapido!*"

Bob and I were being called out of the cell! The Mexicans who had wanted to fight us jeered and shoved us towards the door. One grabbed for Bob's shirt, but Bob wrenched himself from his grasp as we stumbled into the corridor. I was blinded as we walked into the sunlight and open air of the courtyard.

We were led to a car outside the prison, and the guards motioned us to get into the back seat. The plain-clothed man, who looked like a Federale, got behind the driver's seat. Another plain-clothed man in the passenger seat turned to us. Neither Bob nor I had spoken. We were outside—that was all that mattered. We could see the sky and plants and people!

"I know English," the passenger said as the car moved down the street. "Things good now. Big mistake. I talk for you at Federales. No problem." Bob and I sat shocked, our mouths open.

"We can go home then?" we both blurted out.

"*Posiblemente*," the man answered.

"Are you an interpreter or Federale or what?" I asked.

"I speak for you, yes. No Federale … work in *tienda*, store. You know, sell cookies, cake, milk, Kellogg's Corn Flakes … good English, no?"

"Oh, yes," I said, somewhat sarcastically, "cookies and cakes." The man turned to face the traffic as Bob nudged me and pointed toward the back floorboard of the car. Lying on the floor was an unsheathed machete. There was only one visible pistol between the two men and the driver wore that. It would only take a split second to lean forward and attack the driver, but was it a trap?

I wanted revenge, but I was weak and confused. We'd be going home soon. Murder someone? I thought I couldn't, yet I was still frightened of what I might or might not do. The hate and fear made me want to kill them.

Bob and I looked at each other and shrugged. I tapped the store clerk on the shoulder. "Uhhh, I think this is yours," I said as I carefully lifted the machete and handed it to him. Both men's eyes widened and they gasped. They nervously took the machete and thanked us.

"Guess it wasn't a trap," I whispered to Bob. "At least they must know now we're not killers."

We were led back to Malpica's Federale office. Malpica came forward with a large smile on his face.

"You look like you were in the cell for a month, not a few days," he laughed. He waved towards the female clerks. "These gringos are not so pretty now, huh?" he spoke in English. The clerks laughed. Bob and I sat in the chairs, too exhausted and weak to say anything. Malpica reached into his pocket and pulled out a small vial with a tiny spoon attached to the top. He took several spoonfuls and snorted the white powder contained in the vial up his nostrils. He made a face and waved his hands in the air as he sniffed hard several times.

"Good, no?" he asked. I assumed the white powder was cocaine. Malpica walked over to me. He reached into a shirt pocket and brought out a small bag of marijuana. He placed some of the weed in his hand and held it in front of my face.

"You know how to make a marijuana cigarette for me?"

"No," I said.

"I use those little machines most times, but they are hard to get in Mexico. Not too good this way," Malpica confided as he expertly cleaned the stems and seeds from the marijuana and rolled the weed into a well-formed cigarette. "It's good; it's from Culiacan." Malpica walked over to a secretary and said, "*Un regalo para ti.*" He handed her the rolled joint after kissing her hand. She blushed and put it into her desk.

Malpica grew serious. "Now, where is Lucio Cabanas? Where is his hiding place?"

"We don't know. We weren't even sure he got away until you told us," I said tiredly.

"Liar!" Malpica spit. "If you do not tell me the truth, you will be charged."

"Charged for what?" Bob asked.

"Who knows? Gun-running, cocaine, marijuana? Maybe even murder," he said calmly.

"That's bullshit!" Bob yelled. Malpica signaled to some Federales in the office who leaped on Bob and I, yanking our arms behind our backs and pushing us both into the chairs along the wall.

"Sit there until I make a decision." Malpica turned and walked into his office.

We sat in the chairs silently for what seemed like hours, brooding over our fate and watching the office staff going about their business.

Suddenly, the main door to the Federale office was slammed open, and a young Mexican was thrown across the room. He was short, thinly built, and from fifteen to twenty years old. His torn white shirt had blood spattered on the front, and his face was swollen and bruised. The boy appeared terrified. He hung onto a desk, shaking uncontrollably. Two blond-haired, blue-eyed, American-looking men walked in behind the Mexican boy.

Immediately, I was relieved to see someone who might be able to help us out of this terrible mess. The two blond men reminded me of typical Nordic types. "Right out of the Vikings," Bob said later. The taller of the two men was about six foot two, heavy-set, around two hundred pounds but not fat. The other man was five foot eleven and somewhat stockier. Both men wore their hair short. They were dressed in the loose-fitting guayabera shirts that the Mexican Federales wore; the shirts hung outside their pants in order to conceal their weapons. The taller man jabbed the young Mexican in the kidneys with his fist. He slammed the boy's head against a desk and hurled him across the room towards Malpica, who was now standing calmly in the doorway. I winced at the force of the boy's beating.

The young Mexican cried out and was now groveling at the feet of Malpica, who was picking him up from the floor by his hair.

"We found this," the taller blond tossed a glass vial containing a black substance into Malpica's hands. Mallpica placed the vial in his side pocket and dragged the young Mexican into his office and slammed the door behind him.

These men are speaking English! I thought excitedly. *They must be Americans. Yet what are they doing in Mexico, bringing a prisoner to a Federale officer?* I always believed the Mexicans handled their side of the border and the United States took care of its side. I concluded these two men must be mercenaries working for the Mexican Federales. How else could they legally beat people, if beating people was legal anywhere?

Yet maybe they could help us, possibly take us to the border. Bob and I sat watching. We forgot how disheveled and filthy we appeared. The two men either didn't notice us or they thought we were two Mexican nationals.

Finally, the taller of the two blond men looked at us. We nodded, and I said, "Hello."

He squinted his eyes and asked interestedly, "Are you two Americans?"

"Yes," I replied. "Who are you guys?"

"We're customs."

Customs? I thought, confused. I wondered what customs was doing below the border, beating up Mexicans.

"What are you in for?" the tall man asked casually.

"Nothing, we haven't done anything. It's been a nightmare," I replied.

"Nothing? Nothing?" the man said sarcastically. "That's what they all say!" He walked over to Bob and me and started waving his fist in our faces. "Don't you guys ever watch TV? Don't you know when you're busted down here, you're in for the hassle of your life? Damn right it's a nightmare!"

Bob had glared at the two men silently since their entrance, but the cliché set him off.

"Hassle? Hassle?!" Bob yelled. "We haven't done anything and we're in for a *hassle?* We don't sit around and watch the stupid fucking TV all day long like some people who probably don't even have a high school education."

The words bit into the tall blond man, and he whirled on Bob like he was going to hit him.

"Wait a minute," I tried to reason. "Bob's tired and angry. They attacked a village, killed people, dragged us across the country to this place, and we just got out of a stinking jail. We're a little more than freaked out," I said. "Then we see you guys in Mexico beating the shit out of someone. You're supposed to be *our* customs agents. No wonder the Mexican's hate us." I had to hold back the tears. I was trying to make sense in a crazy situation. It was too late though.

"You bastards!" Bob blurted out. "That guy right there," he said, pointing to me, "works for the government, and he's not going to forget what you did to that Mexican. He's a writer too …" The agents stiffened as soon as the word *government* was mentioned. They looked questioningly at each other and then back at us. The tall man signaled the other agent who was sprawled in a chair. He stood up, grabbed Bob by the arm and jerked him from the chair. The agent then shoved Bob to the doorway where Malpica had taken the beaten Mexican.

Malpica emerged with the boy, who looked even worse than before. The boy was transferred to a Federale and led away. Bob protested, but was pushed into the room by the agent. The tall agent remained behind, in the room with me. He seemed to relax and began talking offhandedly to me.

"What's your friend's name?"

"Bob Smith."

"He's got a big mouth."

"You would too if this was happening to you. What is *your* name?"

"Roy Anderson. And yours?"

"Steve. Steve Wilson." I felt exhausted. I looked at him tiredly and asked, "Are you really with customs?"

"Sort of," was the laconic reply. "I used to be, now it's the DEA." I didn't know what the DEA was. I had never heard of it, but I let the abbreviation pass. My body ached and my head swam. I became aware of my appearance, and I was ashamed. Maybe this guy could help? "Could you at least take a message to the American consul?"

"Sure," he answered, "I guess I could do that."

I actually felt some relief.

"So, where are you from?" Anderson continued.

"North Carolina."

"North Carolina?" He seemed surprised. "I used to be stationed in North Carolina. The Fayetteville area for a while, than the Raleigh-Durham area."

"I'm from Greenville," I replied. "But why would a customs person be stationed in North Carolina? I thought customs were only at the borders."

"Oh, no," he said, "We're everywhere. I was working in narcotics there, but they moved us every so often so we wouldn't lose our cover. Nice place, though, North Carolina. Do you really work for the government there?"

"Not really," I sighed. "I work as a counselor for a local mental health center. The extent of my writing has been movie and record reviews for a local paper. Bob was just hysterical. Who can blame him?" I asked. "By the way, what are Bob and your customs friend doing?" I wanted to trust these men but couldn't convince myself.

"Oh," he replied casually, "nothing much. Name. Address. Just routine. I'll be asking you the same questions in a few moments. It's part of our job." Anderson tried to sound sincere.

It was approximately twenty minutes before Bob emerged from the room. His eyes were puffy, and I could see traces of blood below his nose and mouth. His head hung down, and his eyes focused on the floor. I stared at Anderson angrily. "You bastards," I blurted.

"Okay, come on ..." Anderson ordered and forcibly led me into the interrogation room. I was thrown into a chair, and the door was slammed shut behind me. Anderson and I were now alone in the room. From underneath his shirt he pulled out a nickel-plated .357 magnum pistol. He placed the barrel against my temple. I noticed several scratches on the gun, just above the grip.

"Now I want the truth out of you," he snarled. "I don't believe your name is Steve Wilson, and I don't believe you friend's name is Bob Smith. I think you're really ..." He tossed out a foreign-sounding name I didn't understand. This absurd predicament was deteriorating even more, if that was possible. I started to believe Anderson was emotionally disturbed or playing some weird game. This was the same man I had just had a rational conversation with moments before. This had to be an act.

"I never heard of that name," I protested, trying not to look at Anderson like he was crazy. "I'm Steve Wilson. Check all of my papers and you'll see that I'm Steve Wilson!"

"Bullshit!" he screamed at me. "This is your last chance to tell me the truth. Now, where's the cocaine?"

This was too much for me to deal with. Except for what Malpica had been snorting, we hadn't seen or heard of cocaine anywhere in Mexico. The question was so far out in left field that it was ridiculous. I couldn't help myself. I laughed in Anderson's face.

I made a big mistake. Anderson's face turned red.

"What's so funny, you son of a bitch?" He pulled the gun back and jammed the barrel hard into my already wounded temple. This man literally knocked me silly. He grabbed me by the shirt and began shaking me violently.

I was no longer laughing. The situation was anything but funny now as I sat at the mercy of a sadistic man. I kept thinking over and over again, *Be careful, Steve. This guy is really crazy!*

"You over-educated sons of bitches," he yelled as he shook me. "You're not good enough for the United States or for anybody else. We're going to do something about you guys. You're going to fry. I'm going to see whether you're legit or not, and when I find out, I'm going to see that you fry!"

Oh shit, I thought fuzzily, still trying to clear my head from the hit to my temple. *We've got a real live fanatic on our hands.* Anderson motioned for me to stand up as he jerked the door open and shoved me back into the other room at gunpoint. I was pushed to Malpica's desk.

"Hold these two," Anderson directed Malpica.

"I had never planned anything else," Malpica replied as he shrugged his shoulders, looking at me. He seemed annoyed. The two agents, satisfied, turned on their heels and abruptly left the room. Malpica looked at Bob and me with mild pity. He shook his head. "You should have kept your mouth shut. You Americans always too cocky," he said, jerking his head in the direction of the door. "Now, back to the jail."

As we were led away for the second time, I kept thinking to myself, *What in the hell is the DEA?*

Chapter Nine

We were beyond panick when we were sent back to the jail. We had been stupid; we agreed we should have kept our mouths shut, but it was an emotional situation and we lost control. It had happened, and it was too late to correct. We brooded over our fate in the darkness and filth, saying little, hating everything.

The jail was still hot, filthy, and overcrowded. Fortunately, the Mexicans who had wanted to constantly fight earlier were gone, so we were able to pass the next two days without incident.

Then the following day, the store clerk-interpreter returned with a different Federale. There was no machete in the back of the car we rode in this time. The store clerk kept telling us to do what we were told and that we would be all right.

We found ourselves taken to Malpica's office once again. He handed us some papers and told us to sign them. The papers were written in Spanish, and we didn't have any idea what they contained. I felt the situation was getting even worse, if that were possible. Malpica was cold and businesslike. The store clerk would not tell us what was written on the papers. He appeared nervous and tried to reassure us that everything would be all right. He warned us not to anger Malpica.

Malpica informed us that as soon as our signatures were on the documents, freedom was only a matter of time.

"It has all been a big mistake," he said sternly, "but if you do not sign these papers, we will not be able to process you and allow you to leave. It is a policy, no?"

I looked at the document suspiciously. I needed to understand what I was signing. I poised the pen to sign, frantically scanning the document for words I might understand. I needed to find a clue to what the papers did actually say.

Then it caught my eye: "350 kilos" typed approximately three-quarters of the way down the page. I put the pen down on the desk.

"I'm not signing anything," I said, "Not until I have a real interpreter."

Bob was startled.

I turned to him. "Bob, it's a confession," I said desperately as Malpica shoved me towards the wall. "I'm not signing!" I yelled to Bob. He was panicked.

"Me neither," he replied.

Malpica stared at me icily and said, "You will sign one way or another if you ever want to go home."

"No," I told Malpica, "I can't sign to 350 kilos … 350 kilos of what?" I insisted. "C'mon, where would we put 350 kilos of anything, anyway? Would we drag it behind my van, or stack it on the roof? It just doesn't fit. It's not true."

Malpica nodded his head. "Maybe that is too much," he concurred. "I thought about charging you with smuggling guns. Even with murdering Indians. But I thought drugs. Your government has no tolerance for drugs and will do nothing to help." He shook his head as if to indicate that Bob and I were making a huge mistake by not signing his lies. He motioned to the men in the room and eyed us sternly. "Good-bye," he said and turned his back to us. The two Federales led us out the front door towards a partially built, windowless, brick building to the left of the Federale station.

We found ourselves being led through a doorway into a large room where we recognized the Indian villagers who had been brought with us by truck to this place. They were lined up in front of a large trashcan, which was filled with soapy water. Our hands were roughly tied behind our backs with rope. We noticed then that the others hands were also bound behind their backs as well. The atmosphere in the room was ominous. My stomach fluttered. I kept trying to put the thought of a firing squad out of mind.

I felt my body ache as I stood there in my filthy stockinged feet, a large bruise still visible on the side of my head. I tried to glance around the room at the other prisoners. They appeared to be miserable and frightened. I heard Bob's stomach growl. He gave me a weak smile. There were Federales armed with automatic weapons and 9-mm pistols spaced throughout the room. I tried to think of other things to allay my fear. I especially didn't want to imagine the purpose of the large water-filled can in the middle of the room. I thought I might vomit and hoped I would be strong enough not to.

We were lined up with the rest of the prisoners. I ended up on one end of the line with Bob standing next to me. Four or five Federales grabbed a villager standing at the other end of the line and began forcing him to the trashcan. The villager resisted and was clubbed in the side and on his back. He spat out a flow of harsh Spanish words as he tried to kick his captors. The rest of us stood solemnly. I silently cheered the struggling villager. A few more Federales jumped on him and he was dragged, still resisting, to the can. He tried to bite the arm of a

Federale in one last attempt before we watched his head being shoved under the soapy water.

My God, I thought. *They're drowning him. They're going to drown all of us in here!* The room was filled with a palatable fear as the villager's body tensed and then kicked and jerked several times. His head was quickly pulled out of the can. They gave him a chance to gulp some air before they shoved his head back into the soapy muck again. When the man could hold his breath no longer, he was forced to swallow the water. He was pulled from the can and then shoved back in repeatedly, until his stomach bloated up as if he were pregnant. We watched as his body went limp. The Federales threw him contemptuously to the floor, and one of them kicked him hard in the stomach. The man's body jerked and soapy water retched from his mouth. "*Donde esta Lucio Cabanas?*" one of the Federales demanded of him.

This water treatment left the victim weak and sick for days. It was an effective means to break down resistance or get a signature on a fraudulent confession. Most of the villagers looked ready to confess to anything after witnessing this poor man's fate. How could they tell where Frank had gone when, I honestly believed, none of them knew his whereabouts?

My knees were shaking uncontrollably. I felt I would not be able to resist and would admit to anything or sign anything the moment they pulled me towards the bucket. But fortunately I was at the end of the line, so I waited and watched to see what the other men would do. Prior to this I always had a brave image of myself and thought I would react heroically in times of duress. After all, I had been a jock. I was built sturdily and had even won a scholarship to play football in college. I was a muscular two hundred ten pounds, I had been strong, and I could be aggressive. I was now disgusted with my emotions as I stood in line watching another person's pain. My fear was stripping away my self-respect and dignity. I was afraid I would act as a coward.

As the torture continued, man by man, the villagers were all convinced to "confess" within half an hour. A few were tough and fought throughout the treatment, but eventually they too gave in and signed some form of confession. I marveled that they did not go easy ... not as easy as I might ... and there were only four of us left.

The Federales grabbed a tall, thin villager. He twisted and jerked his way to the bucket. As I stood there watching his head being pushed into the soapy water, I noticed Agent Anderson stroll into the room. I assumed someone told him the Federales were in the process of breaking us down and he wanted to see how well we would hold up. Bob had told me, when we went back to the jail, that the name of the agent who had him punched was Mailer. Mailer was not present now.

Anderson stood there and quietly watched the thin Indian gag and then break down and agree to sign the confession paper. Anderson continued to watch as the head of another villager was shoved in the water and held down. When this Indian was brought up for air, he momentarily broke free from the Federales. They were on him in an instant. One Federale punched the Indian in the side of his face and another jabbed him in the kidney. He continued to struggle, yelling Spanish obscenities, but he lost his footing in the soapy spillage and crashed heavily to the floor, carrying two Federales with him.

Anderson just smiled and then walked to the Indian and kicked him hard in the abdomen. The Indian doubled up but tried to grab Anderson's foot. As the Federales struggled to retain him, Anderson kicked him a second time in the chest. The agent had lost his composure—hate was all over his face. His lips curled back and his teeth clenched. He left the room without looking back.

Now it was Bob's turn. I could see him shake as his eyes rolled pleadingly in my direction. He was being dragged to the water treatment when a Federale walked in and shouted orders in Spanish. The men holding Bob relaxed their grip. It was over for some unknown reason; this torture session had been postponed and both Bob and I were spared. I felt giddy and light-headed but my body did not stop trembling until hours later.

We were then both taken back to Malpica's office. Malpica held the papers in front of us and asked smugly if we were ready to sign yet. Reluctantly, we shook our heads. As frightened as we were, we weren't going to sign. We had not done anything wrong. Anderson was sitting at a desk in the office, watching us.

Malpica threw the documents onto his desk as Anderson stood up to leave.

"I checked on these two," he said to Malpica. "They're nobody special. Nail those over-educated sons of bitches real good." He glared at us and walked out of the office. That was the last time we saw Anderson.

Malpica picked up the documents from his desk.

"If you sign this now," he said, "you won't have to go back to the jail, and we will let you have a telephone call. It no longer says 350 kilos. If you don't sign now, you will be held in the jail cell until it is signed." He leaned back into his chair and waited. Bob and I looked at each other. We were physically and emotionally exhausted. We were frightened and broken.

"We'll get a telephone call?" I repeated plaintively.

"Yes," he said sternly, "but only one of you."

I looked at Bob, and then back to Malpica, and whispered, "Okay, we'll sign."

Hands shaking, we both signed the document, which we did not understand. It was quickly agreed that I would be able to call my employer. I was afraid to call my parents for fear of what this information could do to them. I picked up the receiver that Malpica pointed to. I dialed the number, trying to keep myself together. Lee Walton, the coordinator of the center, answered the phone.

"Lee …" I croaked into the phone, trying to hold back my tears. "It's Steve." I tried to tell him what was happening as best I could. "Please try to help us; don't leave us here!" I implored. The call was short but Lee understood the gravity of the situation. He would immediately contact lawyers and our parents. The conversation ended with me sobbing into the phone. When I hung up, Bob and I were herded back to the jail. Malpica was not a man of his word. At this point, we were not surprised. I was never to see him again either, or the Indian villagers who were in the interrogation room with us.

Upon our return to the jail, I felt like a zombie. I lapsed into a partial state of shock and moved in a foggy, gray world. My physical state deteriorated rapidly. We were probably only in the jail for one day, but to us it felt like an eternity.

When the guards did come for us, they told us we were being sent to *un carcel*. I dragged my shoeless feet over the concrete and walked into an outer courtyard, where bright sun soaked into my skin. The courtyard walls were bleached stark white. My eyes glinted in the glare, and I felt sweat trickling down my back. Flies swarmed everywhere, trying to cling to my sticky clothes or fly up my nostrils. I didn't swat at them as I would have before; I didn't care. Faintly, I knew I was being led to my new home and I would have to get used to such things as flies and filth.

We turned to the left in the courtyard, where an iron-barred door was unlocked. The jail had been an extension of the prison. We were pushed roughly through the door and waited in an alcove as another barred door was unlocked. There was another inner courtyard, where the flooring was nothing more than cracked and broken concrete. The high walls were bleached from the severe sun and were scrawled with graffiti. Stretched over the walls, as a roof to the inner courtyard, was chicken wire. A rampart ran around most of the wall so that the guards could walk and watch us from above. Once inside, we were surrounded by prisoners who pulled on our clothes and poked at our bodies. The prisoners grabbed us by the arms and shoulders, and shuffled us toward a wooden door. They were muttering and yelling.

"Hey, gringo, dinero, dinero!" While we were moving toward the wooden door ahead, I noticed small huts made of cardboard and blankets strewn throughout the inner courtyard. The Mexicans, we would learn, called these huts *curacas*.

Sitting in front of a curacas, by himself, was a tall, lanky blond man. He smiled sheepishly and called out, "Welcome to the San Luis Hilton!"

Chapter Ten

The crowd of prisoners banged on the wooden door, and a heavyset Mexican stepped out. He wore no shirt and his belly hung over his pants. He had a pencil moustache. He kept pointing to himself and saying he was the jefe. We seemed to not comprehend what this meant, so he called over an extremely thin Mexican who bore a striking resemblance to a weasel. The weasel called himself Victor and spoke passable English. In a drugged haze, Victor explained to us that the fat Mexican was the boss in charge of all the prisoners. Everything in the prison would cost money—*dinero*. Victor told us we had to pay 200 pesos apiece to keep the prisoners from attacking us en masse, and to keep from doing *talache*, which consisted of cleaning the toilet holes with a brick and bare hands. If we did not have the money, he said, they would accept clothes as collateral. However, our clothes were so ragged that they instead took an IOU from us. A space to sleep in the courtyard would cost us 100 pesos, a blanket was 100 pesos, and a curaca would cost 500 pesos.

"Food cost money," Victor continued. "Drugs cost money. Everything cost money, man. You in Mexico now, and you have the rights of a Mexican. No more, no less. If the Mexican has a right to live as a pig, that what you get. No money, you live worse than a pig." He stopped and grinned a toothless smile. "You not in Estados Unidos now."

After we were roughly searched, we were left to wander around our new environment. My body was extremely tense. I hadn't the slightest idea what to expect. I had heard rumors of the gang rapes and beatings that occurred in prisons and I was imagining the worst. But as miserable as this seemed to be, at least it was better than the jail where we had been kept.

Bob and I walked over to where the lanky blond man was sitting. There were no benches or chairs to be seen in the prison, so the guy was sitting on the hot concrete, cross-legged. He had a cup of ice water in his hands, and my parched throat ached for a swallow of that refreshing fluid.

He smiled at me and offered me his cup. "Weird movie, huh?" he asked. "Wish we could change the channel." He watched me drink his water. "My name is Bradley Speare; what about yours?" I continued to gulp down the water, but Brad yelled at me to stop. "Hey, take it easy with that stuff!" he said. "It costs 1 peso per cup, and money is hard to find here."

"Sorry," I gasped gratefully and passed the cup to Bob, who took a few sips.

"I didn't know they sold the water too," I explained. I introduced both Bob and myself. "Are you an American? Are there other Americans here?"

Bradley nodded, "Yes, I'm American, and there's one other. He's standing over there … Rex Dean Heisler," He pointed to a man across the way. "Watch him, though; he's a con man and hustler. But he's sorta likeable, which makes him all the more dangerous."

Squatting in the hot sun, we told Brad about ourselves and the circumstances that led to our current fate. We were glad and relieved to explain what had happened to someone, anyone. He seemed to be in as much trouble as we were.

Brad was from Southern Carolina. He had an easygoing, sarcastic air about him that put us at ease immediately. He had been arrested one month ago. He was visiting a girlfriend in Arizona when he decided to enter Mexico to buy a small amount of marijuana for himself, "because it was less expensive and the quality was better." A recent acquaintance from Arizona suggested he could introduce Brad to a good connection. That good connection turned out to be Rex Dean Heisler, the other American he had pointed out to us, who sold everything from grass to guns to heroin. The acquaintance from Arizona who helped Brad turned out to be a narcotics agent. Brad never bought any marijuana, but he was in the house with Rex when the arrest came down and was charged, along with four other people, for five ounces of heroin. Before our own misfortune, I doubt if I would have believed Brad, but now I certainly did.

Rex came over to join us, and it gave us an opportunity to learn about him. He was affable, easy to like. We began to talk.

Rex was married to a Mexican girl. He spoke Spanish and had lived in Mexico for four years. Rex was also familiar with the prisons, having served five years for counterfeiting. We would need him to interpret for us, but we would also be prey to his scams.

Chapter Eleven

What was the DEA? Brad thought it meant Defense Enforcement Agency. Rex got little or no information from the Mexicans about what was happening to us, but he was aware of the DEA. "It's called the Drug Enforcement Administration", he said with distaste. Rex began to brief us on the events of the past few years, which influenced the attitudes of Mexicans towards gringos. The story was similar to the one Frank had told us in the mountains of Zirosto.

In 1968, he explained, thousands of Mexican students protested the pre-Olympic games. They were standing up for the poor and mistreated masses. The protest ended in the deaths of over 350 students and innocent bystanders by the Mexican Federales. The family ties in Mexico are extremely close-knit and religious, yet the bodies were rushed into mass graves before the families could claim their dead. The killings came to be known as the Three Cultures Massacre, and bitterness swept throughout Mexico, causing radical elements to mobilize into guerrilla units. Bank robberies, kidnappings, and mountain revolts resulted from the guerrilla movements—something most American tourists knew nothing about, although it left certain areas of Mexico extremely dangerous for tourists.

The man who we knew as Frank was identified by Rex as one of the revolutionaries, and his village was a revolutionary outpost. "Hell, everyone in Mexico knows of Lucio. His full name is Lucio Cabanas Barrientos. He grew up in the state of Guerrero, not far from your village. He used to be a school teacher. Now he's the chief of a small rebel force they call the Party of the Poor. He's the most important single leader of the Mexican guerrilla opposition. One of his reported exploits supposedly occurred in Oaxaca, where he was said to have gunned down a group of policemen from a moving vehicle while they were standing for an inspection. He also shot down the Governor of Guerrero's helicopter. You didn't know I was such a wealth of knowledge?" Rex grinned. "You have to be in my business."

"It didn't keep you outta here" Brad said in a sarcastic tone.

Rex gave Brad a Dirty look as he continued. "Many Mexican officials believe young Americans were providing the money and/or guns to the revolutionary groups in exchange for marijuana. Therefore, there was a policy of brutal harassment toward any American the Mexican officials remotely suspected of a drug connection or attachment to revolutionary groups. This made it even more dangerous for Americans or college-age Mexicans to travel off normal tourist routes."

We had never suspected how dangerous it was for us, both student aged, to be traveling throughout the countryside alone, without political permission. It immediately put us under suspicion. Rex further told us that Americans were given severe penalties for even small amounts of drugs, while Mexicans in possession of tons often received a heavy fine or a short jail term. The U.S. Tourist Bureau and the Customs Bureau did not offer this information to persons entering Mexico. "The Americans enter Mexico blind and are left to discover this by trial and error," Rex emphasized. "They are told by the American Consulate, 'You shouldn't have come to Mexico in the first place,' after it's too late."

"In the summer of 1969, the Nixon administration decided that the current policy was not stopping the flow of marijuana coming across the border into the United States. The Mexicans were having their own internal problems with the guerillas and did not seem too concerned with stopping the flow, so Operation Intercept was set up.

Operation Intercept was literally just that: every man, woman, and vehicle crossing the border was stopped and thoroughly searched. Some two thousand customs and border patrol agents were spread along the Mexican border to harass anyone coming across. Tens of thousands of tourists were tied up for days at a time, trying to get home from Mexico while the lines of cars piled up. The tourist business crumpled.

The Mexican government was hurt so badly by the lack of tourist trade during the time, and American-owned businesses in Mexico complained so much, that Operation Intercept was cancelled."

Listening to Rex explain the political situation took my mind off of my surroundings for the first time since the arrest. It also helped Bob and I to understand what had happened to us.

Rex continued, explaining that the U.S. government then started Operation Cooperation. This was an attempt to aid the Mexican government and buy their cooperation in stopping the drug traffic from the Mexican side of the border. The United States provided money, guns, helicopters, pilots, and training. The Mexican officials could hardly refuse, because this equipment would also allow them to escalate their war on the revolutionary movement. The Mexicans did burn out fields and arrest more people, but tons of marijuana continued to make it across the border. The small-scale smugglers and marijuana farmers were going to prison, while the organized, large-scale smugglers were lining the Mexican government officials' pockets with even more money and getting a clear path into the United States. The profits increased for these large-scale smugglers as the smaller competition dwindled.

It felt like we were listening to a spy novel. The twists and turns had Bob and I entranced. We tried to comprehend what we were learning and relate it to our experience. Somehow, sitting on cracked concrete in the blazing sun made everything all too real.

"With this in mind," Rex continued, "Nixon proposed another plan." He said Nixon decided to reorganize the Bureau of Narcotics and Dangerous Drugs by stripping the CIA and Customs Bureau of its best, most radical, and most vicious agents. Over twenty three hundred men were assigned to the newly formed Drug Enforcement Administration on July 1, 1973. During the time of our arrest, Anderson and Mailer were in a transition stage between the Customs Bureau and the DEA. We were some of the first to be harrassed by President Nixon's newly founded agency.

We learned that the DEA was given almost limitless funds to purchase illicit drugs in attempts to set up smugglers. The DEA was also given a degree of unlimited power. The three hundred DEA agents assigned to the Mexican/American border had the power to seize a person without a warrant, search that person, and forcibly have the person's stomach pumped in search of evidence. The DEA was accountable to the U.S. government, but once the DEA crossed into Mexico, they were considered free agents. The Mexicans had no control over them because they were working for the U.S. government—but the U.S. government had no real control over them because they were on foreign soil.

With every word, Rex's information helped us to understand why Anderson and Mailer acted the way they had. They were responsible to no one. They had power to abuse—and they obviously enjoyed using it.

When the DEA was formed, Rex said, hundreds of agents were dispatched to Mexico and assigned to various U.S. embassies as part of their administrative staff. Therefore, a prisoner who looked toward the American Embassy for help often got a visit from the person who jailed him. The DEA had arrested Mexican citizens, causing more bitterness and hatred towards gringos among the Mexican poor. The DEA was becoming notorious for its forms of entrapment, blackmail, torture, and extortion. What business did they have, as foreigners in Mexico, arresting Mexican citizens?

"How can they be stopped?" Bob asked.

"Eventually, the Mexican people will stop them, not the Mexican government." Rex speculated. "But hell, it's just started. You boys have only seen the beginning. This is gonna be one damn weird movie."

Chapter Twelve

There was nothing to do in the San Luis prison except worry. I was still confused, frightened, and hungry. I managed slightly better with the help of Brad and Rex, and discovered that the courtyard I was in was not the only section of the prison.

To the right of the gate where we entered the courtyard was a large enclosed room, forty feet by eight feet. In the rear of this room were the two toilets—a concrete slab with holes in it that were supposed to accommodate the two hundred to two hundred and fifty men. The toilets did not flush, but buckets of water were poured down the holes to force the feces down. Next to the toilets were two spigots that were used to take showers. Brad explained to us we should never enter the room alone or we would be jumped and robbed.

"There are Mexicans here who blame the Americans for their arrests and their poverty in general," Brad told us. "They hate us and would love the chance to get even, so be careful. Most of them will back down from several of us. Junkies only fight when they know we don't have a chance in hell." The room was eerily dark, and the air stunk of urine and body odor. There was no circulation of air. Sleeping men were strewn on blankets or rags throughout the room. The men turned toward us angrily as we passed. There were no beds in this prison. Either a person slept on the concrete and asphalt floor, or slept in a curaca. It was hot and rivulets of sweat ran down everyone's face. There was no routine or exercise period. There was *lista,* or roll call, at dawn and dusk. The rest of the day was spent trying to endure the heat and avoid getting beaten up.

Brad told us that there was a visitor's day on Wednesdays and Saturdays. Whole families were allowed in the prison to visit and this broke the monotony, even if we did not receive a visit ourselves. Brad finished showing us the toilets and showers, and we gladly returned to the open courtyard. When we had found ourselves a spot to sit on the concrete, we silently watched the prison guards. Brad explained that their only responsibility toward the prisoners was to keep us from escaping and provide us with an allotted 50 centavos (4 cents) worth of food per day. The Mexican government did not provide a salary for the director of the prison, or the guards, or any of the people working inside the prison.

"The position of a director of a prison is a political stepladder," Brad continued as we watched the guards walk by. "The director is assigned a prison. If he can keep the prison running with few incidents, and make money or a reputation for himself with so little government support, he has an excellent chance of being promoted to a high-level government position. That's why they sell everything here. It's to support the prison and the guards and make the director a wealthy man. Some shit, huh?" He smiled. "We're paying them to keep us here." Brad shook his head disgustedly. "They won't even give you a blanket to sleep on or toilet paper to wipe your ass with. You gotta use old magazines or book pages or anything you can find for that." He shrugged his shoulders.

Brad then began to file through some of his things. He couldn't seem to find what he was looking for and got up and walked over to Rex, who was jabbering with two older Mexican men. He interrupted their conversation to ask Rex something. First Rex shook his head from side to side, indicating he was not amenable to what he had been asked, but then he wandered off into the yard. Within minutes, he returned triumphantly with a torn, filthy rag that at one time was a quilt. He crossed over to us and offered it to me.

"Here," Rex said, "I got you two this, so you'd have something to pad the concrete when you lay down." Then he turned to Brad and said, not maliciously, "Now the two guys here owe me a favor." He smiled and picked at his yellowed teeth. Under normal conditions, this "quilt" would have repulsed us. I would not have touched it, let alone sleep on it. But now we took it gratefully and thanked Rex for the favor.

The first night was surreal. We were numb, dazed. Could this be happening? Our nightmare had begun and we were trying to figure out how we could and would adjust. But then, slowly, the days dragged by and the nights came. The routine set in. Nights were comforting; the darkness and the cool air helped make things bearable. Bob and I shared the rag-quilt in the center of the courtyard each night.

A week had passed. It was night. Bob and I lay side-by-side, watching the evening sky. "Do you think your boss Lee will be able to help us?" he asked.

I turned and looked at him, feeling my despair but managing an encouraging smile. "I sure hope so," I answered. "I know he'll do everything he can. He's been a damn good boss and a better friend."

Bob shivered, but not from the cold. Blank eyes looked into mine. "Well," he said, "I sure hope he hurries." Silence filled the air, and it was all we could do to smile and laugh nervously, trying to allay our fears.

Chapter Thirteen

For the next several days we slept as much as possible and waited for a response to our telephone call. I attempted to write letters on the back of old paper bags or paper that Brad had not used for the toilet, but I found myself getting choked-up and unable to finish writing. Nevertheless, I hoped I would be out of this hellhole before the letters arrived at home. Brad said the best way to get letters out was to have visitors smuggle them out of the prison. The guards would promise to mail letters for you, but very few ever made it to their destinations because the Mexicans tried to cut off all outside communication.

So we wrote the letters, and we waited. On approximately the tenth day in prison, which to us felt like an eternity, the guards came for us and took us to the outer courtyard. A man introduced himself to us as Mr. Jeff Richardson, a lawyer my parents had apparently sent to us. He was in his mid-forties, of medium height, with brownish hair. He was wearing a white short-sleeve shirt and khaki pants. As happy as I was to hear that he was a lawyer, at the same time I was not impressed with him. His face was bland and devoid of interest and sympathy. Certainly, anyone looking at us would indicate some sign of compassion. We introduced ourselves to him, hoping we might be looking at the end of our nightmare. Richardson looked around the courtyard slowly and then fixed his eyes back on us.

"Are you guilty?" he asked. His first question.

I was outraged but calmed myself,."Of what?" I answered indignantly. Then I begin to explain to him, in a somewhat hurried manner, about our ordeal—about the village, Pati, and the forced confession. It was like he didn't hear a word I had said.

"The Mexicans say you're guilty of smuggling drugs," he replied blandly.

"What would you expect them to say?" I said, trying to hold back my anger and frustration.

"Well," Richardson continued, ignoring me, "this is going to cost lots of money, and your parents don't think they can help you." He stood in the hot sun, sweat pouring down his forehead and soaking his clean white shirt. He looked nervously at the guards. "I hate this damn country," he confided. "They're apt to throw me in here with you for no reason. I hate coming down here ..." Then he looked at us, as if for the first time. "You look awful," he said. "Have they hurt you badly?" His concern did not sound genuine.

"Not too bad," I mumbled. I didn't like this man. It was instinctive.

"You should have known better than to come down here in the first place." Richardson sighed heavily. "I better get out of here now. Is there anything I can do for you?"

"Yeah," I said numbly, realizing that there may never be any hope. "We need about $30 for protection money ... and tell my parents that I love them." Richardson looked around apprehensively and then peeled off two twenties and placed them in my hands.

He leaned close and whispered, "The only thing I can tell you is to nail your partner—blame everything on him." I was thankful for the money but I didn't have much to say for Mr. Jeff Richardson.

I later found out that Lee Walton had contacted my parents immediately after my call and, having no idea where to turn, my mother spoke to a judge at the country club she managed. The judge referred her to a lawyer in Yuma, Arizona—Mr. Jeff Richardson.

A U.S. lawyer has absolutely no authority or power to do anything of a legal nature in Mexico. Mr. Richardson, knowing this, still demanded a $500 retainer fee from my parents before he would even discuss the case. He warned them that I was in an extremely precarious position and would probably be killed without legal aid. After my parents paid the fee, Richardson told them that I was probably guilty and would most likely be executed unless they came up with $50,000. My parents were grief-stricken. It might as well have been $1,000,000. They were hard-working, middle-class Americans and did not have money like that. The retainer fee alone set them back.

So, like a flash, Richardson was there and then he was gone. Bob and I walked back into the main prison, crushed. Our hopes of possible release were destroyed. Richardson had completely ignored Bob and he had certainly discouraged me. I leaned against the inner wall. Over the wall from the area of the jail cells where Bob and I were initially held, I could hear the wailing and the chants beginning—a new series of interrogations. I felt my mind becoming unhinged.

Brad walked up to us. "You guys all right?" he asked.

"Don't say a word. I don't want to talk about it" I said sternly.

Brad didn't flinch. Instead, his face took on a look of total sympathy. "That's okay, man," he replied quietly, "I understand." Then he walked off and left me to my misery.

Chapter Fourteen

The following day, a guard called us to the main door and told us that we had been found "presumably guilty," as interpreted by Rex, and that we would have to go to Nogales with the rest of the prisoners found presumably guilty to stand official trail. Rex said it could be weeks or months before they made transportation available for the transfer. We were not present at our preliminary trial, if there ever was one. We were not represented by counsel. We never saw the judge, we had no idea when we would be transferred for our official trail and we expected this outcome, just by the farce of the whole situation.

Bob and I gradually adjusted to the conditions inside the prison. After paying off our protection fee, I had $8 left over from the money Richardson had given me to buy food.

Rex, Brad, Bob, and I worked out a guard system to protect each other while we slept. Each night, a different American would stay awake and watch over the others. Strength in numbers became a meaningful expression.

I continued to lose weight and feel weak, but I was surviving. I discarded my filthy socks and made sandals out of a flat piece of wood and a torn belt. I learned to look forward to my 4-cents-worth of beans and flour tortilla each day.

I attempted to write and smuggle out letters to my parents and Lee, but it was difficult to explain to someone who had led a protected life that, first, I was in prison on trumped-up charges, and second, I needed money to survive in this prison. Due process, which I took for granted in the United States was sorely missed.

Since there were no chairs or benches in the courtyard, I learned to squat for hours at a time. I also learned how to squat over the toilet without falling in and how to move around the Mexican prisoners safely.

I also learned other things about this prison … about the heroin, which flowed freely and which half of the Mexican prisoners were addicted to, which made our living conditions even more dangerous. In order to get their drug fix, the junkies would take unnecessary risks and our supposed American riches were a prime target.

I learned to live with fear on a daily basis: fear of being in prison and fear of being forgotten. Being forgotten was my biggest fear. I felt as if I had been swallowed up and no one would care. I would rot away in this miserable prison until I died, and no one would remember me.

And then, to my surprise, someone did remember me! Approximately two weeks after seeing Richardson, Bob and I were called into the outer courtyard again. We were ecstatic. We felt for sure there would be word from the outside, or help, but we were soon disappointed. Five disheveled men, in the loose-fitting guayabera shirts of the Federales, were waiting in the yard for us. I assumed they were Americans, for they asked us our names in English and asked how many times we had been in Mexico. They checked us out as if they were trying to memorize or identify our faces. Then, abruptly, they left.

Later that afternoon, two Mexican guards came into the prison and read a document in Spanish. Basically, as Rex interpreted it, the document said the federal government had not sent the money for food yet, and no federal prisoners were to be fed until the money arrived. The four Americans were the only federal prisoners. Rex and Brad had enough money to survive, but not enough to share with us.

"What do they mean that they aren't going to feed us?" I said stupidly. "They can't do that!"

"They can, and they are," was Rex's laconic reply.

For once the Mexicans were telling the truth: they didn't feed us. I learned a lot about my body in the next thirteen or fourteen days. Bob and I became scroungers. We would either steal or beg for food from the other prisoners. I would swallow just about anything edible. My pants became so loose that they would fall down around my knees so I had to tie them with a tope. We became very weak. When I stood up too quickly, I became dizzy; my head swam, and I would fall or nearly pass out.

Our bodies went through physical changes. My teeth felt weak and soft and my hair began to fall out. My tongue turned grayish black and my breath stank. I could feel what food types were being used up in my body. Some days I would hunger for nothing but starches. My body would cry out for bread or potatoes. Nothing else would suffice. The few spoonfuls of beans I could acquire did nothing. There were days when I felt sick and weak; my stomach would knot and cramp up. Yet there were also days when I felt full of energy and as if I was thinking clearly for the first time in my life.

On one occasion, Bob stole some lard from a prisoner and I had found a cigarette. Bob ate the lard and I ate the cigarette. After much retching and the dry heaves, we agreed that during our salvaging, there were some things best left uneaten.

At another point during our two weeks of not being officially fed, Bob found a stale and soggy graham cracker lying on the ground. He moved to gobble it up, but then looked at me sadly. He split the soggy cracker in half and handed part of it to me. We sat there, the two of us, savoring the taste of a stale graham cracker, tears running down our cheeks as we tried to recall better, happier days of graham crackers and milk in elementary school. We had been reduced to a pathetic state, crying over an inedible cracker, with ropes holding up our ragged pants and only hope keeping us together.

Another week went by and still no transfer from the San Luis prison. Soon we were to get our first glimpse of Mexican democracy. Late one evening, more than one hundred men were led into the prison. At first we thought an enormous drug bust caused this large number of new prisoners. But, as we questioned the prisoners, it was discovered that this was the result of the latest political election. The hundred or more men were members of the losing political party. After the election, the men had been rounded up and imprisoned. They stayed with us approximately three days; then they were divided up and taken to other prisons throughout the state. These men were well dressed and intelligent. Many spoke English. In our prison, the junkies robbed them of their money, clothes, and shoes, yet at the same time they praised the *politicos* for their courage. It was hard to believe this was happening just across the border from the United States ... from home.

Weeks drifted by, and visitor's days passed. I would watch the visitors file in and hope someone would come to see me, but no one ever did. The loneliness was unbearable, and seeing the visitors only made things worse.

One particular visitor's day was a wakeup call for me. If I had ever thought of suicide as a way out of this nightmare, it was totally driven from my mind that day. It was mid-afternoon, and visitors were lounging around, talking to their jailed friends and relatives. Bob and I sulked in one corner of the prison, away from everyone else. Suddenly, one of the women visitors screamed and pointed towards the ground. A stream of blood was flowing out from underneath a curaca. Several Mexicans, as well as Bob and I, ran to see what was happening. The blanket entrance was thrown back and lying inside, in a pool of blood, was a young Mexican. He had slashed his wrists with a broken bottle, and the blood from his left wrist was gushing high into the air. He appeared to still be alive. The Mexicans screamed angrily. They grabbed the bleeding man by the hair and dragged him from the curaca. Other prisoners gathered around and began cursing and spitting on the bleeding man. Several men kicked the man in the groin and face.

"Oh my God," I whispered to Bob as I tried to get out of the way. The man was dragged around the courtyard; the prisoners and a few visitors abused him and shouted insults. The young Mexican was still alive, the blood pumping vigorously out of his arm, leaving a trail where he was dragged. I started to feel sick. These were madmen, all of them! The gushing blood became only a flow and then a trickle, before the guards came in to carry the now dead man away. Then, as the body was hauled off, the prisoners called for help to clean the blood off of the concrete, but I backed off. They grabbed Bob, and he had to help mop up the puddles of blood.

"Why did they do that to the guy?" I asked Rex with a shudder.

"Oh, it's a way to discourage other people from killing themselves," he replied, squinting at me in the sun. "Most people think that if they kill themselves, it will make other people feel bad or leave a guilt trip on the others. You know what I mean? 'Look what you made me do to myself' kind of stuff." He smiled grimly. "Here in prison, the people just get angry at a person for spoiling a nice visitor's day and trying to make them feel bad."

"Oh," I said slowly as Bob finished mopping up the blood and vomited.

Most days, with exceptions such as the above, were indeed monotonous: wake up for lista, try to avoid the heat, wait around, and go back to sleep. There was no formal exercise, no books and no games. Many of the Mexicans occupied themselves by having sex. Homosexuality was rampant in the prison. Although malnourished, I was taller than most Mexicans and still capable of defending myself, so I was usually left alone. Once, while I was squatting on the toilet, two feminine-looking Mexicans stood in front of me, just out of reach, and began to comment about my *buena nolga* (nice ass) while masturbating in front of me. Bob and Brad were protecting me, but they were so amused by the whole episode that they broke into hysterical laughter as I blushed. Many of the Mexicans had what I thought was an odd outlook towards homosexuality. They had a hard time believing that we Americans had never screwed or desired to have sex with another man. They believed it was *puto*, or queer, to be the one having it done to you, but that it was very macho to do it to another man. I would argue with them for hours, saying it did not matter if you were the screwer or screwee; anyone who would have relations with another male was puto. This would always make them extremely angry and they would threaten to fight, although it never came to that.

Bob and I saw our first of many gang rapes in San Luis. In many ways, the prisoners used the gang rape as a means of social punishment. If a man was brought into the prison for a crime that was extremely evil in their eyes, such as child molestation, rape, or harming elderly people, that man was often gang raped. One Sunday morning, a man was brought into the prison and a great commotion ensued. The prisoners pounced on him, attempting to rip his clothes from his body and beat him. The man had been accused of robbing and beating an old man to death. He was carried, screaming, into the large room, where he was stripped and beaten into submission. He was forced to have sex with almost forty other prisoners and was continuously slapped and punched throughout the ordeal. Those of us not participating watched in morbid fascination. After the vicious rape, the prisoner was ostracized. No one talked with him. He was the last to be fed and the first to be blamed. The men taking part in the rape gained prestige in the eyes of the other prisoners. The lesson both disgusted and frightened us. It was a horrible education, but a necessary one we would not forget.

Chapter Fifteen

The weeks dragged into months. Our trial, if there ever was to be one, was not progressing. There was still no word on when we were going to be transferred to the prison in Nogales, which we figured had to be better than the San Luis prison. And what of the fabled American Consulate? Where were they? When would they come rushing to our aid like the U.S. Calvary in Western movies? After being in the prison for about six weeks, the guards called for Rex, Brad, Bob, and me. They said the U.S. consul wanted to talk with us. We cheered and hooted and practically danced into the outer courtyard. We were led through the courtyard into the prison director's office. Outside the main gate of our prison, we had to step over a fly-covered body lying face down in the dirt, a sight that knocked the celebration out of us. It was a grim reminder of where we were.

The director disgustedly pointed to a telephone lying off of the receiver on the desk. The director was a fat, pale man who wore a cowboy hat much too small for his head. I excitedly picked up the phone. "Hello? Hello?" Through heavy static I could barely hear the female voice. Straining my ears, I heard the faint voice said she was a consul and wanted to know if she could tell our parents anything. I yelled my name into the phone again and again but she could not understand me through the static. Frustrated, I handed the phone to Rex. He had no luck either. That was the extent of our first contact with the American Consulate. We were then led out of the office, over the fly-covered body, and back into our prison.

One week after our phone call with the Consulate, I received a visitor. I was escorted to the outer courtyard alone. A Mexican-American from Hawaii introduced himself as a friend of my uncle's. He was with his wife and "everything was getting under control." He said he was there to get me out. In truth, this man, Amiya Jesus, was a vulture, just like Richardson. He conned my uncle from Hawaii into believing he could get me out of prison for $3,000 in bribe money. My uncle fell for the story and gave him the cash. Amiya and his wife used the money to take a vacation to Mexico instead. They only visited me to make it official, and then traveled down the coast to Mexico City, where they had a great time, using me as the pretense for this trip. He did talk to a judge in the state of

Jalisco, but that judge had no authority in the state of Sonora where we were located. If that judge attempted to influence a Sonoran official it more than likely would have made them angry, causing conditions to worsen for us.

The lawyer, Amiya and his wife, leeches bearing false hopes did more to destroy our morale than any other factor. They would tell us not to worry, that we'd be out any day; then they would disappear out the gate with a pocket full of money and never be heard from again. These vultures came often, and we were constantly harassed by their con games. My family was easy prey for them.

Three days after Amiya left, I received another visitor in the evening. It was too late, so they wouldn't let me see him, but I was able to shake a faceless hand through the cell door. He said his name was Alfonso Garcia Gallegas, a Mexican lawyer hired by my parents. Again I heard "Everything is going to be all right." He passed me a dozen apples through the bars. The apples were soft, wormy, and old, but I was extremely grateful. I did not know that this "month's food supply" had cost my parents $400.

Alfonso Garcia Gallegas charged my parents $2,400 to represent me. He was not an *abogado*, a lawyer, but a *licensiado*, a person with a five-year college degree, specializing in law. My parents, in their naiveté and desperation, were being fleeced clean. There was no one to give them reliable advice. They were left to the mercy of these predators. Gallegas was one of many lawyers on a list approved by the American Consulate.

I knew my family cared, even though the men coming to visit gave me an uneasy feeling. I wrote several letters to my parents, trying to warn them of the con games. The information on law and Mexican justice that Amiya and Gallegas offered just did not match what Brad and Rex had told me. "You were guilty in Mexico until proven innocent. There was no easy way out. Even if found innocent, the trail could take years." I began to feel even more helpless and hopeless, if that were possible.

The evening after I received the apples from my newly acquired lawyer, there were loud noises outside the prison walls. The guards ran from place to place, rattling keys and jostling rifles.

"*Translado, translado*." The call was whispered with excitement by the inmates throughout the prison. It was the change, the transfer of prisoners from San Luis to Nogales. We could hear the engines of large vehicles rumbling outside the walls. Apprehensive, Bob and I gathered up our ragged blanket in hopes that we would be called.

We heard rumors that the Nogales prison was large and newly built. It had to be better than the rat hole we were in. Besides, our so-called trial could not proceed until we reached the judicial court in Nogales, which could bring us one step closer to home. We had been in the San Luis prison for almost two months, and nothing had happened. We were in a holding pen.

The guards flung open the main gate screaming, "Lista! Lista!" and the names echoed off the walls. Hard-faced Federales guarded us with sub-machine guns. Bob and I looked at each other and thought, *Please take us.* Brad's name was called. After about seventy names, they called Bob and then me. I almost cried with joy. I was finally leaving here. It might only be a short amount of time before I'd be on my way home.

We were shoved to the outer courtyard, where Federales searched us. Dividing the prisoners into groups, they tied our hands tightly behind our backs with ropes, and we were led to a smaller group on the left. The prisoners to the right of us were also getting their hands tied behind their backs, but they were forced to swallow a pill. I assumed it was a tranquilizer and was being used like a chemical straightjacket. The man administering the pills was fair in complexion and appeared to be in his late twenties. It struck me that he might be an American, but I couldn't be sure. The group on the right was led out first. As we were being led out, I passed close to the man with the pills. I noticed his blue eyes, Western-style shirt, and shoulder-length hair, and I boldly asked, "You having fun?"

"Hey man," he answered defensively. "I'm only doing my job."

"Sure," I replied, "but for who?" I managed to say this before being roughly shoved forward by Federales. We were escorted out the main gate, onto the street. I could see trees! After two months, I could see trees and real people. I took a couple of deep breaths and the air was clean and felt good, not stale and stench-ridden. I was so happy, I wanted to laugh and hug Bob. Then my eyes moved to the loading area for the prisoners. We were being put into camper vans, pickup trucks, cars, and buses with "Yuma State Prison" printed across the side in big, bold letters. Were we being transported in United States-owned vehicles from one Mexican prison to another? Again I asked myself why the United States was so involved within the borders of Mexico.

Bob and I had a chance to stand around for a few moments before we were loaded. "Hey," Bob said, "this is really starting to bum me out. The American Consulate can't even spare the time to talk with us, yet they can lend them transport buses." Standing a few feet away from us were two blond men. At first glance, I thought one was Anderson, but closer inspection revealed they were strangers. No one was watching me too closely, so I took another chance and moved toward the two men.

"Excuse me, sir, could you please tell me how long it will take us to reach Nogales?" I asked as politely as I could under the circumstances.

Both men looked at me curiously for a moment; then one said, "Oh, about seven to twelve hours; it depends on how fast we can travel." Then he asked, "Are you an American?"

"Yes," I answered. "Are you guys with the state prison?" Both men were wearing holstered side arms.

"No, we're customs," he answered in a friendly manner. "We help transfer and guard the prisoners occasionally." I thanked them and moved back to where Bob was standing. I was too mad to say anything for a long while.

Bob and I were not as lucky as the prisoners who were herded onto the buses. The ones in the buses were from the group that had been drugged. We were thrown into the back of yet another open pickup truck, with eight Mexicans, like cattle. Two Mexicans in plain clothes guarded us with AR-15 rifles. A driver and an armed guard sat in the cab of the truck. The caravan started up and pulled out, with our truck positioned somewhere towards the center.

We moved out of the desert and headed towards the mountainous terrain. The temperature dropped and I, in my ragged shirt, started to shiver and my teeth chattered. My hands burned from the tightness of my ropes. Bob's hands were beginning to turn a bluish color. We stopped only once to gas up and for the guards and drivers to eat. One of the guards bought some tortillas and decided to share some with Bob. While we stood up in the back of the truck stretching our legs, the guard motioned for Bob to open his mouth. Bob opened his mouth and the guard shoved a whole tortilla into his mouth and halfway down his throat. Bob gagged and started to choke as he tried to spit the tortilla out. The guard laughed and sprayed Bob with a hot, shook-up Coca-Cola.

Moments before leaving the gas and food stop, a group of young Mexicans came running out of the shadows. They threw stones at the transport vehicles as the Mexican prisoners cheered. I was told the young Mexicans were yelling in Spanish, "Anything we can do for the prisoners, we will help!" The Federales shot a few bursts of gunfire in the direction of the young Mexicans as they ran back into the shadows. I was starting to see some of the political undercurrents in Mexico. The guards hurriedly started up the engines and pulled out onto the road.

It was dawn before we reached the city of Nogales. It was early September, and the chill in the mountain air made me shiver uncontrollably. As we moved through the mountainous area with small dwellings strewn along the way, I was looking forward to seeing the big, new Nogales prison. The caravan drove into a more populated area of the city, bumped down deserted city streets, and stopped in a parking lot next to an old concrete building.

Chapter Sixteen

If all my nightmares of the past, present, and future were ever combined and thrown into one place, it would be in the old Nogales prison. To believe that anything could possibly be worse than what I had experienced in the past two months would have been unthinkable. And here, in the old Nogales prison, the unthinkable was real. The structure, built to hold a maximum of 250 prisoners, was crammed to overflowing with five to six hundred prisoners. Its shape was a box-like configuration that was approximately forty yards long and twenty yards wide at its widest point. The walls were not bleached white as in San Luis, but were a dismal gray and dull green.

There were only thirty cells in the entire prison, with half of them on a tiered level that formed a semi-circle around the top of the prison, overlooking the cement-floored courtyard. More than half of the prisoners were crammed into those eight-by-twelve cells. When we arrived, there were only ten Americans surviving in the prison. There was only one cell set aside for Americans, and only seven prisoners lived in that cell. The other three lived in the courtyard of the prison, on the concrete, in the rain and snow and 100-degree heat. Brad, Bob, and I were to share the fate of those three Americans on the concrete.

To get into the old Nogales prison, a person had to enter the Nogales police station and walk down a long corridor until reaching an iron-barred door. The police station was the front of the prison. To the right of the barred door was the office of the corrupt prison director, Chentana. Chentana was a large, heavy-set man with white hair, who wore Western clothes. He did not speak any English. Chentana was also addicted to heroin. Behind the iron-barred door was a small two-story courtyard, about fifteen square yards. The courtyard and the rooms on the second level, overlooking the courtyard, were occupied by wealthier Mexicans who could afford to pay Chentana for the privilege of not having to live in the prison proper. These wealthier Mexicans were called *trustees*. Trustees not only kept their privileges by paying Chentana, they also enforced the prison rules. They kept the poorer prisoners in the prison proper, took roll call, manned the guard towers, and enforced Chentana's law. In other words, in order to gain privileges, the trustees took on the roles of guard, stool pigeon, and rat. For money, a man could do most anything in the old Nogales prison.

The drunk tanks were located at the rear of the trustee's courtyard and were similar to the jail cells in San Luis. To the right of the courtyard were two large, barred doors made of steel, a small corridor in between, two more sets of the barred doors, and the prison proper, where the five hundred to six hundred men, who could not pay for anything better, were kept. No Americans were allowed to live with the trustees.

I couldn't believe I was in the long-awaited Nogales prison. The section for the trustees was worse than the prison in San Luis. A sickening dread swept through my body. We were roughly pushed through the first set of doors that led to our new home.

The prison proper, the section of the prison for the poor, insane, dangerous, and Americans, was in a state of decay. The forty-foot-high walls were filthy and pockmarked with broken plaster. The prison reminded me of an alley in the slums of an ancient city. At its widest point, it was only twenty feet across, and was about nine feet at its narrowest point. There was also chicken wire stretched over the top, to crisscross the sky, and a guard tower at each end of our alley. As we entered, most of the prisoners were asleep and everything was quiet. We had the opportunity to walk around and survey our new surroundings unmolested. On the far right side of the prison, as one entered the steel doors, were the two cement-holed toilets and one urinal for the hundreds of prisoners. Next to the bathroom was the one cell designated for Americans. The smell at this location was the rankest in the prison.

On the far left, directly opposite the toilets, was a small chapel, and to the left of the chapel was a room for distributing food. A shower area with four spigots was located halfway down the prison alley. The walls of the shower area were covered with green slime, and feces floated in the pungent water on the shower's floor. Across from the shower area were the only stairs leading to the upper level. Clotheslines with tattered garments covering them stretched everywhere from that level.

The gloominess and stench were the most prominent forces in the prison. Bob, Brad, and I walked back to the toilets to relieve ourselves. I had to hold my breath to keep from gagging. A fat, sparsely bearded man in his early twenties, wearing a floppy hillbilly hat, was standing outside the toilet room as we emerged.

"Are you guys Americans?" he asked Brad.

"Sure are," Brad answered, staring straight at the man's hat.

"Whew, are we glad to see you guys." He broke into a grin. "There are only ten of us here, and we sure do need the reinforcements. You can't believe how bad things have been."

"Where are the rest of the Americans?" I asked eagerly.

"Oh, they're over there in cell number one" he answered. "The one right there next to the john." He pointed to the cell. "They're the lucky ones," he continued. "At least they're locked in at night and the junkies can't get to them. The three of us out in the open have been the buffer zone. When the junkies attack, we have no cell to run to and have to fight them off. We have no choice, actually. We've got to stick real close together or we've had it. Those bastards in the cell have really got it made, though. You guys will stay with us out here, so keep alert and be careful!" The fat man had a habit of bouncing nervously from side to side as he talked.

"How do we get into a cell?" Bob asked.

"You have to wait your turn," he answered. "Those who have been here the longest go in as one person leaves. We all have to do our time on the outside."

"How long have you been here?" I asked as I watched him bounce.

"About two months," he replied, looking over his shoulder. His name was Charles Raney and he was from Idaho. Charlie claimed he weighed 350 pounds when he was arrested and was down to about 280 pounds now. He was not a tall man. He was arrested with two other men for "a couple of kilos" of marijuana. Charlie explained that he had never smuggled before, but was just trying to "make some fast bucks."Charlie then led us over to two sleeping men lying on ragged blankets. He carefully woke the men up, so as not to startle them, and introduced us. They seemed excited to see three more of their countrymen. Carl Mayweather and Arthur Johnson had been arrested with Charlie. Arthur was a large, muscular African-American man, also from Idaho. Carl was a thin, mild-mannered African-American college student and former Vietnam medic from Washington State. Both men were in their early twenties.

The three men explained the conditions of the prison to us. It was still early morning, and the cells were locked so we were in little danger, but as soon as the cells were unlocked, they expected trouble. Heroin was rampant in the prison, but there was little money. The majority of the Mexican prisoners were severely addicted to heroin, having been incarcerated for years. The only way to maintain their heroin habit was to extort money or steal, and the Americans were considered the most lucrative targets. Chentana was behind the sale of the heroin, so there was no protection from the prison officials.

At first, the leader of the junkies, a man named Pancho, was satisfied with extorting money in the form of protection fees and a *talache* fee, which kept the payer from having to clean the toilets. Recently, however, the protection fees kept getting more and more exorbitant. Pancho was asking in excess of $40 per man every month. The few Americans had taken a stand and refused to pay any more money. The situation was tense, but so far only a few fistfights had broken out. We, the new Americans, would be the test case. We were broke and could not pay the demands, and the other Americans, as a group, also insisted that we not pay. Charlie figured all hell would break loose. The San Luis prison was looking better to me with each passing moment!

At sunrise trustees who entered our side of the prison unlocked the cell doors. Slowly, the courtyard began to fill with inmates, milling around and talking. At first, no one seemed to notice us, but eventually, small groups of Mexican prisoners began to form. They would point in our direction as they talked amongst themselves. The smaller groups melted into larger ones. All attention seemed to be riveted towards us. We tried to stay as close to the American cell as possible. No Americans had yet emerged from that cell.

Then, it began. Some eighty inmates came rushing in our direction. Screaming, angry Mexicans immediately surrounded Brad, Bob, and me. Charlie flung his large body onto the crowd while Arthur and Carl tried to pull the Mexicans from us. Hands, fingers, and faces waved angrily before me. It was like being in the middle of an asylum—people screaming, pulling on me, jostling me from one person to the next. I was surrounded and being swallowed by a sea of irate Mexicans. I was pulled, along with the other new Americans, from the safety of the American area. Hands tore at my ragged shirt as a fist jammed into my back. I struggled but was overwhelmed. The noise of my attackers drowned out my screaming curses. I saw Charlie fall, dragging several Mexicans with him.

Then the Americans from the cell, led by a large redheaded man, attacked the rear of the mob, hacking at them with fists. The mob wavered. A few wild blows from a fist caught me in the head, and then I was left alone. The mob had suddenly backed off to confront the redhead and other Americans from the cell. The redheaded man, approximately six foot four and muscular with a thick red beard, spoke to Pancho and the mob in broken Spanish. He insisted that no more money would be paid to supply the junkies with heroin. Pancho threatened him and the mob waved their fists in the air, only to sulk away after a few moments. And just like that, it was over.

I was shaken and still recovering when the man who saved us came over and introduced himself. He was a Canadian who had been arrested four months earlier with a few grams of hashish. He was the largest of the American group and the appointed leader. His name was Richard MacDonald. The Americans all seemed irritable and jumpy, and their eyes had a wild look to them. They had sunken eyes with dark rings underneath, as if blackened from a fight or the result of months without sleep.

I soon met a tall American with short dark hair named John Putman. He had been arrested in San Luis three months earlier on "unknown charges." There was Rick Morris, a thin, quiet man in his late twenties with thinning blond hair. Rick, a Vietnam veteran, had a plane crash in the Mexican desert. He had walked to a Federale station to report the incident, where he met up with none other than my pal, Anderson. Anderson and some Federales drove to the site of the plane crash. The plane was empty, but Rick was being held for investigation. There was Bob Lee, a balding man in his mid-thirties, who had been a bartender in Arizona. Bob had been caught with a few kilos of marijuana. There was also Pete, a surfer in his early twenties. Pete was charged with possession of seven marijuana seeds found in the back of his camper truck. I also met two other Americans, Rick Herrick and Gary Don Burke, both married men who owned a flight school near Bakersfield, California. Someone had offered them some big money to make a quick flight into Mexico to pick up a load of marijuana. On the way back to the States, they developed engine trouble in their DC-3. Gary, who piloted the plane, attempted to make an emergency landing on what he thought was an empty road. When the plane neared the ground, they realized that they were flying into the middle of a Mexican street dance! The plane whirled sideways and between some high voltage wires, couldn't gain altitude, hit the ground, and flipped over. No one was hurt, but soldiers and the Mexicans attending the street dance had to dig Gary and Rick out from underneath their load of marijuana. All they had wanted was some quick, easy cash. Instead, they got Nogales.

A mixed bunch of very unprofessional smugglers, soldiers of misfortune, and victims inhabited the American section of the prison.

The atmosphere in the prison was tense, but by breakfast, things seemed to be calming down. Arthur, the muscular African-American, told us they served an oatmeal-like gruel in the mornings, which could be forced down if a person was hungry enough. Carl, the African-American medic, scrounged us up some rusty bowls. We headed down to the other end of the prison, to the food room, and away from the safety of the American cell. There were five of us: Bob Smith, Carl, Arthur, Brad, and myself. We were nervous; the further we moved away from our end of the prison, the more restless and angry the Mexicans appeared. The Mexicans needed their heroin and would kill for it. Suddenly, Arthur grabbed at his throat with both hands and made a choking noise. He had been hit in the throat by a soup bone thrown full-force at him. Arthur rushed at the Mexican who had thrown the bone and crashed his powerful fist into the man's mouth, scattering teeth. Arthur started swinging wildly as fifty or more Mexicans came rushing at us from behind. Glass bottles came crashing down from the upper level of the prison into the middle of our shabby group of Americans. The five of us were by ourselves, cut off from the other Americans. My stomach tightened; I thought I would be sick. My throat became dry and sweat poured from my body. It seemed like I had lost my hearing except for a loud buzzing in my ears. I tried to dodge flying bottles and broken glass, but it did not seem as if my body remembered how to react quickly. It was like I was in slow motion. My vision distorted and everything took on a surreal appearance. As the Mexicans rushed us, I knew there were other Americans by my side, but I still felt totally alone. Knives and other sharp objects in the hands of the Mexicans pushed towards me. I knew I was going to be stabbed, and I wanted it to hurry up and get over with. A bottle crashed down in a blur, and I saw someone drop next to me. I rushed into the mass of Mexicans and gleaming knives to get it over with—an act not thought out, just an automatic response. Dazed, I saw a knife glint, and I knew it would connect my stomach. I thought I felt my side tear. I'm not sure what happened. Everything in my vision seemed to blur and turn gray.

When my eyes focused again, I realized I was holding a small wooden bench in my right hand. The junkies had halted briefly to regroup for another assault as Pancho was yelling orders. We had retreated halfway to the American cell. All five of us were still together and we were relatively unhurt. I looked down at my body and felt myself for blood. There were a few scratches, but nothing serious. I didn't remember picking up the wooden bench. In my stupor, I must have grabbed it and beat my way through the mob of junkies.

The Americans from the cell came running up from behind us with glass bottles in their hands. They hurled the weapons into the mass of Mexicans before they made another charge. As the bottles collided with walls or iron bars, the glass shattered in all directions, slicing through the air and cutting prisoners who were unfortunate to be in the way. Several Mexicans fell beneath the shattering glass, blood on their faces and backs.

A few junkies began backing up the steps, but we had no chance against the two hundred or more of them who would be in the next attack. I looked at the faces of the other Americans, frightened men who found themselves in a situation where they had no control. I wondered if my friends at home would even know if I was dead or if they would miss me. I did want to be missed. I was readying myself for the attack, pondering my morbid thoughts, when I saw Chentana rush into the prison with the trustees. They had clubs and appeared as if they were about to break up the riot. I heard someone laughing and realized it was me. Others cried tears of relief. We had held off fifty or more junkies, and now it was over. We were cheering as a loud rumbling noise rolled through the prison; two trustees fell, cut and bleeding. The junkies, hundreds of them, not just the few who fought us, attacked the trustees.

Bottles hurtled through the air as the trustees tried to drag the wounded from the melee, and Chentana yelled in Spanish to Pancho, "All right, if you want to kill the Americans, go ahead. They're nothing but trouble anyhow!" He whirled around angrily and rushed out.

My entire body screamed. I was standing in the middle of the courtyard with three other Americans: Bob Lee, Pete, and Rick Morris. The rest of the Americans just weren't there. The guards were gone … the guards were gone! The Mexicans came at us, a wild screaming mob. We threw bottles into the mass, but it seemed as if they were just swallowed up. I was out of breath, yet I hadn't run a step. I was trembling all over. Glass and bottles smashed all around us. We sprinted for the cell, but it was locked shut.

"Open the cell you motherfuckers," we screamed. "Open the cell or we'll kill you!" In their fear, the other Americans had forgotten us and locked us out. The four of us were outside, and it was no longer just fifty junkies—it was the whole prison coming down to seek revenge on the hated gringos.

A knife plunged into Bob Lee's back. He let out a dull shriek, lost his footing, and fell to the ground. The buzzing noise returned to my ears. I was kicking at them, beating the mass with the bench again. My back was pressed against the locked cell door. I was yelling. I saw a Mexican's face open up … red. Suddenly I fell into the cell with Pete and Rick. The Americans inside had managed to pull us to safety.

"Someone has to get Bob, for Christ's sake! We can't leave him out there!" I pleaded desperately. The door was open again. What the hell was I doing outside again? Richard swung at the junkies like a madman as Pete grabbed Bob and dragged him into the cell. I think I was screaming. And then we were back inside and safe—or were we?

Gasoline splashed against the cell door and pieces of glass sprayed inward. We put an old mattress in front of the door to shield us from the glass, but the junkies set fire to it. All of us in the cell were in a panic, shouting wild orders at each other. At times, one of more of us would get hysterical and become momentarily useless, but together we managed to get the door safely barricaded and the fire extinguished. Bob Lee was hurt but not too bad. It was three days before the junkies calmed down enough for Pancho to talk over terms with us. In the end, we agreed to meet all the demands he made. Those of us who could not pay at once would pay in installments. This was our introduction, our welcome to the old Nogales prison.

Chapter Seventeen

Pancho and the junkies never stopped harassing us. We had to be totally alert and aware twenty-four hours each day. Even when we tried to write letters or read, we had to constantly watch for thieves or for objects being hurled at us. It was exhausting, especially in an environment where one did not wish to be aware. At night, while we slept, the junkies would stealthily slit our pants pockets with razor blades and search them for valuables with a thin wire. If you glanced in an opposite direction, your food or a blanket would be missing. Often the stress would become so intense that some of us would space out. We were stuck in a bizarre, surrealistic world. Except, it was real.

So in our spaced out condition, we would wander around the prison like robots. We appeared tired and slow-witted, as if we were never sure what was happening. We all got spaced out occasionally and were more vulnerable during these times. The junkies could spot it in a moment. On one occasion, Carl had wandered out into the courtyard with a book he had found. He was excited about having a book written in English and sat down to read it, blotting out the horrible place he was in now. He hadn't been sitting for more than a minute when plastic bags full of puke splattered down on top of his head and over his body. The showers had been cut off, so he had to remain like that for a week. When heroin is strong, it often causes the user to vomit. The junkies would vomit into plastic bags and save it to throw on us.

Chentana had a system for smuggling the heroin into the prison. Each Tuesday and Thursday was visitor's day in the old Nogales prison. On these days, a large pig would be inspected and delivered to a designated pusher of Chentana's inside the prison. This prisoner who received the pig (the Butcher, as we called him) would carve the pig, cook it, and sell the meat—*carne*—and pigskin—*chicharones*—to visitors and prisoners at a high price. The heroin was coming into the prison in the entrails of the pig. The butcher would take the heroin out, divide it into eighty-cent shots, and give it to his main distributor in the prison, the rat-faced Pancho. The junkies did not harass the Butcher too often, because they knew it would anger Chentana and Pancho and endanger the drug supply.

Chentana made a double killing: he profited from the heroin and from the sale of hog meat. It was rumored that Chentana owned a hotel, several restaurants, a clothes store, and a fleet of cars. He had a captive market and the perfect population to addict to heroin. The heroin helped pass the time and numb the intolerable conditions. It also caused many good men to turn into animals. No one cared about the prisoners.

Weeks passed. Bob and I tried to adjust to the Nogales prison as we had done in San Luis, but we couldn't. Every morning was a new episode of ongoing nightmares; we never got used to the conditions. I received a few letters from my family and friends. They were still trying their best to get me out. My parents were still going the legal route, and Lee Walton was attempting to contact political help. Sometimes, a few dollars would come with a letter, and I could buy a piece of bread before getting robbed by the junkies. The mail system was sporadic: sometimes we would receive all of our mail; other times it would be opened and the enclosed money gone. Still other times we wouldn't get our letters at all.

Telephone calls were more frequent in the Nogales prison. Chentana wanted people to receive calls so they could plead for money. In some ways, the phone calls were cruel. The people who called did not know how horrible the conditions in the prison were, or the negative effects of hearing their happy encouraging voice. I would be guarding my rags from the junkies, weak, scared and confused, when I would be called to Chentana's office. I would be led to the phone, where a guard with a Winchester 30-30 would point the rifle at my head. Often, a vaguely familiar voice on the other end of the phone would say, "Hey, Steve, how are things? We are just here having a party and we started talking about you and the good old times, so we decided to try and call, and sure enough, there you are! We'll drink a beer for you, old buddy. Hang in there!" The people who called would then put strangers on the phone, who would wish me well or say they had heard so much about me … or women who wanted to date me after I got out. The voices over the phone were not real to me. They caused too much pain. I couldn't even cry for the voices. With a gun at my head I couldn't explain what was really happening to me yet, I often wanted to scream, "You fools! Don't you know what is happening to me? Can't you see I'm decaying here?" But I told them I was okay or kept quiet. After I received letters or the phone calls, my heart would ache and I would cry myself to sleep at night, trying to remember what it was like before.

A representative from the American Consulate showed up approximately two weeks after the riot occurred. The representative was in his mid-twenties, slight of build, and had sandy brown hair and glasses. The Americans were led to Chentana's office to talk to him one at a time.

Prior to any contact with the American Consulate, I had a romantic view of this U.S. office. I had read about the heroic efforts of Consulate officials trying to aid Americans in trouble in several novels and had seen the consul represented as a noble agent of Americans abroad in movies. I was about to have a childhood conception, and my hopes, smashed.

As I approached the representative of the American Consulate, I noticed he seemed edgy and irritable. I was not a criminal, but I certainly must have looked the part. I took the representative's negative attitude to be caused by my dissipated appearance, but what should he expect? I had been living under the vilest conditions for almost three months.

"Are you Wilson?" he asked as an accusation.

"Yes, I am," I answered shakily, staring at him.

"Listen, you bastard," he sneered. "I don't know who you are or what you think you're doing, but you better not try to make us look bad." When he finished blurting this unexpected comment, I was totally dumbfounded.

"What are you talking about?" I asked, honestly confused.

"You or your friends got Senator Irvin to call us and ask what in the hell was going on down here," he hissed at me. "He wanted to know why we hadn't contacted you and if we could expedite your case."

I was flattered to hear this, relieved, and proud of my friends and their efforts. I suddenly became lost in my own thoughts as this man continued his admonishments. "Listen you." He grabbed me by the shirt, startling me back to the present. "You make waves for us, you make us look bad, and there's no telling what will happen to you. You could be killed in there by another prisoner any day or we could register a complaint to the Mexican officials and there's no telling how harsh your sentence would be!"

I pushed his hand from my shirt. This was not what I had expected. I started to ask a question about Mexican law, but he cut me short.

"Buddy, I can't stand here and talk to you all day. Do you think I like coming here? I've got a wife sitting out in the car in hair curlers. Now, get out of here so I can listen to the rest of you troublemakers."

The American consul never helped me or gave me any advice other than to keep my mouth shut. Most of the American prisoners refused to speak with the consul representatives after a few meetings because of their attitude. They were rude, depressing, and degrading. Their attitude was basically 'you got what you deserved so take it like a man.' Guilty or not guilty, they considered most of the prisoners in Mexico to be longhaired hippie types and strictly low priority. The American Consulate was not about to be bothered with hippies' civil rights.

The DEA and the State Department had made it clear to Mexican police officials that the United States was willing to subsidize them to beat and jail American Citizens. (I was later told that the American government was paying the Mexican government approximately $10 per day for every American prisoner held. The Mexican government paid only 4 cents per prisoner. Arresting Americans was definitely a promising investment!) The Mexicans interpreted this as an official license to hunt down and treat Americans any damn way they pleased. It had escalated to the point where every American involved in a minor auto accident was handled as a major criminal. A great number of Americans in Mexican prisons were being held on non-drug charges, many of them for refusing to pay bills after an argument over inflated repair charges. Of 130 imprisoned Americans investigated by the State Department, only six had ever been involved in narcotics before their arrest on drug charges; obviously, the men sentenced to prison were not the professional traffickers the DEA claimed it was putting out of business.

Person's accused of possessing drugs received the greatest abuse by Mexican and American officials. The State Department did not investigate when an American claimed he had been beaten into signing a confession in a language he didn't know or understand. Nor did the State Department advise prisoners of their rights in Mexico or provide interpreters. The DEA and the State Department were working hand in hand in Mexico; it wasn't by accident that the DEA headquarters in Mexico City is in the American Embassy building. Often, the representatives from the State Department were clerks or held secretarial positions, and they had no knowledge of Mexican legal procedures. They took turns coming to Mexico to do their shopping, begrudgingly see the prisoners, and leave. It was a rare occasion when I saw a Consulate representative more than once. The procedure of sending a different person each time helped add to our paranoia and confusion.

My parents had contacted the State Department. In a letter they told me the State Department denied charges of neglect to the families of the prisoners. They claimed that appropriate measures were taken to insure that all Americans imprisoned abroad were protected from maltreatment. Yet the State Department also claimed allegations of mistreatment were unsubstantiated. The recurring theme of the State Department was "American prisoners are felons, and you can't believe a felon."

For the families, too, it was difficult to believe the word of someone arrested for drugs, even when there was no prior history of drug abuse or use. A person accused of possessing drugs instantly loses his creditability. Most people refused to believe a U.S. citizen could be imprisoned without just cause. Senators and political officials seemed to wash their hands of any person accused of drug charges because it was politically dangerous.

Senator Irvin told my parents the DEA admitted that a lot of the Americans who served jail terms would never have been arrested in Mexico were it not for DEA pressure. The narcotics agency preferred to have people arrested in Mexico because Mexican laws are tougher. The Mexicans gave U.S. citizens six years in cases that would be thrown out of American courts. In many ways, the DEA used Mexican officials and the court to act as front men in subverting the American constitution—and this was supported by the State Department.

It was the other prisoners and a few Mexican guards who attempted to brief me on Mexican court procedures, not the Consulate or my Mexican lawyer. I discovered that the Mexican court procedure involves a series of steps and the signing of documents. The accused is guilty until proven innocent in Mexico. He never has the opportunity to represent himself in court, nor does he see a judge or jury. Each prisoner needed to hire a lawyer "to hurry the paperwork along" Court secretaries processed the papers, but the accused was not shown a copy. We had no idea of the content of these papers. The Mexican constitution reads that each person must complete the trial within a year. There did not appear to be any consequences when that did not happen, so many people who could not afford to have their paperwork speeded up remained in prison for several years before their trial was completed.

Most of the Mexican lawyers did not provide a defense for their clients. The prisoner was told to plead guilty and not to anger the judge, thereby leaving himself at the mercy of the judge. Prisoners who pleaded not guilty seemed to be found guilty with the optimum sentence. The amount of bribe money that could be paid was usually the determining factor in a man's innocence or guilt.

Every few months, a secretary who supposedly represented the Mexican court would come to the prison. He would tell us that such-and-such step was completed in our trial and we must sign his papers or the trial would go on indefinitely. The trial consisted of approximately seven steps. All of the documents for each step were in Spanish. They appeared to be just a page for our signature stating we were aware that a step was completed but there was never an interpreter or lawyer present when these documents were brought to us. As with the content of the papers, we had no idea what comprised these steps.

The final step we were told was the *audencia*. The complete amount of evidence found against the accused, together with his defense, was documented and submitted to a judge. The judge would read the charges and make his decision without ever hearing from the accuser or seeing and hearing the accused. According to the Mexican legal system, the judge had three weeks to sentence a man after the audencia was presented. One day, sometimes after years of waiting, a prisoner would be notified that his trial was over, and he would either be sentenced or released. Many times a man was found not guilty after spending two years or more in prison.

Waiting for each step of the farce that was our trial, and the frustration of having no input into the system that was deciding our future, wore on our nerves. Although we needed and depended on each other, we Americans often argued or fought amongst ourselves. It was the frustration and the hopelessness that gave us a tense, agitated, searching attitude. We were frightened, but not frightened of death. I knew that if things became too bad, I would die, and it was not the thought of death that made me feel sad. It was a fear of this existence. It was the thought of never again being able to see or touch the people and things I dreamed of and remembered. I dreamed every day, through the fights and sickness: I dreamed about going home. I knew that each day I was getting weaker and my chances of ever finding those dreams were getting slimmer. It made me almost want to die because it hurt so bad knowing the Mexicans could take those dreams from me at any second, snuffing me like a bug. In a way, I did die a little each day. Yet I didn't cry, although an occasional tear would run down my cheek, like a last drop of hope escaping from my body. The American Consulate brought one of those tears.

Chapter Eighteen

The old Nogales prison was located in the mountains, and the temperature dropped a few degrees each day. Winter was coming. I had no warm clothes. During the third week, we felt our trial would soon begin. Bob's mother hired a Mexican lawyer for him called Hermanez. Together, Hermanez and Alfonso Garcia Gallegas, the lawyer my parents had hired, whom I had never seen except for his hand through prison bars at San Luis, finally called us into the trustee's courtyard. I didn't trust Gallegas and would have dismissed him immediately if my parents had not already paid him.

Neither lawyer spoke English, but they did manage to assure us that they would bring warm clothes. We begged to bring someone over to interpret, and eventually they agreed. Gallegas wanted me to plead guilty to whatever I was charged with and pay the fine levied by the judge at the conclusion of the trial. I couldn't bring myself to plead guilty to something I hadn't done, so I absolutely refused. Gallegas argued, became angry, and refused to talk to me after a few moments. He stormed out of the prison, threatening to never come back again. Bob reluctantly said he would plead guilty and was assured by Hermanez that he would receive no more than a heavy fine. I looked over at Bob and noticed he was trembling. At least our papers were being processed and we would possibly be getting warm clothes.

That same afternoon, I was called into the trustee's courtyard again. Jesus Amaya, my uncle's friend from Hawaii, was waiting for me in Chentana's office. Amaya assured me that he had been to Mexico City and bribed the proper Mexican officials. He claimed to have talked to the judge and said we would be transferred to a better prison in another state within the week. I wanted to believe him terribly but I couldn't; it was just too much bullshit. He had absolutely no knowledge of the Mexican court procedures. He couldn't remember the name of the judge, and even I knew we could not be transferred to another prison in another state without holding up our court procedure for months. But I was in a condition of deterioration where I wanted to believe anything was possible. I was desperate, grasping at any hope, yet I knew that Amaya was the worst kind of thief. He was preying on my uncle and my parents, as well as my helplessness. He used my inability to communicate with my family to his benefit.

Amaya paid Chentana some money, dialed a collect call, and handed me the phone. On the other end of the line was my Uncle Buck. He asked if I was all right and if Amaya had explained all he had done for me. In fact, my uncle had paid $3,000 for Amaya to visit with me twice and tell his lies. I attempted to tell my uncle that I couldn't understand how the things Amaya claimed could be possible, but my uncle was clinging to any hope and was not willing to believe that he threw away his hard-earned money. My uncle told me to stay calm and assured me it would only be a matter of time. Chentana took the phone from my hand and hung it up.

Amaya left me standing in the office for a few moments while he went to get another man. He returned with a white-haired man in his mid-forties who was introduced as "a big lawyer from Mexico City." Since the court procedures took months, I couldn't understand how a lawyer could take on a case 1,200 miles from his office. When I questioned Amaya about the lawyer, I was told he was doing it as a personal favor.

Amaya left with his lawyer friend. I never saw Amaya again. I was not transferred to another prison in another state. I was not released. I waited three days for word from Amaya, three long, tense days. I was sitting huddled in a corner by the toilet room when I got a phone call from my mother. I walked hurriedly to the gate leading to Chentana's office. My mother told me Amaya's lawyer friend contacted her. Amaya had to return to Hawaii, but everything was arranged, and the lawyer friend would tie up the loose ends. Bob and I were to go to court in three more days. The judge had agreed to release both of us, but only into the custody of our parents, and we were never to return to Mexico. I couldn't believe what I was hearing. I wanted to scream for joy. My mother's excitement was so reassuring that I hated myself for not believing in miracles and doubting Amaya. My mother and Bob's mother were going to fly to Tuscon, Arizona, rent a car, and drive to Nogales, Arizona. Amaya's lawyer friend had arranged everything. They would stay on the United States side until the day of the trial and then pick us up at the courthouse to take us home. *Home!* Heaven! We would be going home in three days. The nightmare would be over. My mother sobbed her happiness into the receiver; my eyes were glazed with tears. When I hung up the phone, Chentana grabbed my arm.

"*No es Avagados o licentiados,*" he leered through a crooked smile. "Your friends are robbers. They aren't lawyers or licensed to act as lawyers in court." Chentana's crooked smile broke into a big, evil grin.

No, it can't be true, I thought frantically. *No one could be that cruel. It has to be one of Chentana's mind games to confuse us.*

I pushed my way through the junkies as I returned to our section of the prison and told Bob about the phone conversation and Chentana's warning. Both of us refused to believe the promise of freedom was anything but true. My joy returned. We were going home! Chentana was a junkie rat.

Bob and I circulated through the prison, joyously telling our story to the other Americans. They were jealous and angry that they were not being released, but they were also happy for us.

"It is good to see anyone get out of this slimy hellhole alive," Charlie said sadly. "Maybe someday it will be me." Bob Lee, the bartender, and Richard Mac-Donald, the Canadian, offered us some marijuana to use as a celebration. We refused. That's all I needed was to get caught with grass a few days before my release. Marijuana sold in the prison for about $40 a pound and was constantly available.

The next three days were almost unbearable. All we had to do was hang on. By the third day, I had bitten off all of my fingernails and paced constantly. I hadn't slept for two days. Today was the day!

Bob and I stared at each other, trying to will it to happen. I wanted to cry out, yet I was afraid to say anything for fear we would not be called to court. By mid-afternoon Bob and I were frantic. By evening we were hysterical. We weren't called. Something was wrong!

Amaya, Amaya, you rotten louse, my mind screamed. How could anyone be so low? I didn't sleep that night, either. I was a madman. My body shook and trembled. No one, not even the junkies, dared come near me that night. I had taken several steps closer to the edge.

The following morning again brought hope.

"Maybe today. Maybe today," Bob and I mumbled to ourselves. Then, just before noon, our names were called. Our blood pounded in our ears as we headed towards the gate and the trustees' courtyard. This was it! We were on our first lap home. The other Americans escorted us to the gate, shaking our hands. They sadly said good-bye to us. I felt guilty for leaving them behind, and found it tough to look them in the eyes. I was lightheaded all the way to Chentana's office. Standing in the courtyard were both of our mothers. Their eyes were puffed and red as if they had been crying, and I knew everything was wrong. My dream of freedom came crashing down around me.

My mother was not with Amaya's lawyer, but with Alfonso Garcia Gallegas. She looked sad, frightened, and crushed as she stood there with two bags of groceries in her hands, glancing from one prisoner to another, trying to recognize her own son. She looked directly at me but didn't know who I was. I was ashamed. I had forgotten how badly I looked and smelled. I didn't want her to see me this way. I didn't want anyone to ever see me this way. I was decayed; I was sick. I wanted to turn and run from her sight. My own mother didn't recognize me. Oh God, what had I become?

I took a few tentative steps in her direction and tried to say "Mom," but I could only mouth the word silently. I tried to put a smile on my face without bursting into tears. My mother looked at the wretched thing barely clothed in rags, eyes sunken, extremely thin, moving towards her, and then she saw that it was Steve, her son. Our eyes met and she managed to breathe, "Oh, my God," before her body was racked with sobs. I ran to her, wanting to hug her and stop her hurt, yet I was too filthy and ashamed to hug her. She dropped the bags and threw her arms around me anyhow, trying to talk through hysterical sobs.

"It was all a trick," she sobbed. "They aren't going to let you go! Amaya's friend was not a lawyer. He demanded $15,000 more from us after we got here. We spent all the money we had left on plane fare. What will we do? What will we do?"

I held her. "Don't cry, Mom. Please don't cry," was all I could manage to choke out. Bob and I stood in the middle of the courtyard, comforting our sobbing mothers amongst the junkies. We were two men and two mothers with no hope and no money, swallowed up and lost in a nightmare without end.

After my mother realized Amaya's lawyer was attempting to con her and Bob's mother out of more money, she tearfully went to Alfonso Garcia Gallegas. Gallegas assured them that we were in good legal hands—his—and took them to the prison "for only a small fee." My mother brought a pair of sneakers for me, along with a shirt, pants, socks, underwear, and a large bag of groceries. Bob's mother had the same for him. It was one of the hardest things I ever had to do—maintain myself with my sobbing mother. I wanted to scream, yell, tear someone apart with my hands … especially Amaya. The longer I held the hatred in, the more broken and crushed my spirit became. It was even more difficult to watch my mother leave, looking so small and timid, wondering why all of this had happened.

The worst thing now was that my mother knew the truth. She saw where I was being held and the conditions of my confinement. She realized that this imprisonment was not like being held in an American prison. It was the gate of hell, and her son was being treated worse than an animal. I wanted so much to leave and go with her. She and Bob's mom were led away, still crying, by the police and Gallegas. I didn't think I would ever see her again. When my mother left, everything left. I felt myself becoming detached and my body taking on a numbness I knew would last forever.

Chapter Nineteen

Bob and I stood staring at the gate. Now we had to deal with the junkies. It would be very difficult to get back into our section of the prison with our new clothes and groceries. Already the junkies were crowding the interior gate, waiting for our return. We picked up the bags and were led back to the gates. The junkies were reaching through the bars and screaming at us like rabid animals. The gate opened. I was larger than Bob, so I went first. The junkies leapt at me, pulling on the bags. I kicked and bit, still clinging to my packages, and tried to charge my way through the mob. A bag tore and plums scattered onto the ground. Some of the junkies pounced on the fruit, giving me a chance to break out into the open and run towards the American cell. The Americans saw me coming and rushed to Bob's aid. Bob was surrounded. The junkies were ripping eagerly at his bags and tearing the food from them as the Americans crashed into the rear of the mob. There was a large scuffle but Bob got out unhurt with about a third of his things. The other Americans hadn't expected us back. They questioned us at first, but when they saw the disappointment and anguish in our eyes, they left us alone.

I was crushed. The depression that followed was like a weight that smashed me to the ground. I was beaten and drained. I became part of the shadows and walked in a gray darkness. I felt like the character Snowden in the novel *Catch 22*, as he lay on the floor of an airplane with his guts blown out, saying over and over, "Help me, I'm cold. Help me, I'm cold ..." And the whole time, it was too late. I had fire inside me that made me think that my guts would spill out. My will to survive was gone. There was nothing left to hope for.

Our court process continued, but it didn't seem to matter. I did not see Alfonso Garcia Gallegas again.

The weather became colder, and Brad gave me an army field jacket. My new clothes helped keep out the cold too. With the cold weather came the lice. At first the Americans inside the cell thought it was due to us living on the outside. They threw the ragged blankets we stored in their cell outside into the courtyard during the day and refused to let us take refuge in the cell. They soon discovered the entire prison was infested with lice. There was no hot water to destroy the vermin, and the shower water was turned on only a few times a week, so we simply had to tolerate the creatures. We learned to take cold showers in freezing weather to keep our bodies as clean as possible under the circumstances.

It was becoming too cold even for Chentana to leave the prisoners outside. He didn't care if we got soaked during the summer rains, when the drops plummeted down through the chicken wire, but he did not want a wave of pneumonia and sickness from the cold. Chentana could lose all of the prisoners and profits if there was an epidemic, so the outside prisoners were slowly crowded into the already overloaded cells, a few more each day.

Bob and I remained outside in the courtyard, waiting for our turn to enter the cell. The Americans in the cell bribed Chentana to let them bring a television into the prison. They also had to continue to pay a monthly rent in order to keep the television. We, on the outside, didn't get to see the television too often, because the Americans inside the cell didn't turn the set on in the daytime when we had access to the cell. They didn't want us staying at length in their overcrowded cell. Instead, they would wait until the door of their cell was locked, then watch TV through the night and cook popcorn on a kerosene stove. We, on the outside, had no means of escaping our reality. We started to hate the men on the inside of the cell. Didn't we guard them against the junkies at night? Yet they would not let us store anything in their cell. We had to pile our ragged blankets outside the cell door and position a man to guard them constantly. We could never relax or let our guard down. My reaction time slowed and I spaced out. The strain was too much for all of us.

Bob wandered off by himself a few days after his mother left. I can't imagine he cared much about the danger of being alone, or perhaps he was in a daze and just forgot what might happen to him. He wandered down to the other end of the prison, away from the American cell, in search of coffee. It was at least an hour before we realized he was gone. Frantically, Charlie, Arthur, Brad, Karl, and I went in search of him.

We found Bob lying face down in a gutter that ran the length of the prison, next to the chapel. He had been strangled from behind until he lost consciousness. We found him with his pockets turned inside out, his sneakers gone, and his shirt torn. Charlie turned Bob over and we noticed he had fallen on and smashed the coffee cup he had been carrying. He was cut superficially. He had been very proud of the coffee cup, which his mother had given to him during her brief visit.

Bob regained consciousness and his color began to return. He glanced pitifully down at the broken coffee cup and mumbled, "Ah, those bastards even broke my coffee cup." Tears dampened his cheeks. We helped him back to our area of the prison. I didn't know what to say. I felt detached and emotionless as I squatted in a corner by myself.

Richard, the redheaded Canadian, walked over to me. "Hey man," he said quietly, "he'll be okay. How about smoking a joint with me? It will make you feel better." I sat there looking at the neatly rolled cigarette and decided, What the hell? If I'm going to be punished or accused of doing something anyhow, I might as well get the pleasure of doing it. I took the joint from his hand and found my piece of sanity in this hell.

Marijuana, more than anything else in the prison, kept us from losing our minds. It gave us back our sense of humor. It helped us travel back to places once remembered, and it took the strain off of us. Marijuana helped me pass the days and see humor even in the worst conditions. It did not distort my reality, nor did it give me a sense of well-being. It made the horrible situation tolerable. It gave me back my will to dream. It made me glad to be alive, no matter what the circumstances were.

All of the Americans smoked marijuana in the prison eventually. It was necessary to survive. It seemed to take the strain off of us and aided in our acting more rational in crisis situations. It helped curb the violence in the prison. No one wanted to fight and ruin the precious high. People were more willing to discuss a problem instead of striking out. Boredom often led to violence in the prison. Marijuana allowed us to drift into our thoughts and memories, alleviating the boredom, yet leaving us with enough paranoia to be aware of our surroundings. The only good things I can remember about the old Nogales prison occurred when I was stoned. The food was more tolerable while stoned. I could pretend I was eating something other than pinto beans or greasy soup ... or at least I could try. One afternoon, I was particularly hungry when I decided to attempt to eat the soup that was served. The man in charge of food distribution slopped an extremely foul-smelling liquid into my bowl. The liquid was dark tan and had globules of grease floating on the surface. A bare bone peeked out of the center of the bowl. I lifted the spoon towards my mouth but gagged at the smell. Charlie began laughing at me and offered me a marijuana cigarette.

"Here, this might make it a little better," he grinned. Charlie could eat anything, stoned or not. I took a couple of puffs and decided to attack the soup again. I held my breath this time and allowed a spoonful of the liquid to slide down my throat, hoping it would taste better than it smelled. It didn't, but I managed to get a few more spoonfuls into my stomach.

"At least it's warm," Charlie said, the grin still on his face. I swished my spoon around, trying to find something more substantial than a bone, maybe a small piece of potato or some other vegetable. I caught something in my spoon and lifted it carefully out of the bowl. Sitting in my spoon, starring back at me, was a large eyeball, complete with eyelashes. It probably belonged to a cow at one time. My own eyes widened and stared back at the cow's eye on the spoon. At first I thought I would be sick, but then I chuckled to myself. I laughed out loud as I began offering the eye to the other Americans who were trying to eat. Charlie screamed and jumped up, throwing his bowl and soup on the ground. No one finished their soup that day. It was so disgusting, it was hilarious. Charlie immediately swore off eating the soup ever again.

It was not too funny though when I began to get a burning sensation in my stomach and the shakes later on that evening. I had not had dysentery since my capture, like many of the other prisoners, but I was aware of its symptoms and knew I would soon be one of its casualties. By mid-morning, my forehead was burning with a high fever and I was shaking from the cold. I began to lose control of my bowels, and I vomited until there was nothing left to throw up and I lapsed into the dry heaves. Bob Smith and several other Americans wrapped me in blankets, but I couldn't stop shaking or hold anything in my stomach. I was weak, dizzy, and barely able to walk. By mid-afternoon I was half delirious. Bob and Richard MacDonald were screaming for Chentana to take me to a hospital or call a doctor.

When we were about to give up any hope of medical treatment, Chentana sent in three guards. I was beginning to believe I might die. My hands were handcuffed behind me, and I was carried to the outer courtyard. In the courtyard, my ankles were chained and I was carried by my shoulders out into the bright sunlight by two Federales and guarded by no less than four more policemen. I was pushed into the back of a black delivery-style truck, locked in, and driven to a hospital. Two policemen stood on the rear bumper of the truck, hanging on, in case I kicked the back door open and tried to escape. In my dazed sickness and weakness, I did think about my chances of escape, only about staying alive. I had never felt so ill in my life and wanted to survive. I was grateful to be taken to a hospital.

I was unloaded at the hospital and dragged into a waiting room. I was pleased to see the staff in their white uniforms and tried to smile my appreciation. The other patients in the waiting room put their hands over their mouths in shocked disapproval as they stared at me, hunched over, trying to stand and not puke all over their clean floor … in my chains. The other patients left. The female nurses stared at me and my police escort in disgust, and we were told to leave the hospital. The doctors were refusing to examine me. I was a dangerous criminal. One man in white questioned a policeman about me. I heard the words "*disenteria y posiblemente pulmonia.*" The man in white shook his head negatively as if to say, "We aren't going to admit him." My heart sank. I wanted to explain to him that I was really a good guy who was in an awful situation and was very ill, but I could only mumble incoherently. The man in white handed a policeman a couple bottles of pills and motioned us out of the waiting room. The policeman stuck the bottles in my shirt pocket, and I was taken back to the prison.

I took some of the pills, and the Americans laid me on the ground under some quilts, outside of the bathroom. Now, this may sound ridiculous, but the thing that began to worry me the most was my sneakers. I knew I was weak and defenseless. I saw the way the junkies looked at me as I was being carried back into the prison. I was worried the junkies would attack me and steal the sneakers my mother had brought me. I didn't want to lose those sneakers, yet I knew I could not defend myself. I remember half-crying, half-mumbling to Bob, "Please don't let the junkies steal my sneakers!" Bob gave me a stick to protect myself and, in my delirium, I would swing the stick at anyone who approached me, Mexicans and Americans alike. Everyone began to look like junkies to me. I lay on the ground under the quilts for about five days before I was strong enough to walk around without help. The outside temperature dropped to twenty-eight degrees on a few of those nights. When I finally did get up and take a few steps, I realized my sneakers were gone.

Chapter Twenty

I suppose I lived in fear throughout most of my time in the old Nogales prison: fear of the junkies, fear of disease, and most of all, fear of being left there. The fear gnawed at my insides and would wake me up at night. Yet there comes a point when you have to tell the fear to go away; you can't take it anymore and still survive. So you learn to deal with that fear, and when its gone, it's gone forever. You've conquered it.

Sure, I've been frightened many times since, and will be again, but I refuse to feel the deep-rooted fear that chills the body and works its way into my bones ever again. I learned that the worst thing that can happen is dying, and it just isn't worth being that scared over. It's amazing how strong the will to live is. It took me a long time to face up to my fears, but I finally did on an October night in the old Nogales prison.

One extremely chilly morning, a young American was thrown into our section of the prison. He said his name was Leon and he had been arrested for a small amount of heroin that had been hidden in his cigarette lighter. Leon was an extremely thin boy, maybe seventeen years old, with stringy, light brown hair. He shook almost constantly, from the fear, the cold, and especially from the heroin withdrawal. We didn't like heroin addicts, no matter their nationality, but Leon was so defenseless that someone had to look out for him. It fell upon us. Leon, Bob, Charlie, Arthur, Carl, and I were the only Americans living outside of a cell by then, so it was left to us to keep him out of trouble.

We instructed Leon on the dangers of wandering off alone. We told him he was to be with one of us at all times, and under no circumstances was he to attempt to score heroin in the prison. If he tried to buy heroin, the junkies would know he had money. He would be attacked, and the junkies would steal whatever money he had and anything else they wanted. Also, there was always the danger of rape, since Leon was small, young, and fair-skinned.

Leon didn't have much to say to us. He was too sick. He would pace back and forth, trembling and holding his stomach against the heroin cramps. The longer he went cold turkey, the more his eyes deceived his desire for more heroin. At night, he did not sleep. He would sit hunched over, scratching at himself and staring into space. We did manage to learn he was from Phoenix, Arizona, and had gone through several rehabilitation programs, only to relapse when he hit the streets. He ended most of his sentences with, "Hey, man, I'm sick. I gotta get a fix!" and we would repeat the dangers of dealing with the junkies. I don't know if he ever heard us.

On the morning of the fourth day since Leon's arrival, we heard a scream and saw a scuffle going on at the upper level of the prison. I took a quick head count. Leon was missing. "Have any of you seen Leon?" I asked the group.

Charlie jumped up. "You don't think he's that stupid?" he asked as he stared toward the upper level. It was bad enough to wander off alone, but to go to the upper level was insane. The junkies controlled the entire upper level, and anyone else who went into their territory was shoved into a cell, robbed, beaten, or stabbed, and sometimes raped. We heard another scream and knew it came from Leon.

The five of us, Charlie, Bob, Arthur, Carl, and I, hesitated for a moment. You could see the doubt in our eyes. Leon got himself into this. We warned him. This wasn't our fight! Charlie suddenly ran toward the stairs that led to the upper level. He made the decision for us. We quickly followed. Bradley Speare came running out of his cell to join us. Charlie took several leaps up the stairs, but stopped when he saw a group of junkies at the top, holding *puntas*. We referred to them as *points*. They were any metal object that, has been ground down on concrete, and formed into a knife or ice-pick-style weapon. Plastic was usually melted around the bottom to form a handle. Charlie retreated down the stairs cautiously. We wanted to help Leon, but none of us were about to go up those stairs. We stood, glaring at the junkies, with them glaring back. We had heard no more screams. Eventually, a group of the junkies came out of a cell and pushed past those at the top of the stairs. They were carrying Leon's limp body. They rolled the body down towards us. The junkies did not say a word. They just stared at us with hate-filled eyes. Leon was dead. His clothes were ripped and torn. Blood oozed from numerous wounds. He lay on the steps like a grotesque, broken doll.

I felt a chill. My veins were filled with ice water. It was so easy to die. We were all so fragile. Bradley let out a deep-throated scream and began cursing the junkies, staring at them through tear-filled eyes. He started to move up the stairs. He wanted to kill them all, and so did the rest of us. Charlie grabbed Bradley by the arms and kept him from going any further. We wouldn't lose another. Bradley began sobbing. Some of the junkies left the top of the stairs. It was over.

From the cell where the murder took place, Pancho emerged. He walked with a limp from an old injury and had greased-back hair. His arms were black from needle marks, and blood was splattered across his shirt. He claimed to have survived in the prison for over nine years and planned to survive many more. He had been sentenced to thirty years, the maximum in Mexico, for robbing and murdering several families. He was a slight man, but that did not lessen his evil. He stared at us over the rail. There was no emotion on his face. He looked at each of us coldly, than walked away.

Something inside of me was changing. My fear was being replaced by determination. I would kill Pancho, even if I lost my own life in the process. Pancho was the leader. He was responsible for Leon's death and much of the misery in the prison. He perpetuated our fear and made the filth in the prison filthier. It was not fear or anger that controlled me now. It was a determination that came out of emptiness. I was about to plan a murder.

My thoughts were interrupted as several guards pushed their way past us to carry Leon's body away. I don't suppose the death was ever reported. Leon had been in the prison only a few days, and the American Consulate would not yet have been notified of his arrest. The body would most likely be dumped in the desert. If Leon's body were found, bandits would be blamed. Chentana could not afford a scandal. There would never be a record of Leon entering the prison … but I would not forget.

Chapter Twenty-One

I devised a plan. There were only two toilets in the prison. Sooner or later, Pancho would have to come down the stairs at night to use the toilet. The toilet area was dark and one of the few places in the prison not visible from the guard towers. Pancho rarely wandered from the upper level during the day; he would wait until night, when everyone was asleep. If I could catch him at night, I might not be spotted, and his murder might go unsolved and un-revenged. It was my only chance.

It's difficult to explain how my mind was functioning then. I had lived a protected life on the East Coast. I had not been in a fight for years prior to coming to Mexico. I had prided myself in being a pacifist, and here I was, planning a murder and taking a cold pleasure in the idea. I guess I had been pushed too far. I could end up dead and broken on the stairs as easily as Leon, but I was going to make someone pay for his death, or at least I'd die trying. I was ashamed of these thoughts. I kept my plan to myself and did not confide in anyone. I was afraid they would feel I was crazy. Even worse, they might talk me out of it.

I did not sleep for two nights after Leon's murder. I lay awake under my ragged blankets, listening for footsteps and waiting. I did not feel I could kill Pancho with my bare hands, nor could I bring myself to use a point. I had found a short rope, and I planned to garrote him to death. I felt this would be more failsafe. I was afraid I was too weak to strangle him with my bare hands. With a point, I might only wound him, and his bloodstains might give me away. All of these morbid thoughts weighed heavily on my mind. My only fear was that I could not actually do it when the time came. Yet, I must!

On the third night, sometime after midnight, I heard someone call for the *jave*, or key, so he could be let out to use the bathroom. A man with a key was stationed between our side of the prison and the trustee's side. The *javero*, or key man, could not see the toilet room from where he stood. My greatest risk would be that he would check on the man before I returned to my place of sleep or someone else would awaken and discover me. I carefully peeked from under my blankets to see if I could recognize Pancho, as I had done without any success many times on the past nights. My heart began to pound in my chest. My mind raced in apprehension and doubt. It was Pancho. I could see him, walking stiff-legged towards the bathroom. He seemed to be half-asleep or semi-drugged by the way he was carrying himself. I turned slowly and carefully, trying to hold my breath and follow his course into the toilet room. I clenched the rope as my mind raced back and forth: *Now! Now, do it! I can't. I can't!*

I cautiously removed the blanket and stood up on my bare feet. My knees felt weak and wobbly. I did not feel as if I had the strength to carry out the assassination. My arms did not feel as if they would work. I was out of breath. I felt as if I was stomping on the concrete and it was alerting everyone. Luckily, I made my way to the toilet room door without incident. I could not see Pancho until I crept through the door into the darkness. His back was to me. He was urinating against the wall and seemed not to hear or notice me. His head hung slightly forward, with one hand pressed against the filthy wall as if to hold himself up and away from it. Except for the urine splattering against the concrete and my heart pounding in my ears, the prison was deathly silent. The sound of the urine concealed my padded footsteps. I had the short rope wrapped tightly around my hands as I moved behind him, lifted the rope above his head, and formed my hands so as to loop it over his head, as I had seen it done in the movies. Pancho must have sensed I was there because he attempted to turn around, but it was too late. The rope slipped easily over his head and down around his throat. It was everything I could do to keep from screaming as I yanked hard on the rope. My teeth were clenched together, and I was trembling uncontrollably. My arms felt so damn weak, and my knees kept wobbling. *Kill him! Kill him!* my mind screamed. Pancho tried to yell, but the rope cut the sound off in his throat and he merely gurgled. He flailed his arms in an attempt to break loose. The urine had soaked his pants. He tried to kick back off the wall to throw me off balance, but I held tight and kept pulling on the rope. I threw my knee into his back, knocking him forward into the wall, using the leverage to pull even harder. He clawed at the rope as small sounds emitted from him. I felt weak and giddy. I was afraid I would break into hysterical laughter like a madman. It seemed too drawn out, over eternity ...

Pancho's struggle became more futile. His knees began to buckle and he blacked out. My mind raced, *Pull tighter! Pull! Finish him, you fool. Finish him off!* But my arms would not obey. I realized I could not kill him, even if it meant my death the next day at the hands of Pancho and his junkies.

I relaxed my grip and Pancho slumped to the floor. I was breathing heavily and could not stop trembling as I slipped the rope into my pocket. I quickly turned Pancho on his back and sat on his chest, with my knees pinning down his arms. I removed his point from his belt loop and held it at his throat with my right hand. I listened intently for sounds of anyone who might be approaching. The prison was quiet. I was sweating as I tried to slow my breathing. I slapped Pancho with my left hand, trying to revive him. I felt exhausted. Pancho began to stir. His body jerked and his eyes opened wide. Even in the darkness, I could detect the fear in his bulging eyes. I pushed the point harder against his throat, breaking the skin and causing a small trickle of blood to emerge. He let out a startled whimper and attempted to move his neck away from the point. Pancho could understand some English. I spoke to him through clenched teeth. "See, see! You can die too, just as easily as anyone else. Do you understand? You can die as easily as Leon or me. *Comprehende?*" I pressed even harder on the point. Sweat was burning my eyes. "I just want you to know that we can kill you like you kill us. Tomorrow, you may kill me, but if that happens, one of my friends will kill you. Do you understand?" I hissed.

"*Si*," Pancho croaked. I cautiously eased the point away from his neck and began to stand. I was expecting him to attack me, but he did not. He lay on the urine-stained floor, rubbing his neck. I stood in the shadows, pointing the weapon at him. Carefully, he began to raise himself up. I readied myself for him to rush me, but he moved to the door, head hung down, still rubbing his neck. Just outside the door, Pancho paused and slowly turned to look at me. He nodded, his face expressionless. "*Si, es easy. Buenos noches, Esteban.*" He limped off to the key man. He could have turned me into the key man. I expected him to turn me in, but he never did. He was led back to his cell and never turned or glanced back. Still shaking, I made my way back to my sleeping spot. *I should have killed him*, I thought. *I'm a weak coward who just signed his own death warrant.* I did not sleep that night from the adrenalin still rushing in my veins and from worrying over my very questionable future.

"You okay?" Bob Smith asked me the next morning. "You've seemed kind of quiet lately."

"I'm okay," I answered, secretly thinking the junkies would be coming to kill me.

The junkies started to treat me with a sense of muted respect after the incident with Pancho. Although I was still subject to their thievery, as was everyone in the prison, I no longer felt my life was in danger from the junkies. I would see Pancho every few days, but the incident in the bathroom was never mentioned by him or by anyone else.

In a way, it was a rule for the junkies in the prison. If another prisoner was caught in the act of stealing or doing something to harm someone, the victim was more than less obligated to take revenge, no matter how small the crime. The junkies believed if they could get away with a crime the first time without retaliation on the victim's part, the victim was weak and deserved to be harassed even more. If a prisoner stole a peso from me and I let him go without a fight, the next time he would attempt to take much more from me. If a prisoner got caught, he deserved to get punished. Yet if that same prisoner secretly stole my shoes and tried to sell them back to me in an hour, I would have no right for revenge. If I attempted to forcefully take the shoes back under those circumstances, junkies would come to the thief's rescue. Since I had not discovered the theft while it was happening, it was considered my fault. A man gained respect in the prison by not being taken advantage of, by taking revenge, and by playing the games correctly. I was learning.

Chapter Twenty-Two

Thanksgiving and Christmas were coming soon. I was desperate to hurry my trial so I could be home for the holidays. The thought of spending Christmas in this nightmare was scaring the hell out of all of us. Lee Walton and my friends at the mental health center contacted a woman from Arizona named Gay. Gay spoke fluent Spanish and previously was the interpreter for the District Attorney of Arizona. They thought if Gay could arrange an audience with the judge to explain Bob's and my circumstances, it might aid in our release before Christmas. I believed the language barrier would be our greatest weakness in the court process and hoped Gay could close that gap. Alfonso Garcia Gallegas, my lawyer, had not shown his face since the visit from my mother. I was tired of being told to sign documents I did not understand. Gay seemed to be the person who might bring some order to this chaos.

Gay came to visit just before Thanksgiving. We discussed all that had happened, starting with our journey to Zirosto. She took notes and tried to formulate what she would say to the judge. I was beginning to have some threads of hope again. At least I might have some input in what would be our fate. It was difficult for me to trust anyone because of the many con men I had already encountered; yet I needed a friend on the outside and felt she was sincere after her first visit. It was easy to see she was most uncomfortable in the prison and appalled by our condition, but she came anyhow and was willing to try.

For all the predators who descended upon us and our parents, taking advantage of our hopelessness, there was also a small group of sincere, caring people who did their best to help. Gay was one of those special people. She was an attractive, proper-looking girl in her mid-twenties. She would travel into Mexico and enter the filth-infested prison just to reassure me that I was going to be all right—a stranger assuring me by saying my friends still cared and would not give up. Gay was a speck of sanity in a world gone mad. Knowing she was on the outside, trying to help, made the days in prison seem easier.

Prior to Thanksgiving, three more Americans were brought into the prison. Joseph Silverstrini was a large man in his mid-twenties from Eugene, Oregon. He spoke some Spanish, wasn't afraid to fight, and added to the defenses of our American block. Silverstrini had been arrested near the border with a truck and a ton of marijuana. He thought he would have to wait three to six months in prison, and then he would be fined heavily and set free. Silverstrini appeared to a man who was worried only about himself. I liked him, but I was never sure whose side he was on.

Richard Kohout, a small, blond man in his early twenties, with sharp features, was brought in shortly after Silverstrini. Kohout was from Tucson, Arizona, and was arrested for possession of heroin. This alienated him from us immediately. We were reminded of Leon, yet Kohout turned out to have much more character than the unfortunate Leon. He quit using heroin, was cautious and dependable, and ended up being a good friend. Kohout was a guy who suffered a lot of bad breaks in life and was finding it hard to keep it together on the outside.

The third American was a deaf mute from Hawaii. Although mute, he could communicate through howls, grunts, and sign language. He was actually a noisy mute. We never were sure of his name, let alone his background. The Americans called him Kong, for he must have weighed 350 pounds. Charlie, who was down to 165 pounds, had lost his heavyweight status. The Mexicans called Kong *Mudo,* meaning mute. Kong had an extremely bad time in the prison. The Mexicans teased and harassed him constantly. The Americans could not understand him and were disgusted with his personal habits, which were worse than even the average prisoner. I would sit with Kong for hours, trying to communicate with him, but he rarely told the same story twice. I was led to believe his affliction was a result of brain damage after a motorcycle accident. He was in prison because he had been a passenger in an auto wreck. The driver ran away, leaving Kong to fend for himself. In Mexico, if you are a foreigner in a car accident, you are imprisoned until you can prove you are not responsible for the accident, which could take years.

Some Mexican prisoners told me it was not constitutional, according to Mexican law, to imprison a mute on anything less than a felony. The next time the American consul visited the prison, I presented Kong's case to the representative and demanded action be taken to help him. The consul said he would look into it.

I spoke with four different Consulate employees about Kong on numerous occasions. Each time an employee would visit the prison, several Americans would argue that Kong should not be imprisoned. The consul usually looked concerned, gave a promise that he or she would look into it, and then we would have to start all over again and remind the consul on the next visit. Three and half months later, the Consulate took action and Kong was finally released.

Kong took ill with dysentery shortly after his imprisonment. He was not given any medical attention, and I was afraid he would die. Karl, the ex-medic, and I begged the Americans in the cell to allow Kong to sleep there with them because it was a little warmer. The Americans objected at first, because Kong smelled worse than most of the prisoners, who ranged from horrible to unbearable. Karl and I played on their humanity, and they finally agreed to allow Kong to sleep in the cell.

The cells were locked down. We prepared to hide from the cold under our blankets. I had been asleep for several hours when I heard Kong bellowing and beating on the bars of the cell door. He was awakening the entire prison! I heard the Americans in the cell telling him to shut up, cursing him, but Kong couldn't hear, so it was no use. Then it dawned on me: if Kong was as sick as I had been, he would have to rush to the bathroom, but he couldn't call for the key man! I started to get up to tell the key man when I realized it was too late. "What's he doing?" I heard one of the Americans ask in a puzzled tone. "Oh, my God, he's shitting all over everything!" I heard someone gag. "Stop him, stop him!" Choked screams came from the Americans in the cell. They were screaming for the key man, cursing and threatening to kill Kong, and complaining of the stench. I glanced in Karl's direction. He was hiding with the blanket pulled over his head, giggling out loud. I decided I better get back to my sleeping spot and pretend I was asleep before the Americans remembered whose idea it was to place Kong in the cell. After the mess was cleaned up, Karl and I had our own private joke: "Where does a 350 pound deaf mute shit? Anywhere he wants!"

Kong was constantly tormented by the Mexicans. They liked to hear him scream. One of their favorite tricks was to wait for Kong to squat on the toilet. Several Mexicans would gather in front of Kong, just out of reach, with a long pole. As Kong relieved himself, the Mexicans would try to knock the dropping feces onto Kong's pants with the pole.

It was difficult enough trying to keep clean without the Mexicans' games. There was no hot water and the weekly showers had to be taken in the cold air. Sometimes we would actually turn blue.

Karl had just returned from the shower one afternoon when the Mexicans were indulging in their toilet trick on Kong. Karl was shivering and shaking, but he was clean. The water had just been turned off for the week. Kong was scream-ing in aggravation as the Mexicans poked the pole at him. He grabbed a bucket of feces and old paper that was sitting next to the toilet hole and flung the bucket at his tormentors. But the bucket missed the Mexicans, hitting me in the back, knocking me down. The bucket was hurled with so much force that it bounced off my back, did a semi-somersault in the air, and landed on Karl's head, spilling the contents all over him. I had never laughed so hard in my life as I did while trying to keep the once-clean Karl from killing Kong.

A sense of humor, no matter how weird, often kept us going. If we could find humor in this nightmare, even in the most bizarre circumstances, then we knew we were going to be all right. When you can still laugh, you know that you aren't beat.

We celebrated Thanksgiving on a visitor's day. Some of the American prisoners' wives managed to smuggle turkey into the prison. Some of the turkey was lost to the guards, and some to the junkies, but the wives and girlfriends managed to bring enough to cover the losses and still leave a good meal for us. I was particularly depressed and lonely that day, when Gay visited me. She brought me some turkey and olives, and best of all, good news. Gay had met with the judge. He could not speed up our trial. We had to wait our turn, as everyone else; yet he did say he understood our situation and the language barrier. My mental health work was a good commendation, and I would probably be released on sentencing. Bob would receive the same. It was only a matter of time and it would probably be before Christmas.

I was elated with her news. Gay left, and I had another visitor. A college friend, Paul Meredith, heard I was in trouble and came from Montana by bus to see me. Paul was my age, but Chentana wouldn't let him into the prison; he said Paul was too young. Chentana finally let me talk to Paul through the bars for about fifteen minutes. I was glad to know I had friends who still cared. Seeing Paul brought back memories from my past; the whole world was passing us while we were trapped behind bars. I was bitter but determined not to let the bitterness change me.

They could hurt me, lock me up, and take things away from me, but I refused to let them control my mind. They could change everything about Steve Wilson except the way I thought, and if I could keep that, I would win. The prison taught me to hold onto and fight for my beliefs. I was no longer a passive idealist. I was becoming a dangerous adversary. The prison was creating a mass of hardcore men bent on fighting for their beliefs and seeking revenge against those who treated them unjustly. The prisons were breeding the revolutionary movement in Mexico. There were no rehabilitation programs, no daily activities, nothing in the prison except revenge. I shook Paul's hand through the bars as he left. I think I frightened him; my eyes gave me away. They were dark, vacant, and sunken. I looked much older since I last saw Paul. He appeared glad to be able to leave Mexico.

The days passed more quickly after the Thanksgiving visits. Gay had given Bob and me something to look forward to. Even the junkies seemed better behaved. Bob and I waited anxiously each day for our names to be called to court. The weather was turning to a freezing cold and it was necessary to move the rest of the prisoners into cells. It was Karl and Arthur's turns to be placed in the American cell. The Americans in the cell protested. They said Karl and Arthur were too filthy and lice-ridden to live in the cell. Instead, they offered the cell space to Bob and me, or Silverstrini. Bob and I became angry because Karl and Arthur were no filthier than the rest of us. It was just that they were black.

After a big argument with the celled Americans, Bob and I refused to ever live in their cell. We would live outside and freeze before we would live with those bastards. Karl and Arthur had been our friends. They helped protect us as we lived outside, they were with us when Leon was killed, and they were part of our group that lived in the elements. We stood by them as they had stood by us so many times before.

The Mexicans finally accepted Karl and Arthur into another cell, and Silverstrini, Kohout, and Charlie moved into cells shortly afterward. Bob and I remained sleeping outside in the courtyard, the only two men in the entire prison without a cell. We slept under a pile of old blankets with a plastic tarp stretched over the top of us to keep off the rain. It was bitter cold, but in ways it was better than sleeping in the overcrowded cells. We gained more respect from the Mexicans during those long, cold nights, and we were considered dissidents from the American community, a label that worked in our favor. A junkie leader woke us one evening to offer us hot coffee. We were bridging the gap.

Chapter Twenty-Three

Bad news came again. The judge Gay spoke with was replaced, but Gay would try to plead our case to the new judge. There would be no indication of the outcome until later. These good news/bad news swings were tearing Bob and me apart. Each time our hopes went up, we would receive bad news, and we would drop into depression, which was getting tougher to swing out of.

There had also been rumors of a mass transfer to another prison to add to our anticipation. The last transfer brought us from bad to worse, and we were not looking forward to moving again. At least in this prison, we knew what to expect. The next prison might be worse, if that was possible.

The temperature dropped sharply the night after we received the bad news from Gay. It was the first week in December. Brad's old army jacket helped, but the cold soon drove Bob and me under our blankets. During the middle of the night, it began to rain. I could hear and feel the raindrops slapping against the plastic tarp that covered my blankets. I shivered and curled myself into a ball, hoping the rain wouldn't drench the ground and soak my blankets.

I woke the next morning and tried to get up, but I couldn't. Something or someone was lying on top of my blankets. I tried to get up again, but I couldn't push the weight off or lift the blankets.

"Hey, Bob! Wake up. I can't get out of here!" Bob was silent for a few moments and then he yelled that he was stuck underneath his blankets too. We began yelling for help. I heard someone knock on top of the blankets. Charlie was laughing and asking if we were okay. During the night, the rain had frozen on top of our tarp. Towards early morning, it had snowed on top of the ice. Bob and I were frozen in under the tarp. It took Charlie, several laughing Mexicans, and a lot of effort to get us out. Winter was literally upon us.

The day was the coldest we had experienced, so we wandered around the prison, trying to huddle in any stray sunbeam. A few of the Mexicans started a paper-and-trash fire in an old oil drum and gathered around it, trying to warm their hands. Anyone who had a kerosene stove, was huddled over the burners, trying to soak up as much warmth as possible. I thought Mexico never had cold weather ... wrong again.

I was stomping my feet on the concrete, trying to restore my circulation, when soldiers came running through the gate. The trustees' section of the prison had been overrun by soldiers already, and they were headed into our side of the prison. I bolted towards the American cell and attempted to warn the Americans and figure out what was happening.

Four soldiers, wearing full combat gear and AR-15 automatic rifles, jogged directly to the American cell. The Americans living in cell 1 were ordered to gather up the possessions they could carry and move to the trustee section to wait for transfer to a new prison. The whole prison population was to be transferred starting with cell 1.

I had never witnessed anything like the evacuation of the old Nogales prison. As soon as the junkies realized what was happening, they attacked.

The junkies believed all along that the Americans were wealthy, with their riches hidden in the cell, and this was the last chance the junkies had at those riches. The soldiers didn't try to stop the junkies, but just stepped aside. The junkies burst into the abandoned American cell; fistfights and scuffles over clothes and food followed. Benches were smashed, and what couldn't be carried or used was destroyed. Bob and I grabbed our ragged blankets and placed our backs against a wall. We each had a point, and we faced opposite directions to protect our few belongings. The soldiers were evacuating the prison by cell numbers, but Bob and I were not in a cell; therefore, we would not be taken out of the prison until all the cells were empty. We could be the last two people to leave the old Nogales prison!

The Mexicans were going nuts. They started smashing bottles and fighting amongst themselves. As the Americans fought their way out of the prison, cell 2 was called out. That cell was instantly attacked by junkies, as was each following cell that was evacuated. Bob and I were the only Americans left after the first few moments of the evacuation. The Mexicans were far too busy looting and destroying the place to notice us. It was a scene from an asylum. People were screaming and running from one side of the prison to another, fighting over rags. I saw several men get stabbed. I felt like I was in a war-ravaged city where the looters were taking over. Someone threw a kerosene stove from the upper level, onto the courtyard. Kerosene splashed everywhere. More stoves were thrown into the courtyard, along with wooden benches and useless rubbish. As each cell was vacated, the prisoners were whipped into a greater frenzy. The oil drum that was used to warm hands earlier was pushed over and ignited the puddles of kerosene.

There was a huge flash and a pile of discarded items roared into flames. Now, anything that would burn was thrown into the fire. The flames licked the walls and plaster cracked and crashed onto the concrete floor. Wooden doors were torn off hinges and thrown onto the fire. The prison was being torn apart. I hoped the heat would be great enough to cave in the wall so we could escape.

The flames illuminated our faces while we stood wide-eyed, gazing at the madness. The prison was burning! This lice-infested, filthy hole of a nightmare was being destroyed, and no one would have to endure being within its walls again. I started to smile. This mad storm began to take on a fantasy-like, unreal atmosphere, and to add to the absurdity, it began to snow—big, beautiful snowflakes. Bob and I looked at each other, and we broke into big grins.

Bob started to sing an off-key rendition of "Chestnuts Roasting on an Open Fire" and I, laughing helplessly, joined in. The entire interior of the prison was being gutted by fire. Bob and I stood smiling, points in hand, singing Christmas carols … "Jingle bells, jingle bells" … in the snow.

Bob tapped me on the arm and pointed to the large wooden door that once protected the Butcher's cell—the man responsible for a large part of the pain and filth. The wooden door stood unharmed. Bob let out a yell, ran towards the fire, and grabbed a piece of burning wood like a torch. He ran to the Butcher's cell door and kicked and beat on it. The cell was empty, but he still set fire to the door. I got caught up in the action too. I would help burn this hellhole to the ground! We joined the Mexicans in tearing up and setting fire to anything we could destroy. I didn't care if I was in the burning prison … no one was going to be sentenced to this horror again!

One Mexican went too close to the wall and was buried under a mass of plaster as it crashed down. Some men dug him out, but the man was badly injured. We were told later that the smoke billowing out of the prison could be seen from thirty miles away. It was like being present at the sacking of Rome.

It wasn't until evening that all the cells were empty. The fire was subsiding, and Bob and I stood alone in the smoldering ruins. Our faces and clothes were covered with soot. A melancholy settled over me. The prison was destroyed, yet I was still a prisoner. The soldiers called Bob and me out. We grabbed our blankets and shuffled to the gate leading out of our section of the prison. I glanced back one final time and watched a few flames continue to flicker on the Butcher's door.

Bob and I were thoroughly searched. A soldier told me they had confiscated two .38 pistols, fifteen hundred grams of marijuana, three ounces of heroin, knives, meat cleavers, and other weapons. It didn't dent the junkie's arsenal. We were lead to an enclosed cattle truck by the soldiers and locked in with the last twenty prisoners to be transported. In fifteen or twenty minutes, after riding over bumpy roads in the pitch-dark, the truck came to a halt, and the rear door slid open. I was at my new home.

Chapter Twenty-Four

I don't know what I expected of the new Nogales prison, but it wasn't what I got. It was beautiful—that is, as beautiful as a prison could be—especially after spending several months in the slums of hell. It had big rock walls with newly painted, yellow, cinder block buildings capped with orange roofs. I stood in of the prison with my mouth open. It was modern and it was clean. Bob nudged me. "Hope we get a cell with a nice view. After the last place, this looks like the Holiday Inn."

"As long as they feed us real food," I heard Charlie mumble.

We were ushered up a low flight of stairs by the soldiers, through what appeared to be an office area because of its plate-glass and lack of bars. We went out of the first building, across an open area paved with stones, and up another flight of stairs. Each time we moved in or out of a section of this prison, the soldiers had to unlock a chain-link fence. We went up a cement ramp, past a large dormitory-type building, and up another ramp. I had counted six guard towers as we moved upward.

The new Nogales prison was built into the side of a mountainous area on five tiered levels. The lowest level consisted of a women's section, the administrative offices, rooms for the wealthier trustee prisoners, guards, and the food processing and kitchen buildings. The next level was only slightly tiered and represented a buffer area between the office and prisoners. The third level was made up of a basketball court, a small building designed as a library, work buildings, and a guard tower in the center. A chain-link fence separated the work buildings and the courtyard. The fourth level contained only a dormitory. A dormitory consisted of a two-level building divided into four cellblocks. The fifth and last level was made up of a basketball court and another dormitory. Each of the tiered levels was separated by a chain-link fence.

Bob and I, along with Kong, were taken to the uppermost dormitory. We were then taken to the second floor, where we moved down a long corridor, with cells on the right and narrow-barred windows on the left. A soldier slid a cell door open and waved his rifle for us to go in. The cell door was slid shut and we were locked in, as another soldier handed each of us a clean, new blanket. It was really exciting to get something clean and new after so long. This would be the first time in six months that I would sleep with a solid roof over my head. The cells were eight by twelve in the sleeping area, and each one had its own separate bathroom with a toilet and a ceramic sink. The toilets were raised cement slabs with a ceramic bowl and no seat, so a person still had to squat, but they actually flushed! The sleeping area consisted of three gray slabs of concrete, which protruded from the wall in a bunk bed fashion, with a metal ladder leading to the upper slabs. To us, it was the Hyatt Regency. There were only three of us to a cell. There was no heat, and the concrete made it colder, but we didn't care. It would be the first night I would be able to rest without the paranoia of being attacked by the junkies.

I reflected on the past months and the violence. Had it been all that bad? Yes. And even worse, I had been learning to live a violent existence. I returned violence with violence; it was the only way to survive. It was becoming second nature. I carried myself differently, always checking out the danger points in a crowd, always keeping one arm free and ready. The violence had become a way of life for me and I was fighting it with an equivalent amount of violence. I was adjusting.

The morning sun gave me my first real glimpse of the surrounding courtside. Through the narrow windows and over the prison walls, I could see red-and-brown, barren mountains, flecked with sagebrush. I could see the outside again, and I could dream.

To the left, I saw a deep blue mountain that was a piece of the United States … a piece of Arizona, so close. Oh, to be over those mountains! I attempted to get a better view of the prison, but could not from my vantage point in the cell.

I wondered how the Mexicans could afford to build this prison when I had seen intense poverty throughout Mexico. I soon found out the nature of the newer Mexican prisons. In early 1974, new modern prisons began springing up all along the border. The Mexicans told me that the money for the prisons came from the United States. For years the Americans had been pouring money into Mexico in order to combat drugs and drug trafficking. The prisons, supposedly, were a result of some of this money. The materials for the new prisons came from the United States. This particular prison was also designed and built buy a U.S. architect.

Running a prison was big business for the Mexicans, and most directors attempted to acquire enough money to retire, in case their political aspirations failed. If the director did well, he would be kept on for approximately three years and then would be placed in more important positions. If the prison ran into problems, or if it became too overtly corrupt, the director would be removed. In a year's time, the new Nogales prison went through four directors, some better than others, but all corrupt in their greed to gain as much wealth as possible in a short period of time.

The prisoners turned into victims as the system bred corruption, drug addiction, frustrations, and violence. Money was always being squeezed from the prisoners and their families. It cost me more to live in the new Nogales prison than it did for me to live in the outside world. The sale of drugs in the prison brought in the greatest profit for the director (confiscating the drugs and then turning around and selling them to the prisoners). With no activities or recreation, the prisoners became frustrated and bored and would turn to drugs more readily. Drugs were not the only profit-making schemes; if a man wanted to sleep with his wife on a conjugal visit, it cost more money. If a man wanted a hot shower, it cost more money. The wealthier prisoners could buy better rooms and more freedom to move about. The food was sold out of a small store and restaurant in the prison, at inflated prices. An auto repair shop, a television repair shop, a watch repair shop, and a furniture making shop were established in the prison with free prison labor. The director would solicit customers from the outside by cutting prices. He had no overhead and would make a 100 percent profit. Everything was used to make money.

It was not that a person could not survive in prison without money, but a person who tried *looked* like they were surviving without money. They were dirtier, suffered from malnutrition and were often sick. Prisoners even had to pay for medical help and medicine.

The Mexicans told me many times that the United States allotted $10 per day to help feed and clothe each American prisoner in Mexico, but only 4 cents per day was spent on food for each prisoner. For each day an American was in prison, twenty-four Mexicans could also be fed. The American prisoners became pure profit for the Mexicans. Meanwhile, Nixon felt he was keeping the drug traffic down.

The American prisoners confronted the American Consulate with this knowledge, but the Consulate said they knew nothing of this practice of paying support money, and I was not able to officially substantiate such payment. However, I got my information from the director of the new Nogales prison. If such payments were made, it would influence the Mexicans to give longer sentences and higher fines to Americans.

Even in the new and modern prisons, the treatment of the inmates remained the same as in the old. Extortion, cold, hunger, physical abuse, and coercion were still the games of the day, unless a prisoner had money. The guards conveniently forgot to feed us for the first two days we were in the new prison. The junkies didn't get their heroin either, and we could hear them screaming and breaking windows in another part of the prison. We finally did get food. A large pot of pinto beans was placed in front of each cell door, and a few spoonfuls were scooped out for each man. It was like feeding time at the kennels.

On the fourth day, I was called out of my cell and led down to the lower basketball court. Gay was waiting for me. She was quite upset, for the Mexicans had done a thorough body search before they would let her speak with me.

She had spoken with the new judge and everything was fine. Bob and I were to be sentenced tomorrow. We were to be fined for a misdemeanor and set free! Gay had such faith in the judge's word that she made plane reservations, telephoned my parents, and bought me a new set of clothes to travel home in. My heart pounded in my chest and my eyes filled with tears. Home! I was really going home—tomorrow! I started to laugh and jump up and down as I yelped. It was going to be over tomorrow! When I got back to my cell, Bob and I hugged each other and hooted while we danced a North Carolina Clog and cried with relief. Home!

Chapter Twenty-Five

The day arrived. We weren't sentenced. We weren't called. Nobody came, and we heard nothing. We paced up and down like animals, biting our nails and clenching our fists. It *had* to happen! Maybe tomorrow ... This was the worst mind game yet. Our hopes had been so high and now I felt I would go insane. Why were they doing this to me? Had we been lied to? Had Gay been lied to?

Nothing happened for four days. Neither Bob nor I slept. We were irritable and on the verge of hysteria. What was happening? If I never had ulcers, I was certainly working on some.

On December 11, 1973, in the early afternoon, we were finally called. We were the first prisoners sentenced by the new judge. Days before, as I gazed through the bars, the Mexicans pointed out the judge to me. He had only been a small speck in the distance. I wondered if I would ever get to meet him face-to-face.

I felt like I was floating again as we were led by guards down to the office building for our *sentencia*. I was giddy, and I had a big grin on my face. Home! Bob and I raised our arms in the air like boxing champions as we were led past the cells of the other prisoners. They all cheered. This was it!

The best that we hoped for was to stand before the judge, have our fine pronounced, and eventually return to our homes. The guards allowed us to have an interpreter who was a fellow prisoner. The three of us, with two guards, walked into an office on the lower level of the prison. There, four other guards were positioned around the room. The judge was not in the office. What we got was a dwarf holding a stack of papers. The dwarf smiled and began to speak directly to us in Spanish. The interpreter translated.

"He says he's the judge's secretary to the court. The investigation is over and the judge has heard all the evidence for the preliminary trail. The judge will sentence you shortly."

The dwarf fidgeted with some of the papers, smiled, and continued.

"Before the judge makes his final decision, the secretary here would like to know if you have any money." The interpreter was starting to hesitate as he translated.

"For what? The fine?" I asked, still hopeful that this just might work out.

"No, not the fine. To help the judge out in his decision."

"What?" Bob yelped nervously as his voice cracked. "We have nothing! They've taken everything we have and everything our parents had. He's got to be kidding!"

I affirmed we had nothing left. The dwarf said something else, put the papers he was holding under his arm, and left the office.

"What was that last thing he said?" I asked the interpreter. He shifted uneasily and did not make eye contact. "He said, 'It doesn't sound good.'"

We stood in the office, not talking, left to our own thoughts for almost an hour.

The dwarf returned, this time carrying fewer papers. He smiled, held some papers in front of himself in an official manner, and began to read.

The Interpreter looked pained. He winced as the words were read. "The judge has found you guilty, and the sentence is five and a half years with no opportunity of parole and a 2,000 peso fine."

"Guilty? Guilty of what?" I was losing control. Bob stood next to me mouthing the words "five and a half years" over and over. "What about our friend who talked to the judge? What about their agreement?" I asked.

The interpreter asked the dwarf and then replied, "He says it doesn't say what you were convicted of, only the sentence. He also says that someone else convinced the judge to change his mind after he had talked to your lady friend."

"Who, who would do that?" I was practically yelling. The dwarf took a step back.

"He says he doesn't know. He's sorry. There is nothing he can do about it. He says you can request an appeal to your sentence if you so wish."

"Of course we want to appeal! This is crazy! What do we have to do to appeal?" I now yelled out.

The interpreter asked the dwarf and then answered, "He says all you have to do is say you disagree with the sentence and request an appeal."

"Tell him we disagree and want the appeal!" My head was spinning.

The interpreter did so and the dwarf asked a question. The interpreter shook his head in disbelief. "He wants to know if you have any money to help the judge in his decision on your appeal."

"What is he nuts? We just told him they have all of the money! This is just too fucking weird!"

The dwarf quickly tucked the papers under his arm and practically ran out of the room, but not before he said something to us.

I looked at the interpreter and mumbled, "I know, I know: it doesn't look good."

We stood in the office, not talking, left to our own thoughts for almost an hour.

The dwarf returned with the same smile and demeanor. He began to read.

The interpreter's mouth gaped open. "He says, 'The judge has reviewed your appeal, and your sentence has been overturned.'" Before a shred of relief could hit me, he continued, "It has been converted to thirty years and a 5,000 peso fine."

I couldn't help myself. I laughed out loud. "What happens if we appeal this? The firing squad?" I glared at the dwarf, who did run out of the room this time.

"Sorry, guys." The interpreter actually had a tear in his eye.

"It doesn't matter. They were never going to let us go anyway. It's just one absurd fucking day after another. We're never going to get out of here." I was tired and just wanted to lie down.

Bob was mumbling to himself, "What are we going to do?" over and over.

All hope of release was gone. The circus was over. Thirty years was the maximum sentence allowed in Mexico. It would be our death sentence.

Bob, the interpreter, and I were ushered back up to the cellblock. A few of the Americans yelled encouragement as they saw us returning. Then they saw the blank expressions on our faces as we shuffled along, and everyone grew silent.

The guards locked us in our cellblock, but did not lock us in our cell. They actually looked like they felt sorry for us and were kind enough to allow us some space to walk off our shock and frustration. I tried to get control of myself, keep myself from punching walls or screaming to God. I had no energy and needed to be alone. At the end of each cellblock corridor, there was a shower room. I walked to the shower room, not looking at or talking to anyone. I *had* to be alone. I could not face up to my sentence right now or face up to anyone else. The nightmare was never going to end, and I was afraid I was not strong enough to survive. I sat myself in a corner and huddled against the wall; self-pity overwhelmed me as I broke into sobs. Thirty fucking years ... I should've choked that dwarf!

Bob came in later and tried to comfort me, but I still wanted to be left alone. Whenever I was weak, it always seemed Bob was strong. When Bob weakened, it was I who maintained the strength. We kept each other going; we kept each other alive. I came to depend on Bob greatly, and I loved him like a brother. We were a team. We were in it together, whether we liked it or not. I had to keep it together to help him, and he had to do the same for me. I just couldn't lose my cool for good; he wouldn't let me. It was just my turn.

I sat in the shower for a long time. I finally stood up and decided to go back into the cell. I was still in a state of despair, but I could feel myself getting angrier and more determined to get out. *They aren't going to keep me here! Those bastards! I won't let them break me!* I was trying to convince myself.

Our sentence shocked the whole prison. As yet, Bob and I had been the only Americans to receive a sentence. The other Americans were now sweating their upcoming sentences, and they were trying to figure out a hustle that might help. We all started planning different ways to escape or increase our chances of getting out. For Bob and I, it seemed too late for anything but escape. The desperate look in most of the Americans' eyes kept the Mexicans suspicious and wary.

Before Christmas, a few of the wealthier prisoners were invited to pay $20 for the privilege of eating a meal in the library building with the new director, in celebration of the holidays. The new director was Señor Robles. Silverstrini, the large American from Oregon, had the money to pay for the meal. He attended the dinner in an attempt to hustle his way into the confidence of Robles. Silverstrini was determined to get out of the prison at any cost. He knew he could not depend on a lawyer, the United States, or the leniency of the judges. He would be helpful to the director and this could be his way out. Silverstrini spoke the most fluent Spanish of all the Americans. He had a way of making the Mexicans think he was having a good time and enjoying himself, so they began to trust him. The rest of us were too bitter and showed our desperation. Most of the Mexican guards liked Silverstrini and offered him food and special privileges. Silverstrini seemed to be having so much fun, they didn't think he would want to escape. The director started inviting Silverstrini and some of the wealthier Mexican trustees to small parties where they would get drunk and smoke marijuana. The Americans began to despise Silverstrini, yet he would try to help us with medical aid, communicating with the office, getting out mail, and getting us visiting privileges.

I was too bitter to devise a plan. I would sit in my cell, hating, wanting to destroy anything that got in my way. How would I tell my parents? I tried to write letters but was having a hard time keeping myself together, and I would become more depressed in my grief and frustration. My thoughts were too fuzzy to write. I was not sleeping at night, and each day seemed a little harder and longer. I didn't like to be around people, yet I could not sit by myself for long.

My hands were no longer steady, and I would often stare into space with tears dribbling down my face. I was angry for letting myself sink to such a dreadful state, but I couldn't seem to pull out of it. What had I done to deserve this? I had respected the Mexicans and their land, and I had tried to play by their rules. It had just been Bob and his surfboard, me and my camera, and, for such a short, sweet while, a beautiful Indian girl named Pati.

Bob and I worried about our own sanity. We could see the strain on ourselves and see it in the other Americans. Bob and I made four solemn promises: We would never become homosexuals, junkies, or Jesus freaks, or lose our sense of humor. To let any of these things happen was a sign that a person was giving up totally. Already, some of the Americans were using heroin. Charlie was frightened because the "queers were looking better all the time," and Brad, who had no previous religious affiliation, was quoting from the Bible.

These acute personality changes were a symptom of defeat. Bob was to beat the hell out of me if he saw any of these changes taking place, and vice-versa.

On Thursday December 14, 1973, two Americans came to visit me. They were friends of Gay. Gay had done everything she could to help, but she wasn't about to give up. She sent Wally Love, a ranch owner from Nogales, Arizona, and his ranch-hand, Bobby, to see if they could help. I was paranoid and distrusted these two men when they came to see me. I had been let down too many times. I was afraid of getting burned again. Wally Love was a tall, gangling, blond man who spoke with a down-home accent and wore a big smile. He was hard not to like. He appeared to be about twenty-eight, and he raised thoroughbred horses on his ranch. Bobby, the ranch-hand, appeared to be in his mid-to-late thirties and looked like he could handle a tough situation. Bobby was quiet and wore a tall cowboy hat like "Hoss" Cartwright used to wear in the TV show *Bonanza*. Wally and Bobby told me that they were working on a plan to get me out, and they were also checking the chances of bribing someone into letting me go. The plan was only a vague idea now, but they thought they could pull it off. They had already talked to a few lawyers, and Wally was going to try to speak with the judge. Wally kept trying to assure me, in his relaxed manner, all hope was not lost, and I should not give up. Which seemed worse? Letting your mind grasp at the slightest, smallest hope, or drown in the realization that there was nothing left and you may never see home again? I went with the hope. What did I have to lose, except a little more of my sanity?

I lost many a night's sleep over the next few months, waiting for Wally and Bobby's schemes to materialize. I would pace in anticipation. I wanted to believe, but I had been deceived so many times. Each disappointment wore me down all the more. It was tearing me up inside, yet I did know they were trying.

Bobby traveled hundreds of miles over the next several months, trying to find they key person to bribe. He spent more of his time trying to help me than he did working on the ranch. Wally turned out to be one of those "golden" people. He came to see me faithfully, and he kept me informed. He brought me food, clothes, sleeping bags, basic necessities, and even some games. He never forgot me. At times, it was hard for me to believe he was real. Wally didn't really know me. He certainly didn't owe me anything, and I was not a likeable person while in prison. So why was he helping me? He was an unbelievable surprise to me. There were still good people around! Not everyone had cruel and selfish motives. Wally instilled within me the will to go on. He was a bridge back to sanity, and he became my compass point back to the real world. I don't think we had much in common; I was becoming more radical, and he was conservative. He didn't like coming to the prison. He used to say it was worse than even visiting a hospital. I'm not even sure he believed I was innocent. Nevertheless, Wally kept my parents informed. He would send them a bill for the items he purchased for me, as my parents had requested, but he never took so much as an extra penny for himself. In fact, he lost time and money visiting me while trying to keep my head together. I don't think I will ever really understand him, but he helped me survive.

Chapter Twenty-Six

Christmas was horrible. It was the first Christmas I had ever spent away from my family. A guard came to our cellblock and told us that he felt sorry for us, being so far away from our families in another country. He said he would go into town and buy us some tequila if we could come up with the money. The guard wanted $16 per bottle, but we figured, why not? Wally had given us $20 on his last visit. However, the guard took our money and got himself drunk. We never saw the tequila.

New Year's Eve was a little better. Silverstrini talked the director into letting us have an FM radio and leaving the individual cell doors open so we could wander around the cellblock. Silverstrini, meanwhile, partied in the office with the director and the trustees, but he did bring us a large marijuana flower-top to help us celebrate the New Year. Thirteen Americans huddled together in the corridor of our cellblock, stoned and listening to the Allman Brothers concert live from San Francisco, hoping for a better new year.

There was little to do in the prison except worry or sleep. We had a Monopoly game and a game of Aggravation. We played these games into the ground. The food was slightly better, but not much. In the morning, we were served an oatmeal-type substance that worked well as glue or sealer for envelopes. In the afternoon we were given "grease soup." This soup was so loaded with grease that I would strain it through my now-long moustache in order to protect my stomach. I would take a spoonful, sip it through my moustache, wipe my face, and then start over again. Bob said I looked like a walrus. We were given a substantial bowl of beans in the evening. The poor food, the cold, and the boredom were definitely getting to many of the prisoners. Many men finally gave up. First they would stop taking showers, then stop shaving. These prisoners would try to sleep their days away by not getting off their concrete bunks. Then they would miss meals. Soon, the men would be too weak and too sick to move around, even if they wanted to. I forced myself to shave and shower every day. I would try to keep my clothes neat, and I tried to keep regular hours of sleep and exercise. I knew if I stopped, I would die.

My physical condition deteriorated anyway, and I began spitting up blood and experiencing severe stomach cramps. I had some problems with ulcers before coming to Mexico, but now the worry and frustration were taking its toll on my stomach lining. If only I could get into a hospital where the chance for escape would be greater ...

I paid $10 to see a doctor who visited the prison. He examined me and said he would send some medication by way of a guard. The medicine was stolen before I had a chance to see it.

On an afternoon when I was notably sick, I received an order to report to the main office. Two guards led me down to a room where an American waited. I had severe stomach cramps that day, so I apologized to him as I half-leaned, half-squatted against the wall. The man said he was the consul in charge of the American Consulate in Sonora. He was tall, thin, wore glasses, and had a dark hair with gray flecks. The man stated it was policy for a Consulate representative to visit with all the recently sentenced Americans. He said he knew of my thirty-year sentence and asked if there was anything he could do. I told him about my stomach and my medicine; then, I looked at the consul sadly and reflected on my fate.

"Thirty years. What did I do to deserve that? I had a good job before. I was a counselor; I helped people. Thirty years is so very long. What will I do? What can I do?" Tears blurred my vision. I hadn't expected this man to give me any answers. I just wanted a little compassion. Instead, I got bitter sarcasm. The man looked at me coldly.

"Thirty years is a long time to survive in a Mexican prison. More than likely, you'll die here. There's not really much you can do. You should have thought of that before you came into Mexico. There's nothing much we at the Consulate can do either, unless you do die," he said matter-of-factly. Then he added, "Don't worry ... we'll ship your body home in a wooden crate—if anyone still wants it by then." Something inside me snapped. I stood up slowly, staring at the man with hate-filled eyes.

"You dirty, rotten, son of a bitch!" I yelled at him as I sprang for his throat. I was going to strangle the bastard! He grabbed his briefcase and tried to dodge out of my way by running behind the desk.

"Stop him!" he yelled frantically to the two Mexican guards in the room. The guards ignored his pleas as they looked up at the ceiling with silly grins on their faces. I leaped across the desk, scattering papers and pencils as I grabbed him by the shirt.

"You lousy bastard!" I screamed as I began shaking him. I drew back my fist to smash his nose in, but the guards finally ran over and grabbed my arms. The man was definitely shaken and ruffled. He attempted to straighten his shirt hurriedly as he moved to get out of the office.

"Your kind deserves to be in prison!" he said shakily as he left.

"*Chinga su madre!*" I shouted behind him as the guards grinned and patted me on the back. "Fucking Americans!" It was a very long time before anyone from the American Consulate wanted to talk with me again.

My parents had already lost their life's savings, and we were not about to appeal our appeal. Within the prison, there was a man named Jorge Issachts Corrales. Jorge was an extremely intelligent Spaniard, a regal-looking man in his late forties, who had spent several years in Israel before coming to Mexico. In Mexico, Jorge became very interested in politics and ran for the governorship of Baja California. When it appeared that Jorge had a very good chance of winning the election, the present government had him arrested on trumped-up gun charges. They sent him to prison in a neighboring state, Sonora, to put distance between Jorge and his supporters. Jorge had not given up. Secretly, he was writing an exposé on Mexican politics and he had been smuggling the completed works to friends on the outside. He had been waiting in the prison for two years for a sentence that never came. Jorge became our friend. He attempted to teach us about the Mexican legal system and the proper procedures to try to get our sentence reduced. Although Bob and I had little hope, it did help to pass the time.

Jorge also liked to sit and talk with us about his book, *Los Derecho de los Fuertes* (The Rights of the Strong). The manuscript was almost finished, and he feared the political repercussions, but he was determined to see his book in print. Through Jorge, I was getting my first real glimpse of a country where there was no freedom of the press. He could be killed for words written on paper. I had always taken the freedom of speech and freedom of the press for granted. I began to feel guilty and ashamed of myself for not realizing how free I actually had been in the United States.

Meanwhile, the junkies were getting worse. We had to station guards at our cellblock to keep them out. To the right of our cellblock, there was a cafeteria that was not used, except to house a small store where food and coffee were sold to the prisoners. The junkies attacked and robbed the store on numerous occasions. A guard was placed at the store most of the time, but the store was finally forced to close down after a guard was hit in the face with a broken bottle and lost an eye. Visions of the old Nogales prison began to return. Heroin would be the destruction of us all.

Richard MacDonald, the large redheaded Canadian, and I decided to talk to the director of the prison and plead for his aid in combating the junkies. We felt that if he must let drugs in the prison, then he should keep it to the nonviolent drugs like marijuana. There was a shortage of marijuana in the prison, and an abundance of heroin. He was creating a powder keg that could explode at any time. The director listened, but he did not act. Marijuana smoking was too obvious, whereas heroin use could be concealed if political officials paid a surprise visit. The director did not see the danger of heroin. While he was safe in his office, surrounded by guards, we were left to protect ourselves.

Richard was called for his sentencia a few days after we approached the director about the heroin. Richard first thought he was being called to discuss the drug situation again; then he found he was to be sentenced. Richard expected to get axed, as we had. He was caught with several grams of hashish, and he had been waiting seven months for his sentence. He laughed most hysterically as he was being led down to the office. The only thing he had in his favor was his Canadian citizenship. The Canadian Consulate seemed genuinely concerned about their citizens. They had given Richard a good recommendation and had spoken favorably for him to the Mexican government. The Canadian Consulate had requested that Richard be returned to Canada. Richard came back with tears in his eyes and in semi-shock. He received a bondable sentence. He would be fined and allowed to go free. It paid to not be an American citizen. It proved that the Consulate *could* help a prisoner.

Seeing Richard leave didn't help my spirits. I was glad for him, but I was resentful. *I* had to stay behind. My physical health declined even more. My parents and friends were having a hard time understanding how prison life could cost so much money; I worked to eat in between my visits from Wally. I washed the dishes and cleaned the cell for John Putman for a share of his food. Putman was better off monetarily and helped us out whenever he could. He was not an easy man to get along with; however, he did realize it was necessary for us to stick together.

John would walk up and down the cellblock with me, devising plans and urging me to find a scheme to get myself out. We used to scope the prison constantly to find a weak spot in the security or a possible opening for escape. It was always self-defeating, because our desperation always seemed to give us away; we couldn't help but be obvious. It seemed that if one American noticed a possible escape route, all the other Americans would notice it at the same time. Our frantic eyes and the inept attempts to check out a section of the prison we thought was weak always tipped off the guards and brought tighter security. Soon that particular area would be sealed off.

I had to keep trying. In mid-January, the guards began leaving us out of the cellblocks and in the courtyards for a few hours a day. Two young Mexicans had tied together a number of blankets and attached them to a metal bar bent in the shape of a hook. One afternoon, the two Mexicans smuggled their blanket ladder into the courtyard.

The guards were preoccupied and did not notice the Mexicans as they snagged the bar onto the top of the wall. One of the Mexican boys shimmied up the blankets as the other steadied the bottom. As discreetly as possible, I moved to the blanket rope and took hold of the bottom to help the second boy make his way up. The first Mexican reached the top of the wall and was waiting for his friend when shots splattered along the wall. We had been spotted! I immediately dropped to the ground, and the Mexican boy, halfway up the rope, lost his grip and fell. The boy on top of the wall was hanging on and afraid to jump. The wall was approximately thirty feet high on the inside. On the outside, a trench had been dug around the prison, making the wall at least fifteen feet higher than the inside. A few more bursts of automatic fire came, and the Mexican lost his balance. He fell to the outside of the prison. I tried to crawl on my belly, away from the wall and back to my cell, but I was grabbed by the guards and thrown into solitary confinement.

The attempt was stupid, ill-planned, and doomed to failure, but I had to try when I saw them going. In order to escape from prison, you can never let yourself forget you are in prison. The more miserable you keep yourself, the more determined your will to escape. Many people adjusted to prison life. They forgot their priorities. The prisoners got accustomed to small privileges, and they often did not take risks for fear of losing those privileges. Which is more important: an extra bowl of beans and a book or an attempt at freedom? I never forgot I was in prison. I purposefully made myself more miserable, if possible, and I was always looking for a way out. Each time I was placed in solitary, I was all the more determined to try and escape again.

I was told later that the young Mexican boy who fell from the wall broke his legs and the guards used him for target practice as he tried to crawl away. His body was never brought back into the prison. I never knew his name. I wondered if he had any friends in the prison or on the outside.

The cell used for solitary confinement was large enough to stand in, but not large enough to lie down. There was a hole in the middle of the floor for defecating. It was dark and cold in the winter, and dark and hot in the summer. Water and beans were shoved under the door. There was no water for washing. I spent almost two weeks in the solitary cell. It was my first time, but not the last. Bob,

Charlie, or some of the Mexicans would sneak me magazines, writing paper, and pens. I would sit in the shadowed darkness and write letters. I never told the people to whom I wrote that I was in solitary at the time. Instead, I sketched cartoons and composed poetry to try to cheer myself up. But the unwritten message was in the letters: "I'm in solitary again, doing fine. I'll get out of here yet." When I was not straining my eyes over pen and paper, I would reminisce and fantasize. I would try to remember places I had driven; I would pretend I was in the car again and retrace the route. I would recall people's faces, their voices, and what they felt and smelled like. I would not let the Mexicans break me. I would not give up. I would not let them change the way I thought!

I was determined, but I was also losing. My poor physical health and my depression were breaking me. I was too confused to come up with a good escape plan, and too weak to carry out anything that would require much physical agility. I had to get out of the depression so I could think more clearly. I could feel myself sinking further away from freedom. I needed a miracle.

Chapter Twenty-Seven

It was now mid-February, and I was once again out of solitary. This time it had been for trying to smuggle a letter to a newspaper detailing our predicament. The store that was set up in the cafeteria section of the prison had been robbed by the junkies so many times that none of the Mexicans wanted to run it; it was too dangerous. Out of desperation, Director Robles put Joe Silverstrini in charge of the store. He had not given an American a position of authority before, but Silverstrini was big and could possibly protect the director's profits.

On the first day Silverstrini took over the store I was pacing up and down the cellblock corridor with Bob Smith and Brad Speare. Brad was quoting the Bible, so Bob and I ignored him. We saw Silverstrini enter the cellblock. He barely had time to unlock the padlocked door that led to the store when he was attacked by a mob of junkies. Silverstrini yelled for the Americans to help him, but many of the Americans did not like him. Some were jealous of his ties to the director, others went as far as to call him a collaborator. No one but us seemed to hear the call for help. No one else wanted to risk his neck for Joe.

Silverstrini was fighting in the middle of the mob, throwing Mexicans in every direction, and holding them at bay as he swung the padlock in defense. Silverstrini's eye and mouth were bleeding, and there was no way he could hold out much longer. Brad, Bob, and I looked at each other.

"He's always treated me fair." I said

"We're all God's children." Brad replied

"Besides, I'm bored." smiled Bob

All three shrugged our shoulders, and ran down the corridor as fast as we could go. We slammed hard into the back of the mob and began beating junkies, pulling them off Silverstrini. It caught the junkies with such surprise that they panicked and scattered. Bob, Brad, and I hadn't even been hit. We were out of breath but laughed triumphantly. It felt so good to be able to fight back and win! Silverstrini was noticeably shaken. He was bruised and bleeding and looked like he wanted to cry.

"Why didn't the other guys help?" Silverstrini's feelings were hurt more than anything.

Silverstrini needed some help. He needed someone who he could trust and who would cover his back. He needed all the friends he could get. The junkies would not forget they had been stopped from looting the store. Silverstrini offered Brad, Bob, and me the job of store guards. We would guard the store against the junkies in two-man shifts, and through Silverstrini's connection with the director we would receive more freedom to move about and food from the store.

It was a deal, although we knew there was no way we would stay and fight overwhelming odds to protect the director's store; at the first sign of a junkie attack, we would turn and run, but maybe we could eat well until that happened. Even better, we would not be locked up all day, and our chances of escape would increase.

Silverstrini had the store moved outside of the dormitory building to increase security. Somewhere, the director had found a metal Pepsi-Cola stand, the kind used at American football games, and we moved the food into the tiny stand. Silverstrini situated it on the lower courtyard, against the fence that separated the basketball court and the work buildings. We would be two gates closer to the main gate ... closer to the outside. The prisoners were only allowed out a few hours each day to come to the stand and buy food. The rest of the time, food was purchased through *mandaderas*, or runners. A Mexican assigned as a clerk handled the orders and the money. We were the only guards. The stand sold cookies, rolls, cake, candy, coffee, soda pop, dates, crackers, jalapeno peppers, sardines, and, of course, beans. There was not much of a selection, but it was better than what was being served upstairs. Bob, Brad, and I staggered our shifts so two of us were on guard throughout the day. I managed to grab a candy bar or a soda just about every time I went on duty. The Mexican clerk in the stand was swiping food and money by the armful. Silverstrini ate constantly too. The junkies were not the only danger to the stand's profits.

I could tell something odd was going on. I could sense it, and at other times I could see it. The junkies did not attack the stand. We were left alone for a week or more. The junkies would gather in groups outside the stand to glare at us and talk among themselves. I could feel a tension building up inside the prison. The junkies were interested in something much larger than raiding our tin stand. There were hushed words spoken of a revolution building on the outside. The name Lucio Cabanas—our Frank, and the leader of the revolutionary army that was forming—could be heard reverberating off the walls.

"Fifteen hundred soldiers went searching for Lucio Cabanas in the jungles of Michoacan, and no soldiers returned," we overheard the Mexicans saying.

"Lucio Cabanos will open the prisons and form an army of convicts. Cabanos and the Army of the Poor are heading toward Sonora." The rumors flourished, and a solemnity covered the Mexican prisoners. Secretly, the prisoners were preparing and waiting. "Revolution!" was whispered fervently and floated expectantly in the air.

The Americans were eyed with distrust and were excluded from the conversations of Lucio Cabanas. Bob and I told some of the friendlier Mexican prisoners that we knew Lucio, but they laughed, or called us liars. From the stand, I could watch the secret meetings and the plots being formed: a whisper, a passed word. I warned Brad and Bob that I thought the junkies were stirring themselves into a frenzy. We all felt uneasy. The junkies would hang around the fence of the work buildings and threaten and coerce the workers to give them gasoline-soaked rags. The junkies would then inhale the gasoline fumes, become intoxicated, and stagger around the prison, belligerent towards anyone who stepped in their way. The ritual of inhaling the gasoline fumes continued daily, until the junkies were like mad, drunken undead. The gas fumes deprived their brains of oxygen. Silverstrini would not walk anywhere in the prison alone.

Around noon, on March 4, 1974, Bob came down to the stand to relieve me. I grabbed a bunch of candy bars and headed back up to my cell. A guard opened the gates for me as I passed through the different sections. I was jumpy and glad to leave the store. The junkies seemed even edgier than usual and were again spaced out on the gasoline fumes. I wandered into our cellblock, where all the Americans were sitting in one cell, smoking a few joints. They had to roll the marijuana in toilet paper, paper bags, or strips of comic books, because rolling papers were illegal in Mexico, as if marijuana wasn't. I passed out the candy bars and squatted down to gossip and inhale some of the sweet marijuana smoke. At about one thirty, I heard the faint sound of firecrackers in the distance. Nobody else seemed to pay it much attention, so I ignored the noise and settled back to relax and enjoy my marijuana high.

Charlie, who now had the munchies from the weed, decided to go by the stand and try to con Bob or Brad out of some more free candy. There seemed to be a lot of movement in the prison as Mexicans hustled past our cell door and moved about nervously. Only moments had passed since I had first heard the firecracker sounds, when Charlie came bouncing back into our cell, wide-eyed, out of breath, and pale. "The junkies have got guns!" he screamed. "They've shot some of the guards and are attacking the main office! It's an escape … it's a big fuckin' escape!" he yelled before turning and running out of the cellblock and into the gunfire.

It took a few minutes before what Charlie had bellowed sunk in. He had to be kidding! We all jumped up and scrambled over each other to get out the cell door. It was a mad dash for a chance at freedom. What a rotten time to be stoned!

I ran down the corridor and out onto the upper-level basketball court, where I tried to clear my head. People were running in every direction. I heard five or six loud cracks, which sounded like gunfire, but I could not determine where the shots were coming from. The gates to the lower levels were still padlocked. There were no guards in sight; the guards in the towers were not visible. Some prisoners flung themselves against the gates, trying to force them open, while others tried to climb over. There were more shots, but I still couldn't tell where the gunfire was coming from, and I didn't see anyone falling. It was like being in a stoned dream. My knees began to tremble as I hurried to the locked gates. Three junkies came running up from the lower level with M-I carbine rifles. I noticed the glazed gasoline look in their eyes as they lowered the carbines at the locks and began to fire. I threw myself on my belly to avoid ricochets. The gates burst open as Mexicans cheered and rushed forward.

I scrambled to my feet and followed the mob as they headed to the level where the stand was located. It appeared as if the prison was completely taken over by the prisoners. I heard gunshots, but I could see no resistance from the guards. In fact, there were no guards anywhere in sight. Then I saw the stand. It was smashed. Food was strewn about the ground and there were bullet holes riddling the tin. Bob! Brad! What had happened to them? Instead of heading directly for the main gate, I ran to the wreckage of the tin stand to look for any signs of them. A few of the Mexican prisoners were still trying to salvage some of the food. I grabbed one of them by his arm and screamed, "Roberto? Brad?" The Mexican shrugged his shoulders and pushed my arm away.

Prisoners were running in all directions. Two younger junkies were standing next to the library building, arguing over an M-I carbine. The one junkie punched the boy holding the weapon in the face and tried to tear it from his grasp. The boy who had been hit swung wildly with a fist and pulled the trigger of the rifle. The other boy grabbed his forehead and screamed. He swayed back and forth, and then fell to his knees, still holding his head. He let out a low moan as the blood covered his face and he hit the concrete. The boy with the gun looked horrified. He stared at the unmoving body, dropped the carbine, and ran. I cursed my knocking knees and focused on the weapon. I had to find Bob. I had to escape, but not without him. I *had* to have that weapon! I crossed the distance swiftly, running hunched over, but others had the same idea.

A Mexican I knew only as Jessie reached the carbine first. He snatched it up and aimed it at my chest. I stopped short, watching his finger on the trigger, and wished I were somewhere else. Jessie, who was wearing a gray Western hat, stared into my eyes, and a big grin appeared on his face. He had the power of life and death over a gringo! He tilted his head slightly and then began to laugh. Without saying a word, he lowered the rifle and waved for me to follow.

Jessie and I ran cautiously to the gate leading to the office buildings. Through the office and out the main gate was freedom. The gunshots were more distinct and frequent now. I could finally see the guards on the lowest level. There was a great commotion coming towards us from the offices. Twenty-five or thirty prisoners burst out of the office and ran towards us. At first, I thought the guards were routing the prisoners, and I almost ran with the mob back to the cells. Then I saw the prisoners were carrying toasters, irons, radios, and other appliances. They had ransacked the offices but were *not* trying to escape! Instead, the Mexicans were running back to their cells with their plunder. "What the hell is going on? Are they crazy?" I yelled to Jessie. Jessie looked as confused as me.

It was appearing most of the junkies and Mexican prisoners were attempting to take over the prison and hold it like a fort. Already, gunmen were positioning themselves in the upper floors of the dormitories to await a siege. The Mexican prisoners had planned this day for months! A sympathetic guard had discreetly smuggled M-I carbines, .45 caliber machine pistols, and .38 revolvers in. (In Hermosillo, the capital of Sonora, there was a similar battle going on, which I was to hear of much later. The inmates of that prison set fire to the buildings and awaited the revolutionaries also.)

Jessie motioned for me to stay put as he readied to rush the office. I was sorry he had the gun; yet I was glad too. I was afraid to have the gun; it would make me a better target. I could follow after Jessie while he drew fire. My only thoughts were to survive unharmed and find Bob. Jessie looked into my tense face and smiled. He took off his gray cowboy hat and handed it to me.

"Here, hold this for me," he said in Spanish. "It's a good luck hat and I wouldn't want anything to happen to it." I took the hat as we squatted by the fence. Jessie winked, stood up, and bounded through the gate and down the stairs. I poised, waiting for a signal from him. He disappeared into the front office, and I heard gunshots echo through the building. I pressed myself hard against the concrete and waited as the seconds dragged on. Jessie suddenly backed out of the doorway in a half run. He stopped, fired three more shots from the hip, and turned towards me. He sort of gave me a sly smile and raised his hand in an "okay" gesture. I stood up, clutching his lucky hat, and ran towards him.

Bullets slammed into Jessie's chest. His mouth flung open violently, and his arms were thrown back as he dropped the gun and was lifted off his feet. There were more gunshots. Simultaneously, he was hit in the eye and throat, flipping him over backwards into the air in a bizarre ballet with death. I stood on the steps, frozen, as the life oozed out of him. I was still holding his lucky hat. I felt I was an observer in an indestructible bubble and not actually a part of this. A few more bursts of gunfire brought me back to reality. I tried to throw my body on the ground, but it seemed to be dropping in slow motion. I tried to melt into the concrete and out of the line of fire. I was wondering if Bob had ended up like Jessie. Yet, in the back of my mind, it seemed that this was only a game or part of a movie; nobody would really want to shoot me!

On the first-level basketball court, some of the junkies were organizing to rush the main office again. A few of the armed junkies had convinced many of the unarmed prisoners, in their gasoline stupor, to rush the office en masse. The junkies with guns would follow behind and use the mob as a shield.

I scrambled and crawled up the steps onto the court. There was no way I was going to rush in with the first wave of unarmed men! I flattened myself on the concrete again and waited for the results of the charge. The wave of prisoners readied, let out a yell, and charged through the main gate. A few stumbled and fell, while the men with the rifles kept behind the crowd, trying to pinpoint the position of the guards.

Pancho, the leader of the junkies, came limping in my direction with an M-I carbine, but he didn't seem to notice me. He had a pistol in his belt, and he held the carbine low at the hip with his right hand. He fired the carbine ahead of the rushing mob.

Suddenly, I saw Silverstrini appear around the corner of a building. He was carrying a shotgun. He crouched on one knee behind the building, leveled the shotgun at the mob of escaping prisoners, and pulled the trigger. He was shooting at the escapees! Silverstrini was trying to stop us from getting out!

Pancho spotted Silverstrini and blasted the wall around him. Silverstrini let off a second shot, jerked his head, and slithered out of sight. Pancho limped after the mob, into the office building.

Why was Silverstrini shooting at his fellow prisoners? I asked myself.

Meanwhile, in the office building, the mob had overrun the front office, wounded the guards, and captured the director. Pancho was behind the director, holding him around the throat from behind and pointing a pistol at his forehead. The guards and trustees attempted to make a counter-attack just as Pancho pulled the trigger.

The director flinched in fear ... and nothing happened! The pistol jammed. Pancho pushed the director out of the way as he lunged for the doorway leading to the main gate. The guards and trustees opened fire and hit one of the armed junkies in the spine, killing him. Pancho and approximately thirty prisoners stormed out the main gate to freedom. Only a few of the escaping prisoners had been armed.

Located a mile or more from the prison was a Mexican army barracks and, unfortunately, most of the escaped prisoners ran right into the oncoming soldiers. The military had been notified of the outbreak and were rushing to help the prison officials. The prisoners didn't have a chance. Those who weren't shot were brutally beaten with rifle butts.

As the army arrived at the prison, guards and trustees were holding the lower offices. Armed junkies secured the dormitories and upper levels. The majority of the prisoners, myself included, were somewhere in the middle, frantically looking for a way out. The guards and trustees rallied around the soldiers and then laid an intense barrage of fire on the courtyard and upper levels. The remainder of the armed Mexican prisoners in my vicinity retreated to the cellblocks and higher positions in the buildings. The junkies began to panic and take pot shots at anyone who was visible. I never knew which side was shooting at me.

Bullets splattered on a wall above me as I crawled on my belly and attempted to make my way back to my cellblock. I saw Karl, the medic, crawling along the top of an inner wall near a dormitory. A spray of bullets etched its way up the walls towards him and connected, shattering his arm, knocking him off the wall. He was smiling as he fell, like he couldn't believe it was he who had been shot. Karl crumpled to the ground like a broken doll.

I attempted to stand and run, yet I tried to look inconspicuous. My heart was racing, and I was unbelievably excited. I just wished my knees would stop shaking! I was fascinated by what was happening around me. I would run several yards, then flop down on the pavement as the bullets sped overhead, and rejoice that I was still unhurt and making it back to the cell block ... although I didn't know quite what I would do after I reached it.

I reached the upper level and threw myself down to catch my breath. A Mexican who had been running next to me yelped and grabbed a bleeding hand. I leaped to my feet and made a sprint for the dormitory and the relative safety of my cellblock. The junkies were firing back at the army from upstairs. I practically fell into the building. I made my way down the corridor and found most of the Americans in a few cells. I asked about Bob and Brad, but no one had seen them.

The soldiers began indiscriminately spraying the building with machinegun fire. Chunks of brick and glass scattered as the bullets ricocheted in and out of the corridors and cells. The junkies continued to battle.

The barred cell doors faced the corridor windows, which were targeted by the soldiers. I decided to crawl between the concrete pillars of the corridor to avoid the ricochets that were bouncing off the bars into the cells. Charlie moved out with me, and we dodged the bullets together. I could not sit and hide in a cell, waiting to be shot. It was my macho side coming out. I had to play the masculine game for myself. I also gained the utmost respect for Charlie. I always liked Charlie. You could count on him. Most of the Americans considered him an oaf because he could not read or write. That day he showed he had heart. We would look at each other sheepishly and smile as bullets slammed by.

The siege lasted for two or three hours. Bullets would echo against the bars and rip apart concrete. Someone would be dragged, hurt, into another building. Charlie and I would play our dangerous games as the soldiers advanced slowly, scarring the building with huge holes as they came, shooting anything that moved and a lot of things that didn't. More glass shattered and tear gas canisters flew into the corridors. We didn't know what the soldiers would do to us, so we placed wet towels over our noses and tried to hold out against the tear gas. More tear gas canisters crashed into the building. My eyes burned and watered, and I couldn't keep myself from rubbing, which only made things worse. A Mexican panicked and ran blindly out of the doorway. The soldiers promptly fired at him, so he scrambled back into the building.

The guards began to shout to us over megaphones, "Come out in single file and we will not harm you!" No one wanted to be the first to go out. Hesitantly, two Mexicans moved out of the doorway. They were instantly shot at. I thought of how the Mexican soldiers had shot 350 unarmed students in the demonstrations to protest the Olympics. I started to edge my way to the back of the line. The guards shouted for us to come out again. This time several different prisoners walked into the open. No shots were fired. I walked out of the dormitory with a knot in my stomach. We were shoved and pushed into lines on the basketball court. The guards, trustees, and soldiers were screaming angrily and waving their weapons threateningly. I was not convinced we would not be massacred on the spot. Silverstrini was nowhere around; maybe he had been wounded or killed.

Bob and Brad were still missing. The guards walked through the lines, angrily identifying the instigators of the riot. The soldiers struck and beat those identified men with their rifle butts and dragged them toward the prison offices.

A formation of soldiers led a string of prisoners towards us. I could see Bob and Brad strolling along in the midst of them. I broke into a big smile knowing that we would still be together and that he was unharmed.

When the riot broke out, the stand was one of the first places to be hit. Bob was standing next to the stand when bullets tore through it and the office buildings were first rushed. Bob and Brad took off into the office complex with the first wave of Mexicans. They turned a corner and were intercepted by a small guard with a very large pistol. In broken Spanish, Bob tried to explain he was only trying to see what was going on and report the destruction of the store. The guard must have believed him, for he took Bob and Brad to an outlying section, where they waited out the battle.

There were many casualties, and there would be more. Jorge Issachts Corrales, the author, rushed from the lower dormitory during the tear gas attack and pleaded with the soldiers and junkies to stop the insanity and call a truce. However, the strain had been too much for him; he suffered a stroke, causing paralysis of the left side of his body. He was dragged to the offices for medical attention.

The prison became a quarantined military camp. The soldiers were ordered to stay indefinitely, and we were thrown into the cells where the tear gas lingered. My eyes watered and my skin burned. All but four or five of the escapees were shortly captured. Miraculously, Pancho got away! The prisoners held directly responsible for the riot were kept in a section of the office complex. Their screams would drift up to us as they were interrogated for information and confessions. It went on for days on end. Their screams would run through me like chills. The prison officials and the soldiers did not want to have a hand in the torture. They left the interrogations up to the trustees. Prisoners were to torture other prisoners, for favoritism. Ears were beaten off, fingers were broken, toes were shot off, and bodies were burned. A favorite interrogation method was to lay a prisoner on his back, blindfolded and tied. A trustee would place a foot on the prisoner's throat to hold him down, while seltzer water was shot up the prisoner's nose with a hypodermic needle to gag him. Meanwhile, another trustee beat the prisoner with a flat board. At night, many of the prisoners being held for interrogation were slipped razor blades and encouraged to commit suicide; many of them were persuaded and succeeded.

The screams echoing throughout the prison brought on a silent mixture of fear and insanity for those who could do nothing but listen helplessly and imagine what horrors must be going on.

Days passed with little change. Occasionally, the soldiers would return to the dormitories to drag another suspect from his cell, while most of us waited to be next. We were not fed during this time.

The fourth day after the riots had been put down, two guards came to the cellblock and called for Bob Smith and myself. We both thought it was all over for us. My stomach felt as if it had just experienced a sudden drop in an elevator. The guards silently led us to the first courtyard, to Silverstrini. I was confused. I thought we were to be interrogated; instead, Silverstrini, who was whistling and happily cleaning up the mess that had once been the store, met us. Silverstrini turned to us with a big grin as he waved the guards off. They left us alone with him. Silverstrini had a deal.

Chapter Twenty-Eight

When the riot broke out, Silverstrini was in the office, smoking marijuana with the trustees. He knew the junkies hated him and they would probably shoot him given the opportunity. So, he chose to take sides with the director. Afterward, the director felt indebted to Silverstrini and gave him a semi-private room in the office area as well as control of all food sold in the store. In some ways, I disliked Silverstrini. He was a hustler and his only loyalty was to himself. If we were drowning, he was the type to stand on my shoulders to save himself. Yet, he helped us and I owed him. The remainder of the prisoners already knew of Silverstrini's part in preventing the escape. Some prisoners vowed to kill him. The American contingent now despised him. Silverstrini needed someone he could trust and depend on, so he chose to trust Bob and I; He knew we were indebted and loyal.

Silverstrini wanted Bob and I to work in the stand after it was rebuilt. He wanted us to select a trusted Mexican to help, and the three of us would be given food and more freedom for our efforts. If we proved ourselves trustworthy, there was a good possibility we could be moved out of the cellblock and into the office section. Bob and I took the offer; we were hungry. We cleaned up the store area and banged the tin walls back into shape.

Silverstrini would take care of the money, take inventory, and order supplies. We were to be clerks and guards. We had to improve our Spanish quickly!

That evening, Bob and I sat in our cell, discussing our new job. It was worth a try. We approached a Mexican from the Southern regions of the country, who had seemed friendly and wealthy enough. We felt he wouldn't have to steal, and he didn't use heroin. Horatio Munoz of Guadalajara quickly accepted our offer, and we shook hands. Things were changing for the better.

Each morning, we would get up early and open the stand. Horatio Munoz would teach us Spanish, and we helped him with English. I began to learn the Spanish words for *cookie, crackers, cherry, soda,* and *Kellogg's Corn Flakes*. I was becoming the opposite of the Mexican grocer who had attempted to interpret for us when we were first arrested. I was definitely not a conversationalist.

Silverstrini stocked the stand with bread, cakes, peanut butter, tuna, coffee, and nutritional supplies, so we ate better. We would also try to give out bread and other food to the poorer prisoners at the end of each day. The prisoners would send their money and their orders with a runner, and we would fill them. The stand kept me occupied and healthier. There was still a lot of resentment towards Silverstrini from the prisoners, and some of the resentment transferred to Horatio, Bob, and me for helping him.

At night, when we would return to our cells, we had to be on guard constantly. The atrocities in the office sections continued, so most prisoners were hesitant to do anything that would attract attention to them, but we still had to be careful. I saw a result of the interrogations one morning as I was walking to the stand. I passed a man wearing bloody, torn rags. He was under heavy guard. One of his ears was gone, his arm appeared to be broken, his head was shaved, and his face had been beaten beyond recognition. I didn't know who it was, although I later learned I had lived with the man for more than nine months. It was the Butcher, seller of heroin in the old prison. The Butcher had been an evil man, but not even he deserved that fate.

The prison began tightening its security; chain-link fences were stretched from guard tower to guard tower on top of the high walls, and electrified barbed wire was placed on top of that. A guard building was placed on top of a water-storage well that overlooked the prison, and manned with automatic weapons. With these extra precautions, the prisoners were eventually allowed out of their cells during the day, and visitor's day was reinstated.

Chapter Twenty-Nine

I had to figure out a way to get our sentences reduced. Working in the stand was a start, but it was not enough. I began to write letters to everyone I thought could help. I wrote the *Los Angeles Times*, *Playboy*, *Time*, *Newsweek*, *Penthouse*, the *Philadelphia Bulletin*, and many more. People had to know about our plight. I had to smuggle many of the letters out, and I also had to be very conservative in what I said, in case the Mexicans intercepted the letters. I also wrote letters for the Americans as a group. Wally Love continued to visit me regularly, so I gave him a few of the letters to carry out. I did not want to endanger him, so we often gave the letters to Mexican visitors who seemed sympathetic, or to strangers.

I had to keep as busy as possible. The strategy of the Mexicans was to make us lose our self-respect from the moment we were first arrested. We were treated like animals and spit upon. I kept busy at working on being a human again. I was fighting to keep my health and my sanity, to keep from being broken. I had to tell myself I would be home soon. I wanted to be home so bad it hurt, and I wanted to scream, but I couldn't even admit that to myself. So, I wrote my letters, worked in the store, concentrated on Spanish, and tired not to dream of freedom.

I wrote the State Department a long, lengthy letter describing my situation and asked a lot of questions as to why nothing was being done. I had received no reply from any of my other letters, and I expected none from this particular letter as I handed it to a Mexican visitor to be mailed. Approximately three days later, I was called to the office section of the prison, and I was told three Americans were waiting to see me. I was ecstatic! I hoped I was getting a response from my letters. At last, something might be done to help! I practically skipped down to the office.

Three shabbily dressed men waited for me. Their appearance took me by surprise. They wore casual, dusty clothes, needed shaves, and appeared to have been on the road for some time. I only identified them as Americans when they spoke to me in English.

"Are you Steve Wilson?"

With a large smile, I nodded. Two of the men grabbed me by the arms and held me tightly; the third man began hitting me hard in the stomach with his fists.

"We read your letter," one of the men said calmly. "We don't want to read any more." I struggled and tried to kick out at them, but it was useless. They let me slump to the floor and left. I didn't write any letters for a long time afterwards. I was paranoid to even write to my family for fear of repercussions. I suspected those three men had something to do with the U.S. government, maybe the DEA. Don Orelio, an Indian and sergeant of the guards, lifted me off the floor. He was a heavyset man with a large grey walrus mustache, who always wore a straw cowboy hat.

"You are no longer an American," he said to me sadly in Spanish. "You be good, and I will no longer let them speak with you. You are a Mexican now."

I still wouldn't give up. I would just have to use a different approach. I began to write and translate a rehabilitation program into Spanish for the prison. If I did something to benefit the people of Mexico, my sentence might be reduced.

The prisoners wounded from the riot slowly began to return. Jorge Issachtts Corrales was paralyzed on the left side and had to move about on crutches. He continued, however, to write the final chapters of his book, and he still advised Bob and me about our sentence. Karl, who had been shot off the wall, spent several weeks in the hospital. He was weak and his arm was not completely healed. The bone had separated, and he needed a vital operation and a pin to keep his arm in place. The Mexican doctors feared gangrene would set in if the operation were not completed soon. The operation cost money, Karl was poor, and the prison refused to finance it. Silverstrini and several Americans approached a representative of the American Consulate and begged for the Consulate to help Karl. The Consulate refused. They said there was no money allocated for such circumstances, and there was nothing they could do. "Besides, he shouldn't have gotten himself into that situation in the first place." The reply of the American Consulate so angered the Mexican and American prisoners that a collection was taken among the prisoners themselves and the money was raised. Even the poor contributed what little money they had. The Consulate had a way of making us feel all the more lost and alone. Didn't anyone care? Were we that bad a group of people? I wasn't sure anymore.

More prisoners arrived continuously, including more Americans. Bob Champion, a retired Air Force mechanic, was brought in. He was a novice pilot, and had been moving some things to a new home in Tucson using a small chartered plane when he somehow flew off-course during the flight. Champion never admitted it, but we suspected he probably had a beer or two before getting lost. He landed at the nearest landing strip and was soon told he was on a customs runway in Mexico. Champion asked a policeman for directions and then caught a taxicab to the nearest Federale station to ask for advice. The Federales asked Bob to spend the night while they straightened out the paperwork. Bob Champion spent the night in a local hotel and returned to the station the next morning. He was placed in a car and taken to the Nogales prison, where he was accused of carrying contraband. The plane was the contraband and Champion was facing a minimum of six years in prison ... for getting lost.

Other Americans entering the prison were Pat Rhondo, a bald-headed Californian who was arrested for an ounce of marijuana; Steve Caudle, another North Carolinian, who was arrested for a gram of heroin; and Leland Hare and Nancy Craig, who were arrested for several pounds of marijuana.

Nancy was placed with the female prisoners and refused to cooperate with the Mexican officials. Nancy was a strong-willed girl who adapted well. She resisted the Mexicans' sex games; she was offered a more comfortable life, booze, drugs, and privacy if she cooperated. It not, she would be fed poorly and put in a cell with the worst of the female prisoners. Nancy managed to hold out and gained the respect of the Mexicans and Americans. Leland came from a wealthy family in California; he was spoiled and had a penchant for attracting trouble. The Mexicans kept making things very difficult for Leland, who spent most of his time in solitary confinement. He was continuously trying to escape and getting caught. Bob Smith and I sent food to Leland whenever we could.

With the new prisoners, came new rules. The Mexican prison officials no longer wanted the prisoners to have beards although moustaches were permitted. Therefore, every few weeks we were forced to have a mandatory shave. We were not allowed to have razor blades, so those of us without electric razors were shackled, both on our hands and feet, and shuffled down to an outer office by a guard, where a prisoner-barber would shave us with a straight razor. It was my turn, and I was shackled and placed in the barber chair, then strapped in. My barber was a Cuban prisoner who had a reputation of being loco. He lathered my face up and began to slide the razor across my stubble. I heard a snap and the barber took a deep sigh and began laughing uncontrollably. Another snap and more screams of laughter as he wielded the straight razor. I felt the razor nick my cheek as I tried to glance up at the barber. He had two amylnitrate capsules stuffed up his nose. I tried to jump out of the chair, but I was strapped in. I felt another nick. "Whoa! No! That's enough!" I yelled. I heard another snap and he shoved a broken amylnitrate capsule up my nostril. I felt a tremendous rush of dizziness and began to scream with laughter as I continued to yell, "No! No!"

About this time Leland was led shackled into this weird scene for his turn in the chair. He saw the barber screaming with laughter, making wild swings with the razor, and me, sitting in the chair with tiny flecks of blood coming through the lather, laughing just as crazily.

Leland's eyes popped wide and he threw himself to the floor. "No way! No way am I getting in that chair!" The guard tried to lift him up by the shackles to no avail. Leland struggled and continued to yell that there was no way he was getting a shave. The guard finally gave up and urged Leland out the door ... and back to solitary confinement. The amylnitrate wore off quickly. The Cuban showed me a mirror. My face reflected back clean-shaven with only a few minor razor cuts, until the next few weeks.

Another man who entered the prison was Daniel Ruiz, a large Mexican-American Indian. Daniel had been a heroin addict for years and his arms were black from needle marks. He stole a truck in the United States and drove it into Mexico, where he had planned to sell the truck to support his drug habit. Ironically, the truck had previously been stolen in Mexico and taken to the United States. He had returned a stolen truck to Mexico and was arrested for it. Heroin was still available in the prison, but one day Daniel approached me and asked me if I would help him stop using the drug. I agreed. We agreed that any time I would see Daniel attempt to use or buy drugs, I would hit him. We would fight or wrestle until both of us were too exhausted to do much else. I worked off my frustrations, and he worked off his addiction. I could fight with Daniel and know he wouldn't really try to hurt me, although his huge, six-foot-four frame often provided me with many bruises.

It took several months before Daniel was completely free of heroin. He had a tough time kicking the habit, so I got him a job in the stand to direct his attention away from heroin and so I could keep a closer eye on him. The Mexican nationals hated Mexican-American *pochos*. These were Mexicans who left Mexico in hard times and supposedly came back to show off. In many ways, Daniel had it harder than me.

Weeks passed, and Daniel and I worked well together. As the heroin addiction faded, Bob also grew to like Daniel. Daniel had a good sense of humor, acted as an interpreter, and told us he was a semi-professional boxer before his drug troubles. It was hard not to like this huge Indian.

One day, while working in the stand, Daniel asked me if I would become his brother and join his tribe. I agreed half-heartedly, not understanding. After lock-up, Daniel led me to a cell in the Indian section of the cellblock. A blanket was draped over the front of one cell, closing the cell off from the corridor. Two men guarded the entrance.

Daniel pulled back the blanket, crouched down, and let me inside the smoky cell. My eyes burned and watered as I gazed at a dozen or more men sitting around a kerosene stove with a boiling pot on top.

Sitting on top of a concrete bunk, a young man beat on a taught stretched T-shirt that covered the top of a bucket—a makeshift drum. I was motioned to sit in the circle next to Daniel.

"Esteban, in this ceremony you will be given a sign and a chant. Look for these things." Daniel handed me a palm-sized peyote button. I was instructed to chew the spongy button. It tasted horrible! It was acrid and made me want to gag. Daniel encouraged me to continue chewing, so I did, with effort.

The cell was hot and stuffy. The drum thumped in the background. My stomach churned, and I wanted to throw-up. Daniel shoved several more buttons in my mouth.

A man passed a small pan for members of the circle to puke into. I threw up on the floor, not caring, as I noticed the colorful hues that spewed from my mouth. I knew I was very stoned and thought it was really neat; I didn't mind throwing up again.

The buttons tasted less bitter as I continued. My body took on an unnatural feeling. I forgot where I was. Daniel talked to me, but I couldn't remember what he said. Sounds echoed in my ears. I was frightened, then ecstatic. I noticed things and people in the cell, and then I was lost. I was very high. I began to make chanting sounds. "Hey ya ya, hey ya ya".

Someone grabbed my hand and cut my palm with a knife. I was too confused to be frightened now. Daniel grabbed my right hand as another Indian gripped my left. The circle of men held each other's bleeding hands.

I was lost again. I cried real tears and babbled to a day-glow Indian standing in front of me. He told me I would be all right and the others in the room would help protect me. He vaguely resembled Daniel as he drew a design on the floor in front of me. It was a winged serpent. This would be my sign and help protect me. The peyote continued to take effect, and I drifted to many places. At one point I felt like I was outside and looking down upon the prison and the surrounding area from a great height. At another I could hear the ocean and smell sea air. I felt free.

I was eventually aware of the cell and my surroundings again. I was still not in control of my senses as Daniel lifted me by the arm and led me back to my cell. I noticed it was morning. I was back from some strange place, and I was glad to be alive. It was a new day, and I was alive! It felt good, even here in the prison. My new brother and I would survive! I tried to explain my euphoria to Daniel, but he only smiled and helped me to my bunk, where I fell into an exhausted sleep.

Daniel's miracle cure worked. It was good to be alive ... and sane. The drug wore off, but some of the euphoria remained.

Chapter Thirty

Gradually, my health and my emotional tolerance improved. Daniel, Horacia, Bob, and I became a team, with Silverstrini as our coach. We often found it hard to tolerate Silverstrini. He could be very demanding, but we owed him a lot. We were no longer sitting idle in a cell. Our work in the store kept us active and forced us to learn Spanish.

Silverstrini approached me one afternoon and asked if I ever played a game called Blitzkreig or Stalingrad, by Avalon-Hill. The army colonel in charge of the prisoners had confiscated the games when someone tried to send them to an inmate. Now the colonel was demanding that someone teach him how to play. I had been playing these military games since I was ten years old. My status in prison was about to increase measurably ...

Silverstrini took me to the office, where I slowly, painstakingly taught Silverstrini and three officials to play the games. The Mexicans included the colonel; Alejandro Teran, a presidential policeman who was in disfavor and serving a minor sentence; and Jorge Cachon, an undercover agent also in the same predicament as Alejandro. I became an instructor and arbiter of rules, and I slowly began building trust among the prison officials as they excitedly played out the part of Hitler and his blitz. They learned to play the games faster than I expected, yet they played the way I would expect a Mexican to wage war: the object of the games was to acquire cities, but the Mexicans kept abandoning the cities and taking to the hills and deserts. The colonel said I could keep the *pinci* (fucking) cities; it was safer in the hills. He also was too macho to resist attacking, even when he was on the defensive.

I won many of the games, and they gave me much more mobility in the prison. They were my keys to the office section and gave me an excuse to be out of my cell at odd hours. Frequently, I would hear a megaphone bellow out for Herr Wilsonski, and I would go to the office section to play or to umpire a game. I could be called at any time of the day or night, so the guards became accustomed to seeing me wander around.

The games would last for hours at a time and the players took them seriously. Often, large bets would be placed on the games. Cochon, Alejandro, Silverstrini, and the colonel would divide into teams, and the director and other officials would be spectators. The stakes ranged from large sums of money to bottles of cognac, and on one occasion an ounce of cocaine. I was given cognac, beer, and marijuana, and gained respect for my efforts.

I didn't actually realize how seriously the games were being taken until I was called to the office one afternoon to be Silverstrini's advisor. Cochon was to play Silverstrini—the Americans against the Mexicans. Alejandro was to be Cochon's advisor. There were many spectators, and the stakes were four bottles of cognac. Silverstrini played an excellent game and had Cochon surrounded and near defeat after five long hours. Cochon suddenly stood up and screamed, ripping the board from the table and flinging it against the wall, scattering the playing pieces on the floor. As Cochon ranted and raved, Silverstrini calmly pulled out his penis and urinated on Cochon's few remaining soldier pieces and then danced and stomped on the rest of them.

Cochon's face turned scarlet red. He stammered curses at Silverstrini as he leaped towards him and tried to strangle him. They fought and wrestled for another thirty minutes until they were too exhausted and lay panting on the floor. The game was called by default. The spectators helped a tearful Cochon attempt to tape the board back together and wipe the urine off his soldiers. I was careful not to win too many games afterwards.

I felt the games helped Bob and me from being switched to another prison; we were already sentenced, and sentenced prisoners were to start being transferred to other prisons. The transfers, or changes, had been rumored since I had arrived at the new Nogales prison, but they remained only rumors until some months after the riot when the first change came. It was late at night, and all prisoners were locked in the cells. I was lying awake when I thought I heard the sounds of engines idling and boots marching across the concrete. From my cellblock, I could also hear the sounds of cell doors opening and closing and people yelling or pleading. I tried to stretch myself up so I could look out the window and down into the courtyard, but I was too short. The Mexicans in our cellblock became very nervous as they whispered among themselves, "The change." I could hear voices pleading and begging more distinctly, so I crawled on the top of Bob's shoulders and strained at the barred window to see.

In the courtyard were men in plainclothes—Federales. They were leading men, naked or only in the underwear, to the center of the courtyard in very rough manner. Those who tried to resist were hit with rifle butts. I could just barely make out a man without clothes, on crutches, being pushed along. It was Jorge Issachts Corrales! A Federale grabbed Jorge's crutches, and Jorge fell to the ground. Another man kicked him several times, and I couldn't restrain myself as I hung onto the window. They were making Jorge crawl to the trucks that would take him away.

Jorge had been our friend. They would cause him to have another stroke, killing him. I screamed to him, "Jorge, no!" I screamed his name over and over again, "Jorge, Jorge!" as I watched his frail body trying to move along the concrete. The other prisoners began to chant his name. The Federales were trying to kill him, for words he had written on paper. They were trying to destroy him for his ideas, for his book. I fell off Bob's shoulders as a guard slammed open the cell door. I started yelling at the guard, "They're killing Jorge!" The guard pointed his rifle at me ominously until I broke into tears of frustration. They took Jorge away for his thoughts—a good man gone.

The next morning I felt like I was a survivor at the aftermath of a battle. Who was left? Who had they taken? Since the riot the junkies and more dangerous prisoners were segregated in a separate dorm. The prison felt safer. Regular Mexican prisoners didn't fear reprisals from the junkies, so they interacted with us more. We traded with them, joked and talked of home. I had my Indian brotherhood, my regular customers at the stand who I spoke with every day, and the poor prisoners who we gave food from the stand. People I had lived with for months and grown to like were suddenly gone. Over a hundred prisoners had been moved. Would I ever see them again? Were they all right? I would wander from cellblock to cellblock, trying to see which of my friends remained. We wrote the prisons where the missing men would most likely be transferred, but many of them were never heard from again. Prison officials and guards insinuated that many of the transferred prisoners were killed in escape attempts somewhere in the desert. They never reached the new prison. Interestingly enough, many of the instigators of the March 4th riot were never heard from or seen again.

Losing my friends in this manner only increased my feelings of alienation and loneliness. I knew it would be the loneliness that would finally break me. It was that feeling that broke us all. I had lived through emotional periods that were laced with false hope, and each period was a trial where I had to fight to live as human being, to keep it together. I made it through the panic and the fear, the despair and the depression, but it was the staggering loneliness that could destroy me. Pati was gone, my old friends were gone, and now my new friends had disappeared. It felt that I was absolutely alone and no one really cared … and I stopped caring as well.

Although Bob and my conditions had improved we were still in a prison. I hurt deep in my throat and deep down inside of my chest. Sometimes I would cry for no reason. I had not been touched tenderly by another human being in over a year. I had been shown no affection; I had not hugged or touched a familiar face. How I wanted to be hugged, just for a little while, and be told I would be all right. I needed that so desperately. I dreamed of paying some girl just to hold me for a while, so I could live in the ecstasy of that lie, yet I knew it would only remain a lie. I had written more than 127 different people from the prison, asking for a hello and a little reassurance that I was not alone. Only a handful of people replied, and the longer I remained in prison, the fewer they became.

Daniel, Horatio, Bob, and Silverstrini were all still with me, but they were as desperate as I, and therefore didn't count. My life was caught up in some cycle of fate that I believed I could not control.

Silverstrini continued to exploit his hustles on the director. He convinced the director that the prison population would benefit if a restaurant were constructed inside the prison—operated by Silverstrini, of course. I completed my rehabilitation program and submitted it to the director. The director took the program to Hermosillo, the capitol, where it was favorably received, in the director's name. The director showed his gratitude by moving Bob Smith, Horatio, and me into the work area of the prison; however, the director would not move Daniel because he was a pocho. The section was adjacent to the first-level basketball court and much more comfortable. The director completed the restaurant, gave control of it to Silverstrini, and gave Bob and me complete control of the tin stand. The director also wrote Bob and me a recommendation of good conduct for the court. Bob and I hoped that our sentences might be reduced.

The work section contained a long building that housed a TV and electronics repair shop, a body shop for cars, a furniture-making shop, and a watch repair shop run by Bob Champion. The privileged workers and those who could pay the money were allowed to live in the shops. The long building also housed the wealthier trustees, who could pay for private rooms constructed in this area. The prison was definitely a profit making institution. The director also had hot-water showers built for those who could pay for the convenience. And of course, there were still the drugs.

We ordered food and kept the stand well supplied as Silverstrini worked the restaurant. I was able to convince the director to get fresh fruits. At the end of each day, we would distribute the leftover fruit to the poor and hungry and report to the director that it had been spoiled or crushed. We tried to be fair about running the stand, and we gained many allies amongst the prisoners for our efforts.

Chapter Thirty-One

It had been over a year since our arrest, and I continued to change and adapt. Don Orelio, my sympathetic guard friend, who I referred to as Deputy Dawg, asked me one afternoon why I never had any female visitors, or if I was married. I explained to Don Orelio that I had no one on the outside, and I told him about Pati. He seemed saddened by what I related to him and shocked when he realized that I had not had sex in over a year. He must have told the female prisoners, because each time I would pass the area where the women were taken to make tortillas for Silverstrini's restaurant, the women would hoot and point at me, saying, "*Un ano, un ano*," one year, one year. They would laugh and make wild sexual gestures. I started to feel like a eunuch. The women and Don Orelio were plotting to change my fate.

Don Orelio marched up to the store with two guards one afternoon and gruffly ordered me to pick up the new supplies. The two guards led me down to the supply closet, where I had to pass by the women prisoners. The women were quiet and only stared after me with big grins. I began to feel very uncomfortable. The guards stood behind me as I unlocked the supply closet door. As I opened the door, the guards shoved me in and locked the door behind me.

Standing in the middle of the closet, naked, was a very pretty, petite, young Mexican girl. She smiled at me slyly and whispered, "*Un ano, gringo!*" My mouth fell open and I gawked in disbelief. Don Orelio had arranged a present for me, for my one year anniversary of celibacy! He had waited until a very pretty girl with an open mind was picked up by the police and explained my situation to her. The girl came willingly. Two guards were posted outside the door so we wouldn't be disturbed, and the women making tortillas acted as lookouts.

I felt awkward; I didn't know where to start or how to act. She came closer to me, hugged my waist, and began to unbutton my shirt and pants. I was definitely aroused. I kissed her and caressed her breasts as we slid down onto a pile of flour sacks. I felt as if I was moving in a dream, in slow motion, and yet watching myself.

I had missed so much during my imprisonment, and I tried to fantasize that she was Pati, suspended in time in a supply closet. We explored each other's bodies time and time again; yet, in the back of my mind, I felt more and more resentful. I was being reminded of what I had lost and what I was missing. I had been given the taste of a fine jewel, only to have it taken away from me.

A knock came at the door much too soon. Reluctantly, we dressed. It was dark now. We had been in the closet for hours! The girl, whose name I had forgotten to ask, kissed me tenderly one last time. She quickly fondled my penis through my pants and then returned to the women prisoners. I couldn't conceal my pleasure. I felt as if I was walking on highly elevated shoes with soft, spongy soles. I couldn't stop smiling. As I passed the women, where the girl was explaining our exploits in detail, I saw her for the last time as she blew me a kiss. Now someone else had been taken away from me, although I kept the scent of her body with me for days.

Don Orelio tried to hide a grin behind his gruff exterior as he led me back to my cell. Finally, he burst out laughing and slapped me on the back. "You were in there so long; I thought maybe she killed you!"

I blushed, laughing. It was a sweet bitterness that brought a smile to my face. I had to get out soon! I didn't want to wait another year before having sex let alone thirty.

Chapter Thirty-Two

Changes continued to alter the prison. The director was thrown out for political reasons and replaced by a new director, who was a homosexual. The soldiers gradually left, and Silverstrini was sentenced. Silverstrini was given the option of a three-and-one-half-year prison term or heavy fines, for possession of thousands of pounds of marijuana. He paid $50,000 and gladly left. Horatio received a similar sentence for tons of marijuana and was also waiting to go home. At least some people were going home. We hoped the pressure from the United States on Mexico was easing off.

It was August 8, 1974. Richard M. Nixon was forced to resign. Maybe things would change ... it was *his* policies that were making things for Americans so difficult, wasn't it? The Mexicans wheeled in televisions so we could watch the resignation. I felt humiliated by and ashamed of Nixon. The Mexicans jeered him *and* us. But maybe things would get better ...

On September 1, 1974, I was called down into the office to interpret Pat Rhondo's sentence; by now I was relatively fluent in Spanish. The sentence was read to me and I felt sick all over. I turned to him and said sadly, "They've got you, man—five and one-half years for a handful of marijuana, without bond ... while the real smugglers and dealers buy their way home. They got you like they got me. I wouldn't appeal if I were you."

As we turned to walk out the door, we passed a Mexican by the name of Don Govinda, who was going home. He had been arrested for five kilos of heroin and was going home after paying a $2,400 fine. I couldn't look at Pat anymore.

They destroyed him! They destroyed one of our tribe, just as they destroyed me, the inside of my head roared as I numbly walked up the steps. I didn't want to think of anything right then; it was too heavy, and I didn't want to blow any fuses. So I went back to the work area and walked into the watch repair shop, where Bob Champion was. I said casually, "Hey, Bob they just ..." and my mind couldn't take it anymore. I tried to start over again, but my words caught in my throat and I broke down into tears.

"They got Pat," I managed to strangle out. Champion started crying too. We were both ashamed of our country for allowing this to happen. The United States was still encouraging the Mexicans to treat us more harshly. The situation narrowed down to one question: How much justice could an American afford? Hardly any of us had the amount of money as did Silverstrini.

Chapter Thirty-Three

The insanity of prison life continued. A young Mexican, who had been placed in solitary confinement, was found hanging from a makeshift rope in the cell when a guard happened to check on him. The new director rushed to the scene and cut the boy down. The boy was still alive, so he was revived. When the boy seemed to be all right, the director became hysterical and decided to teach the prisoner a lesson. He would teach him not to attempt suicide again in *his* prison!

The director ordered the guards to rehang the boy. The boy fought violently, so his hands were tied, and he was hanged for the second time. The director would wait until the boy was near death, then haul him down, wait for him to recover, and re-hang him again. The prisoner was hanged at least four times. After the final time, the director grabbed the boy and threatened to skin him alive if he ever attempted suicide again. The boy believed him, and so did everyone else. There were no more suicide attempts.

Bob and I were constantly looking for means to escape the prison, but we tried to be as discreet as possible. Bob was befriended by a younger guard and started to gain his confidence. Bob thought we could bribe the guard to let us escape from his guard tower. I didn't trust the plan and felt the guard would simply take our money and turn us in, but at least Bob had a plan; I had nothing.

We worked in the stand each day, lived and slept in the work area, and nervously prayed we would find a way out. The new director was unpredictable and he worried me. He did not molest us in the stand and he appeared to trust our business judgment. Nonetheless, he was cruel and he seemed to hate Americans in general. He had a white streak in his hair, so we dubbed him *Pluma Blanco*, or White Feather.

Pluma Blanco approached me one evening and offered me a marijuana cigarette. I refused; my nerves had been on the edge, and I had not felt comfortable smoking for some time. Pluma Blanco became extremely offended, saying I thought I was too good for him. He said all Americans thought they were better than Mexicans, and Americans would not accept even the friendliest offer. I felt threatened, so I apologized and said I meant no offense while accepting the joint.

After three or four puffs, the director pulled a pistol from his belt, cocked the hammer, and pointed it between my eyes. His lips were curled and his nostrils flared. He had an insane look in his eyes as he said, "Do you know that it's illegal to smoke marijuana in Mexico? I could kill you right now, or I could give you an additional sentence." He stared at me with hate-filled eyes and then burst into hysterical laughter as he lowered the gun.

"Just remember, senor," he said threateningly, "you are still a prisoner, and you shall always be one. You are mine to do with as I wish. Your life is mine, gringo!"

I felt sick. I tried to avoid Pluma as much as possible after that. He enjoyed playing mind games as much as he enjoyed re-hanging the boy who attempted suicide. I never thought I would miss the other directors. I didn't know how much longer Bob and I would be able to maintain the stand and our freedom inside the prison.

A few days after my unpleasant event with Pluma Blanco, it was Bob's turn to be down. He stood in the stand, staring off into space. A one-legged homosexual in drag, wearing a pink chiffon dress and falsies, hopped by the front of the stand. He had a crutch under one arm and a bunch of eggs in the other. Occasionally an egg would start to roll out of his arm, and a large homosexual following the one-legged queen would hurriedly waddle up and attempt to catch the egg before it hit the ground.

"See those guys?" I said to Bob, nodding towards the homosexuals. "They were normal when they were put in here." Bob started to laugh through his sad-dened mood. We would make it. We would have to; our lives were very different now. Maybe Mexico would be our home from now on, but we couldn't give up. I hoped I could convince Bob … and myself.

Shortly after the queen and his friend passed, I noticed the Mexicans were bringing up another wheelbarrow full of supplies, and I was glad to know we would be busy for a while, stocking the stand. A junkie suddenly walked up to the wheelbarrow and stole a carton of cigarettes when he thought no one was looking. I saw him, and all of my frustration rushed to the surface. He picked the wrong day to get caught. I leaped over the counter and confronted the thief.

"I want the cigarettes you just stole," I said with a threatening smile on my face. I knew it would be stupid to fight the junkie. There were other junkies lingering around the courtyard. They were not known to fight alone. I would be outnumbered and wouldn't stand a chance of winning. Already, a small crowd of junkies was beginning to form around the thief and me. It was a dangerous risk, but I wanted to fight. I wanted to hit someone and beat my frustrations out on him. I spotted a few American faces in the background, and I hoped they could keep the rest from jumping me.

"Fuck you, foreigner, I don't have any cigarettes!" the thief hissed. I gritted my teeth, pulled back my arm, and smashed him in the face with my fist. It felt wonderful! The bottled-up hatred was escaping. The junkie was sprawled on the ground, and the cigarettes spilled from underneath his shirt. He looked shocked. The crowd murmured its excitement and disapproval as they closed in. The thief swayed to his feet and hit me in the forehead. We traded facial blows for facial blows. I was enjoying myself. The junkie was a good fighter, and I was surprised at how well he withstood my anger-filled punches. I noticed Bob still in the stand, trying to protect it. I noticed that there were no other Americans around me and the crowd was getting dangerously close. I saw the glint of puntas as I grabbed the Mexican around the head and began to pound my fist into his nose. He could not last much longer; neither could I. The crowd would not let me win; already I could feel feet trying to trip me and arms shoving me off balance. I could hear Bob screaming to warn me, as I yelled back to him to protect the stand. The thief was bleeding but still fighting hard when the crowd closed in. I saw the points coming, but there was nothing I could do to avoid them. I felt my skin burn from the points as I was tripped. I lost my balance and fell. The crowd backed away and waited to see what I would do.

I was bruised and bloody. I looked down and saw my torn shirt and blood seeping from my skin. I had been stabbed in six different places, but only superficially. The blood looked impressive as I swayed to my feet. I looked at the faces in the crowd, seeing contempt on some and puzzlement on others. The cigarette thief stood bruised and winded. I shook my head and smiled. I took a step towards him, my hand extended as if to shake hands with him. "You put up a damn good fight," I said. What did I have to lose? I decided to throw the thief and the crowd off guard. I let out a deep laugh, withdrew my hand, and smashed the thief in the face with my fist as hard as I could. The junkie toppled to the ground. I laughed as I looked around at the crowd. I stood in the midst of them, laughing, face bruised, body cut, hands swollen, and bleeding. The crowd began to laugh also as they picked the thief up from the ground. This was one crazy gringo! One of the members of the crowd told me later, "I thought you were either completely loco or you had more balls than anyone I have ever seen."

Bob came out of the stand and grabbed me. He said he felt horrible that he had not helped me fight, but we knew he had done the right thing in protecting the stand. However, at the onset of the fight, the other Americans had abandoned me. I would not forget that.

"Remind me not to do that again," I said to Bob. "A guy can get hurt that way."

I also had to report the thief to the office. I fought to show my honor to the Mexicans, and I would report the thief to protect myself from having to fight every day. If I didn't report the thief, I would be opening myself up to all challengers. Don Orelio was dispatched with me to locate the thief in the upper dormitory levels. He was not difficult to identify; he was bruised and swollen. The Mexican prisoners called me a *finger*, an informer, and some threatened to kill me if I pointed out the thief. After finding the thief, Don Orelio asked me in front of an angry mob if I wanted to file charges. I said I did not; I only wanted to report the man to protect myself. The thief and I shook hands, and I no longer had any problems. I was learning the way of a macho Mexican. I was gaining the reputation of being a fair, yet harsh, man.

Don Orelio walked me back to the stand, shaking his head. "You are a strange man, Esteban. Are you hurt from the fight?"

"I'm all right, I guess. I sure do ache. I'm getting too old to fight."

We reached the stand, where Don Orelio stole a candy bar and began to leave. He shook his head again, looking confused. "You are a strange man. I think that is good."

Chapter Thirty-Four

It took over a week, but my soreness from the fight was almost gone. Bob and I stood in the stand, looking across the courtyard at Charlie. Charlie was sitting in a corner, shoving raw potatoes in his mouth.

"That's amazing!" Bob mumbled.

Bob and I had helped Charlie receive a fifty-pound bag of potatoes through the stand. Don Orelio had informed us the potatoes would be confiscated unless the other guards were told to deliver them to the stand. So when Charlie's mother brought the potatoes to the prison, we had the guards deliver them and then turned the potatoes over to Charlie. The amazing thing was Charlie had eaten almost the entire bag by himself … in three days.

"I can't stand to watch this. Take over for a while, will you, Bob?" I hopped out of the stand. The temperature was close to one hundred degrees; I wore only cutoffs, sandals, and a loose shirt. I took off the shirt and wrapped it around my head as a bandana. Few prisoners were moving around because of the heat and boredom. Charlie sat eating his potatoes as a few younger boys played with something near the library building.

I walked to Charlie and squatted in front of him. "How can you eat all those potatoes?"

Charlie tried to talk and swallow at the same time. "Hey man, these are Idaho potatoes. I *love* Idaho potatoes, and if I don't eat them fast, they'll get stolen. Want one?"

Something landed on my left shoulder. Charlie yelped, losing his footing, and fell on his side. I froze in terror. A large scorpion was sitting on my shoulder. The play toy of the younger boys was a scorpion. In their boredom, the boys had made up a game: a thin string was tied to the scorpion, and then it was spun around. After it was spun, it was flung into the air and onto an unsuspecting victim. The object of the game was to yank the scorpion away before it could sting the victim. If the victim was not stung, the boy won. I was the present victim. I was too shocked and frightened to move. I didn't breathe as I watched the tail and stinger arch in the air. The boy yanked. I was safe, but still so frightened that I wanted to kill the boy. Shaking, I jumped up to look for a board to beat the boy.

"You little son of a bitch!" I raged. "I'm going to kill you!" The boys giggled and ran for the upper levels of the prison. Charlie was gone, leaving the remainder of his potatoes spilled on the ground.

Chapter Thirty-Five

It was visitor's day in early September. Bob, Daniel, and I were working the stand since there were an unusual number of visitors on this particular day. Pluma Blanco had arranged a special event. A wrestling ring had been erected on the basketball court. Professional wrestlers had been brought in to entertain the prisoners and their visitors. One tag team match was performed by dwarfs, and Bob wanted to see if one of them was the secretary to the judge. "If that dwarf is one of them, I'm going to figure out a way to choke him," Bob said only half jokingly.

After the wrestling match, a Catholic priest and several nuns held a religious service. Then some homely strippers were brought out to do a strip tease for the crowd. Yes, strippers. We could never figure out what Pluma was thinking. It was just another day in paradise.

While I was working in the stand, an exceptionally pretty girl with pigtails, wearing a sundress, caught my attention. She appeared to be in her mid-twenties and was missing a front tooth. She was talking with a girl in her teens, and they kept looking at Bob and me curiously. This was nothing new, because Americans were still an oddity.

Eventually the older of the two girls came up to the stand counter, and I asked her in Spanish if I could help her. She stared at me shyly and finally said in English, "Frank sent me." Bob heard her and took a step back. I must have appeared startled because the girl took a step back too. Throughout our time in prison, we had heard rumors and reports of Frank, the fabled Lucio Cabanos, but never thought we would ever receive a message from him. Still in shock, I ran out of the stand and grabbed the startled girl by the hand. "What?" I said as I led her away from the stand. Bob still stood behind the counter with his mouth open.

Her name was Billie. The younger-looking girl was her sixteen-year-old sister, Kornie. They had recently moved to the Nogales area and had received a message from Frank to look in on us. They were cousins to Pati. Billie spoke fluent English, but Kornie knew only a few words. I asked a flurry of questions about Frank and the attack on the village, but the girls either did not know or weren't telling. Still, it was nice to have two pretty girls around to just sit and talk with. The girls asked if there was anything they could do to help, but there wasn't much they could do for me. Billie said she would come back to visit ... and she did, sometimes with Kornie, sometimes alone; but over the lingering months, she would return at least once a week, bringing home-cooked food and occasionally an article of clothing. Once she brought me a mouth harp that I learned to play on the lonely nights. Many times we would not even talk, but rather sit and enjoy each other's company in silence. She was attractive, with darker skin then Pati. Her smile, with the missing tooth, was contagious. I looked forward to the visiting days. I was attracted to her, but in a way she was more like a sister. Frank had sent us a gift.

Chapter Thirty-Six

Over the next few weeks I continued to work in the stand, look forward to my precious visits with Billie, and occasionally do something stupid and risky. The nights were the most difficult, and boredom set in. Since we were no longer in a cell, but in a padlocked area in the work section, we had more room to move about. One night, Bob whispered, "Come on, we're going for a ride." He stood up and walked to the padlock. I followed, asking if he had a plan.

"No plan. I've just been thinking about doing something." Bob popped the lock and carefully opened the door. "There's an old abandoned car at the lowest work area. The engine's gone, and it's up on the cinder blocks, but it's got seats. Let's pretend to go somewhere. If they don't shoot us, what's the worst that can happen? Solitary again?"

I shrugged my shoulders as we slipped into the warm night. We stayed close to the walls in the dark shadows, moving slowly. We cautiously passed one guard tower, barely breathing as we went, and then another. Silence. After what seemed like an eternity, we rounded a corner and faced the ruin of an old Chevy. In the darkness, it was just a silhouette. Bob silently squeezed the handle on the driver's side door and eased the door open. He slipped into the seat and gently closed the door. I did the same on the passenger side.

Bob placed his hands on the steering wheel. "Okay, now where do you want to go?"

"Anywhere you want to take me." The windows were up and trickles of sweat were running down my back.

"Okay, we're on Tenth Street, heading towards 33 South. Oh look, there's the university on the left, and the girl's dorm. We're heading past Piggly Wiggly and are coming up on Cliff's Oyster Bar. Man, do they have good seafood!"

"Hey, let's turn on the radio!" I made some noise as to imitate static and started to sing "What's Your Name?" in an off-key version.

"Next time, I'm the radio," Bob mumbled. And so it was. Two lonely, desperate men, sitting in a car, pretending to drive and listen to the radio. Relieving old memories, fighting the boredom, and trying to remain sane.

After an hour or so, we made our way back to our work area without incident. We went back several times in the next month, taking turns on who was the driver and who was the radio, remembering a life that was gone.

A few days after our first road trip, as I worked in the stand, Don Orelio came shuffling across the courtyard. I handed him his obligatory candy as he told me to grab a wheelbarrow and come with him to the supply area, where he wanted me to bring up some sacks of sugar.

I pushed the wheelbarrow behind him as he unlocked several gates and went down various ramps. At the open door of the warehouse, he pointed in the direction of the sacks of sugar. The warehouse was dark, and my eyes had trouble adjusting from the bright Mexican sun. I threw several fifty-pound bags of sugar onto the wheelbarrow and turned to head back out. Then, to my right, I noticed something in the dim light, hanging from a ceiling beam. There were several things hanging. I strained my eyes and let out a horrified scream. It was naked children ... or dwarfs. I could see their little penises. Terrified, I dropped the wheelbarrow on its side, spilling the sacks of sugar, and ran for the door. I slammed right into Don Orelio, who had run to the door to see what all the screaming was about. I had almost knocked him over, so he grabbed my shoulders more to steady himself than to stop me. I pointed a trembling finger toward the little bodies. Don Orelio looked confused as he stood trying to figure out what I was pointing at. He started to smile, which led to a grin, which changed into an out-and-out laugh. He was slapping me on the back as his belly moved up and down from laughter. "*Tortuga!*" he choked out through the laughter. He was actually coughing and crying now, he was laughing so hard.

I was very confused and a bit humiliated. I stared up at the bodies. "Tortuga?" Then it slowly hit me: they weren't babies, nor dwarfs. They were sea turtles that had been stripped of their shells and were to be used for food.

I blushed and said, "Never mind."

Through his coughing, tears, and laughter, Don Orelio said, "Esteban, you are a very strange man."

For weeks I would see him relating that story to others in the prison, and he would laugh just as hard every time he told it.

Chapter Thirty-Seven

A couple of days after the turtle incident, Daniel stood swatting flies on the store counter with a fly swatter. The flies were exceptionally bad that day, and he was killing five or six flies at a time with a single whack. Daniel referred to the fly as "the national bird of Mexico."

Daniel made himself a cup of coffee and scooped a large spoonful of sugar from an open sack while waving the fly swatter to drive the flies away. He liked his coffee sweet while I liked mine black. He dumped the sugar into the cup and blew on the coffee, then got a curious look on his face.

"Look at this," he grinned.

I stared into the coffee cup and saw several marijuana seeds floating on top. "I'll be darned. So Pluma Blanco is smuggling his marijuana into the prison in the sacks of sugar?" I said slyly.

"Sure looks like it to me. I was wondering why the sugar always came in from the body shop. He must be hiding it in the sugar sacks and bringing it into the prison in the cars that come and go." Daniel picked out the seeds and sipped at his coffee.

Leland Hare, the wealthy Californian who had a penchant for trouble, sauntered up to the store. I hadn't seen him since the scene in the barber shop. He was wearing only cut offs and sandals. His long blonde hair stuck to the back of his neck from sweat. He swiped at a swarm of flies. "Can I have some bananas? I'll have to pay for them later."

I reached below the counter and handed Leland a bunch of six bananas. He immediately peeled one and started gorging on it. Then he quickly ate another until they were all gone. Over against the far wall, some workers were doing repairs and had a ladder leaning against the wall. It was a tall extension ladder that reached maybe four feet from the top of the wall. Leland was pacing back and forth and kept glancing nervously toward the workers and the ladder. No one was on the ladder, but there were five or six Mexican guards watching over the workers. The guards were unarmed, which was not unusual since there were armed guards in the towers.

Leland looked at me matter-of-factly. "You know, I heard a rumor that Pink Floyd is playing in Tempe, Arizona tonight." He suddenly kicked off his sandals and bolted in the direction of the ladder. He sprinted across the courtyard and passed two guards before they realized what had happened. Daniel and I stood open-mouthed and dumbfounded. It was one of the most stupid, suicidal, and insane acts we had ever seen. Didn't he know how high the other side of the wall was from the ground?

He passed the other guards before they could react and grabbed a rung on the ladder, then another, and he was on his way up. The guards reacted and rushed after him. One guard caught his ankle, but Leland jerked his leg and kicked him away. He continued to scramble up the ladder. One guard started up the ladder after him. Leland was about a third of the way up its height. The remaining guards grabbed the inside bottom of the ladder and shoved it away from the wall, causing it to tumble over backwards and slam both Leland and the guard on the ladder onto the concrete. Leland lay there. The guards who had pushed on the ladder descended upon him and began kicking him and pummeling him with their fists. Pluma came running up from the office area. Briefly, I thought he might stop the kicking and beating, but when he reached the melee, he started stomping on Leland's head with his foot.

Daniel moved first. I quickly followed. We ran the distance to the guards and Pluma Blancho. We pleaded with them to stop, but they ignored us. Leland was bleeding from the ears. I touched Pluma Blanco on the arm to get his attention, and he flung his arm back at me, snarled, and then lifted has foot to smash another blow to Leland's head. Someone else grabbed Pluma's arm this time. Pluma Blanco turned with insanity-filled eyes to strike the person who had grabbed him. His eyes seemed to focus and he stopped. It was Don Orelio.

He was simultaneously barking orders at the other guards. They too stopped. Don Orelio bent over Leland and shook his head. He ordered two of the guards to get a stretcher. Pluma was breathing heavily and we weren't sure if he wanted to start assaulting Leland again or not. He suddenly turned on one foot and headed back toward the office. Leland was loaded onto a stretcher and hauled off. We didn't see Leland for many months. He had received several cracked ribs and major head trauma. When he did come back, he was no longer Leland; he was brain damaged.

Chapter Thirty-Eight

It was around the first of October, 1974. The sweltering heat had subsided and somehow Bob, Daniel, and I had managed to hold onto our jobs in the stand. I credited this partially to Don Orelio, who would come each day for his customary bribe of a candy bar or a cup of coffee and conversation.

I could see him slowly heading to the stand, and I looked down to see what kinds of candy we had in stock. As he got closer, he looked pensive and had worry lines on his forehead. Even his moustache seemed to droop.

He approached the counter, saying, "Esteban, it is bad." He motioned me out of the store and pointed to a crude wooden bench.

We both sat as I asked, "What's up? What's bad?"

Don Orelio sat hunched over, head down, clasping his hands. He did not speak for a long time. Then, slowly, he deliberately formed the words on his lips. "Pluma Blanco. I have seen the papers, the *ley de fuga*. Pluma has signed the papers on you. He doesn't like you. He doesn't like any Americans, but he says you are a troublemaker."

"What the ..." I started, but he shushed me.

"You are to be transferred to another prison, yet you will not make it. You will be killed on the way. There is no death penalty in Mexico, so there is the ley de fuga. I am sorry there is nothing I can do. I'm so sorry!" Don Orelio's eyes clouded over with tears.

I was both incredulous and frightened. I was aware of the term *ley de fuga* and knew what it meant. I was to be put to death sometime in the near future. If anyone inquired about me, they would be told it happened while I was trying to escape. "The papers? Bob, Daniel, any of the other Americans?" I felt nauseous.

"No, you are the only American for now," he said quietly.

"When?"

"*No se*. There was no date on the papers. It could be soon or it could be many months. Esteban, I'm so sorry," he said again, tiredly.

He then looked thoughtful for a second and reached into his shirt pocket. With his right hand he pulled out what appeared to be a Mexican silver dollar.

"Here, take this. It is the only thing I have that might help you. It is silver; silver carries magic. It will help protect you from spells and evil. It will also keep your *bad* inside you and help to make you a better person. It acts like a mirror and reflects harm back to the way it came." Don Orelio paused for a moment and then continued, "By me giving this to you as a gift, all of the magic I've gathered up in my life now is yours. May it always help to protect you as it has me." He placed the coin in my right hand.

I believed Don Orelio was sincere in his beliefs, but I was distraught and thought to myself, *I'm going to die, and he is going on and on about magic! Please, give me a gun or a key, not some stupid coin.* I glanced down at the coin in my hand before placing it in my shirt pocket. It was .900 silver 5 peso coin from 1948—the year that I was born.

I didn't know what to do or say. I wanted to run. I wanted to run and never stop running. I just kept shaking my head. What was I going to do?

Don Orelio slowly stood up, looking old and tired. He touched my shoulder before he turned to walk back across the courtyard. He hadn't even gotten his candy. I watched as he shuffled away, shoulders sagging … a sad old Deputy Dawg, wiping tears from his eyes.

I don't know how long I sat on that bench. I don't believe I had any thoughts. I was blank.

Daniel came up to me and broke my trance. "You all right? Why aren't you in the store?"

I slowly explained to Daniel what Don Orelio had told me. He punched a concrete wall and yelled, "Shit!" Bob walked up, and Daniel related the events to him. Bob looked obviously shocked and questioned Daniel of the credibility of the information. When Bob got upset, the pitch of his voice got higher. He was almost squeaking. I no longer felt like talking and walked away.

That night, when I did sleep, I slept restlessly. I was more than disturbed by the day's events and hadn't bothered to undress. I drifted into a semi-conscious state. I dreamed I was in a coffin; I dreamed that I was on fire; I dreamed the dream that would wake me in the middle of the night screaming, sitting up in bed, drenched in cold sweat. I glanced around. Everyone else was still sleeping.

I lay there thinking, *What am I going to do?* over and over again. I accidentally touched the coin though my shirt pocket. Then slowly an idea started to form, an idea that could be worked into a plan. Why hadn't I thought of it before?

Chapter Thirty-Nine

I knew the director smuggled drugs into the prison. Cars brought into the prison body shop had false compartments in them, and Pluma Blanco used the compartments to bring in the sacks of sugar that hid the drugs. If five kilos of marijuana could be smuggled into the prison, why couldn't 150 pounds of Steve Wilson leave the same way?

I needed someone to build a false compartment for me. I needed a car that could be driven in and out of the prison without the compartment being discovered in searches by the Mexican guards. I needed someone I could trust, someone on the outside, but whom? Who would be willing to take on such a risky project? I thought of Frank and wished he were still with us. Then I thought of Billie. I had to work fast; time was growing short before I would be transferred and dumped in the desert.

Tuesday, visitor's day, came and passed with no sign of Billie or Kornie. I was almost relieved; I had mixed feelings about asking Billie. In how much danger would I be placing her? Would she even agree? I knew my plan probably wouldn't work. There were too many variables that could go wrong. Yes, I had broken out with Bob to work our way down to the auto shop area and take our imaginary journeys, but we had to put a stop to that; they had installed more lights in the prison. Our path to the old car was no longer in shadow.

If I was caught trying to escape, I expected I would be horribly beaten or tortured, then killed. Yet I wanted to die while trying to get out. I didn't want to die like a cow going to the butcher. In reality, my plans were a suicidal attempt at freedom.

On Thursday, Billie showed up by herself. I practically ran to her, but held back. I also had to fight not blurting out my plan to her right away. I escorted her as far away from the other prisoners as I could and carefully attempted to explain Don Orelio's news and the plan I had in mind. She sat and listened intently, with a worried expression on her face. I attempted to explain the dangers. Maybe if she could find someone to build the compartment, we could try to find someone else to drive the car. Billie expressed grave doubts about my plan, but she too knew of the ley de fuga. Worriedly, she shook her head and said she would have to think about it.

"No matter what you decide, I can't tell you how much you've already helped me." I kissed her good-bye on the forehead.

The following Tuesday, Billie was back with Kornie. We greeted each other, and this time they led me from the crowd. "We want to help. Kornie knows a man who smuggles contraband, and he has made small hiding places. The trouble is, it will take time to make such a larger compartment," she said without a smile.

She stared in my eyes. We both knew I might not have much time. Yet I had no alternatives. "Do what you can."

The three of us spend the rest of visiting hours trying to work out the details of the plan. I spoke to Billie and she interpreted Kornie's questions for me. I felt the Mexican guards were too familiar with American cars, such as a Ford or Chevy. They would spot any alterations. We agreed a foreign car—or, even better, an older foreign car—might be our best bet.

Billie believed she could find a driver who was not registered as the owner of the car, who would deny any knowledge of the compartment if I were discovered. He could show a fake receipt that he was paid to deliver the car to be painted at the prison. I think we all knew the plan was shaky at best.

The girls came the next Tuesday and Thursday as we continued to adapt the plan. Kornie's friend was searching for an appropriate car. Time was racing by.

On this last visiting day, Billie said she would not return until everything was ready. They hoped the car would be ready in approximately three weeks. She would give me last minute instructions at that time. I hugged them each good-bye. "Good luck and be careful!" I nervously smiled at them.

Chapter Forty

While I waited, my nerves became frayed, I lost more weight, and I was constantly high-strung. I needed to tell somebody, but I couldn't: not Bob, not Daniel, no one. Discovery was almost certain if just a hint of suspicion about my plan leaked to the Mexican officials.

My behavior was becoming edgier. My nervousness was hard to hide from those around me. I feared torture more and more, and death was looking better and better. I needed an alibi in case my altered behavior caused suspicion or I was caught trying to escape.

The only defense I could think of to tell the Mexicans was that my mother was deathly ill. I thought that might put things in a merciful light. I'd explain that she was dying from a terminal illness and I wanted to see her before she passed on.

Pluma Blanco cornered me one day after noticing my jumpy behavior and asked if something was wrong. "Hey, Esteban, *que pasa?*" I told him the fabricated story of my mother and it stirred what little sympathy he was capable of. Even Pluma held his mother in high esteem. I further admitted how guilty I felt knowing that I would never see her again. Pluma fell for it; he told my sad story to other Mexican officials. My strange behavior was then looked upon as grief.

As days dragged into weeks, I still had no word from Billie; I searched for her every visitor's day. My behavior was becoming increasingly more erratic; I had to get out, but so far all my efforts added up to nothing.

At night, I eased my stressful state by sweeping corridors and pacing wall-to-wall in my cell. The Mexicans thought I was losing my mind over my dying mother; I thought I was just losing my mind.

I was fighting against time and expected to be transferred any day. A month had passed without word from Billie or Kornie. Then, one humid day, I received a postcard with the message: "I hope you are still doing your exercises and dieting." I wasn't quite sure what this meant, but I assumed my escape was still on! They hadn't forgotten me!

It seemed like the plan was taking forever. A total of seven weekends had passed since Billie and Kornie left the prison that last time. I had heard nothing since the postcard. During that time Wally Love visited me; I didn't tell him of the ley de fuga. I didn't want my parents to find out. I wouldn't tell him of my escape plan. I did give him my belongings so he could mail them to me, explaining that I might be transferred to a new prison. I said I was afraid my belongings would be stolen if I waited till my transfer. One of those items was Jessie's gray cowboy hat.

After Wally left, I went looking for Daniel. I found him sitting against a wall near the prison store, and I squatted next to him. I felt the weight of my thoughts. I made small talk with Daniel, and he could tell I was not holding up well under the threat of the ley de fuga.

"Daniel, I'm going to leave here soon." I wanted to tell someone of my escape plans.

"Sure, sure you are, Steve," Daniel replied. I could tell by his concerned look that Daniel thought I was talking of the ley de fuga. I had second thoughts and said nothing else.

Anticipating the escape, I frequently checked and rechecked my preparations along my escape route within the prison. If I was to sneak into the car's compartment at night, I had to draw one of the guards down from his sentry tower long enough for me to sneak into the work area unseen.

Although the days were still hot, the nights were getting cold. The sentry towers had open windows, and the guards would frequently huddle below the windows to avoid the cold desert wind. Knowing this, late each night, I would yell up to the sentry tower closest to the work area and ask the shivering guard if he wanted a cup of coffee. They always took my offer. Bob and I then brought a filled coffee cup to the fence that separated the tower from the working area. The guard walked down a three-story flight of stairs inside the tower to meet us at the fence. After thanking us for the hot coffee, the guard would return to the top of the tower, and we would go back to the work area to sleep.

For the several minutes the guard was inside the tower, climbing down and back up the stairs, he was unable to see outside. It would be during this time when I would sneak my way into the area where the car was kept and enter the escape vehicle.

A few days after I spoke with Daniel, the one of the guards I'd been giving coffee to came up to me while I was working at the prison stand in broken English, he asked, "Hey, Esteban, how much you pay my watch for?" The guards occasionally wanted to trade or sell personal items for food or cash. Their salaries were barely enough to live on. The guard handed me a twenty-one jeweled Univer. The guard wanted $16 for the watch, but I shook my head no. We bargained back and forth until we both settled on $8, which I swiped from the stand cash box. The young Mexican was going to use the money to buy liquor and women. I was going to use his watch to help me escape.

The following night, I timed the guard; it took him two minutes to climb down the stairs. For two minutes, he couldn't see the work area—enough time for me to run from the fence to the concealing shadows.

I couldn't complete my escape plan alone. I needed help getting into the car's hidden compartment, and my time was growing short before my transfer. I had to tell someone; I couldn't just disappear. I had to say good-bye to somebody.

Late one night, Bob and I were talking, when I asked him to follow me into a bathroom. The bathroom was deserted, and I whispered my plan to Bob. When I finished, Bob was quiet for a few minutes. Then he looked at me grimly. "I figured you had something going. It's not like you to give up. That's why we've been doing the coffee routine each night, isn't it? But the plan is suicide, Steve … too many flaws in it. They'll find you and kill you, man."

He tried to persuade me to go along with his old escape plan of bribing a guard and going out through a sentry tower. I wouldn't agree. Bob realized I was determined to go through with my escape scheme, win, lose, or die.

Looking at me sadly, Bob shook his head. "Well, one of us free is better than none of us free. I hope you make it, man, but I think you're going to get killed." His eyes filled with tears. "I'll do anything to help you, but I'm sure going to miss you." Leaving Bob behind would be one of the most onerous actions I had ever taken in my twenty-six years; I had to find a way to protect him so he wouldn't suffer repercussions from my escape attempt.

To deceive the Mexicans and keep Bob innocent of my plan, Bob was to wait as long as possible until my escape car had left and then report me missing to Pluma Blanco. Bob would explain I had been acting strangely ever since I received the news of my dying mother and that he hadn't seen me all day. Bob would relay his fears that I might be attempting to escape and felt I was hiding somewhere in the prison, waiting for a chance to go over the wall. He would explain that he would rather see me in solitary than dead. Hopefully, this ruse would erase any connections with my escape.

Lista, or roll call, still presented a problem. Late each night and early each morning, Don Orelio and his guards entered the sleeping quarters and took roll call. If someone didn't answer to his name, a search would immediately begin to find the missing person.

Bob contrived a "grunt plan." Before the guards entered the work building for roll call, Bob and I would position ourselves in our bunks with a blanket pulled up over our heads. When Don Orelio called my name, Bob answered in a single muffled grunt. When Bob's name was called, Bob would again answer with a double grunt in a different tone. It worked! The guards couldn't distinguish which bunk the grunts were coming from. The head count would come out correct. On the night of my escape, Bob would grunt for me, but my bunk would be stuffed with blankets.

December came and I started to wonder if Billie and Kornie were all right. The three weeks had turned into nearly three months. Then it happened: Billie and Kornie showed up on a visitor's day. I almost threw up I was so relieved. Bob gave me a sheepish smile and a barely noticeable thumbs up.

Neither girl gave us the usual smile and wave when they saw Bob and me. Their eyes were puffy, like they had been crying. My anxiety rose as I immediately thought something had gone wrong with the escape plan. I hurried to them. "Thank God you're here! Is everything all right?" I was trembling.

Neither girl made eye contact. Billie did not say anything; instead she handed me a Mexican newspaper she was carrying in her hand. Confused, I scanned the paper, but I did not immediately see what she wanted me to read. The paper was dated December 3, 1974. Then I saw the bold print. "Lucio Cabanas! Muerte!" Under the article, there was a photo of a bloody body lying on the ground. The face was unrecognizable, but the man was wearing a bloodied white suit. Next to the body, on a rock, was a pair of broken glasses with overly thick lenses. Frank had been caught in an ambush on a dirt road somewhere in Southern Mexico. The fabled Lucio was dead. Our Frank was finally with his daughter and Pati. As I read the article, both girls were openly sobbing. My throat hurt and my chest ached, but I did not cry. I put my arms around the sobbing girls, and all I could manage to say was, "Oh, Frank."

Eventually the girls stopped crying. I took the paper to Bob, who sadly read it.

"What's this going to do to the plan?" Bob said as he looked up from the newspaper.

"I answered sheepishly. "It's probably the ley de fuga for me."

I walked back to the girls and we sat in silence. After a while, I looked at Billie and sighed. "Well I guess that's it for me too."

"No, it is done," Billie whispered as I stared at her in shock. "It took so long because Kornie's friend got a car with a brand-new paint job. He had to ruin the paint so we could use that reason to get it painted here. It is a Volvo. We were very excited about the results, than we read about poor Frank."

Billie said she could not stay. She had to return for last minute preparations. I asked her if she had found a driver. She stared into my eyes and spoke softly in Spanish this time. "Don't say a word or make a sound until you hear me call you. Enter at night, after the car is painted, and I will meet you in the morning."

I was startled. Apparently Billie had not found a driver. She was going to drive the car herself.

The girls hurried away. In my grief, and anxiety, I hadn't asked when the car would arrive or how to get into the compartment. They told me where the compartment was located, but in their sadness over Frank, they forgot to tell me how to enter it. The news of Frank and the confirmation of the plan were like a hard punch in the gut. This time, I did throw up.

It was Saturday morning, and I was in the work area, smashing large pieces of concrete into smaller pieces, when an old car drove through the prison gates.

It was an old Volvo. This was my car; it was finally here. My plan was going to happen! Little pieces of my sanity began to flake away. My face paled, my blood raced to my stomach, and my heart pounded. I had the urge to run to the car and scream, "It's here!" just to help my mind believe what my eyes were seeing. But I had to get out of the area and not bring attention to myself or the car. I saw the guards swarm over the car as they searched it. I prayed, "Please don't let them find it."

An hour later, the car was driven up the ramp to the work area. Bob and I were in the prison store when my "look of lunacy," as Bob called it, came over me. I was flipping out just looking at the approaching car. Bob quickly walked over next to me to quiet me down. I wanted to assure myself the compartment was in the car. I wanted to find it and to know it was there, waiting for me. Bob calmed me while we walked to the work area, where half a dozen prisoners were looking over a reddish-gray station wagon Volvo. Kornie's friend put much thought in choosing the car for my escape: a blotchy, gray, rust-colored 1958 Volvo station wagon that needed an overdue paint job.

Bob and I discretely examined the car to find a clue to the compartments whereabouts. Kohout was also looking at the car, sizing up the paint job he was going to give it. "Looks like they got some more work for you, Kohout," I said, trying to sound light about my interest in the car.

"Yeah, it'll give me something to do," Kohout sarcastically replied.

Looking closer at the car, I touched its blemished hood. "This car is in really bad shape. How long do you think it'll take?"

"Ah, not too long. This one is supposed to leave Thursday morning."

"Thursday morning is pretty soon." I kneeled to the ground and examined underneath the car. "Will it need an undercoating?"

"Naw. Who cares? I won't have time, anyway."

Squinting, I thought I could see the bottom of the compartment. I felt my face turn pale again. Lightheaded and shaky, I tried to calmly stand up. The compartment was well camouflaged so no one would notice unless they were told about it. In the rear or the Volvo was a covered tire well compartment. The tire well had been enlarged and made to resemble a gas tank when viewed from underneath the car. The original gas tank was ripped out to make room for my escape compartment, while a small gas tank was hidden in the chassis, holding enough gas for one trip across the border and back.

I still had no idea how to enter the Volvo's hidden compartment, but I needed to find out by Wednesday night. I suspected I'd have to enter from within the car, but the work area was lit up at night. I'd be visible through the car windows. I had to find a way to get the windows credulously covered so I could freely move about inside the car.

I approached Kohout Wednesday morning, the day before the planned escape. I told Kohout I knew the owner of the Volvo and that there were two fifths of cognac carefully hidden in the car. I explained the cognac was a Christmas present. I knew where they were hidden and I would give him one of the fifths. All he had to do was leave the paper on the windows until Thursday morning so I could retrieve the bottles unobserved. Kohout could have spent hours tearing the car apart in search of the bottles, but he was basically lazy, so he happily agreed.

Later that night, my panic and paranoia magnified, and I had second thoughts about Bob helping me escape. I knew I needed help to enter the Volvo's hidden compartment, but it would put him in danger. I told Bob about my reservations. He smiled a sad smile and said, "We're partners to the end. We got in this shit together, and we'll help each other get our asses out of it. Even if it does sound crazy, we've got to try. If you get out, then maybe you can help me out … help all of us. Tell everybody what's been happening to us down here. Make them believe, brother." He added, with a grin, "Even if your plan is stupid and suicidal."

We both thought I was going to die in my attempt, but I knew for sure I was going to be killed when they came for me for the ley de fuga. If I were going to be killed, I would do it trying to escape.

I knew if I was in the Volvo's compartment for any length of time, I would need a drug to help me relax and stay immobile or even unconscious. In the prison, there was a muscle-relaxant called Mandrax, sold as a heroin substitute. I tested it several weeks earlier and it made me feel groggy enough to push me into unconsciousness.

Taping seven Mandrax on the left sleeve of my shirt, I pocketed an ice pick knife and pulled on my boots. I dropped six Milky Way candy bars into my jacket pockets and cut a hole in the waistline of my jeans to hold the rolled up money I had stolen from the prison store earlier that day. I gave Bob $24 to buy Kohout a bottle of cognac and reminded Bob to report the stolen money when he turned me in to Pluma Blanco.

We walked into the moonlit alley with the coffee for the tower guard. I yelled up to the guard, and he left the tower to meet us at the fence. We handed the guard his coffee, and he thanked us. The night was cold and he was visibly grateful for the hot drink. While the guard was making his way back up to the top of his tower, Bob slammed the barred gate to the work building to make it sound like we went back inside to sleep. We ran silently in the shadows of the building and around the rear of the workshop before the guard reached the top of his tower.

In the twilight darkness, we crawled on our bellies to the Volvo and quietly opened the rear door. The windows were stilled papered over. We quickly climbed on the rear seat and carefully closed the door. Holding our breath, we waited. Nothing! So far, so good.

Bob brought out two screwdrivers he'd stolen from the workshop and handed me one. My body was trembling while I helped Bob search for the compartment entrance.

We searched the back of the Volvo with our hands while our eyes slowly adjusted to the dim light through the newspaper-covered windows. Bob occasionally lit a match to help us see in the dark corners of the car, but we couldn't find the opening. The compartment hatch was too well disguised. We knew we had to be crouching on top of the compartment, but we didn't know how to get into it.

Finally, Bob suggested we unscrew everything. My hands were shaking so bad now that I couldn't hold on to my screwdriver. Kornie's friend used wooden strips to cover the rear compartment. The wooden strips were screwed into the metal floor, making them seem original to the car, because they matched the wooden strips on the sides of the Volvo. We started removing the wooden strips. I was so frightened I had difficulty concentrating. I was having second thoughts about the whole plan. Bob would have to return soon to act out the grunt system for the evening lista.

In a panicked tone, I said, "Let's go back. It's not going to work. It's taking too long; we'll both be caught if you're not there for roll call." Tears of frustration welled up in my eyes, but Bob wouldn't quit.

"We've gone too far to go back now, Steve. The hell with the fuckin' roll call. I'll deal with that later."

Afraid of being discovered, Bob wouldn't light any more matches. We had to find the screws to the wooden strips by touch. Working in darkness, Bob and I removed all twenty-four screws that bolted the seven wooden strips to the Volvo's rear floor. We had to be careful not to lose the screws or jumble up the sequence of the wooden strips. Each wooden strip was individually cut and fitted flush only to a specific area of the rear floor. Trying to remain noiseless and not alert a guard, we worked for a half hour unscrewing the strips.

We found the metal hatch to the compartment under the wooden strips. Lifting the hatch, I felt around the inside of the compartment and was startled by the smallness of it. I tore the seven Mandrax off my shirtsleeve and re-taped them to the arm of my jacket.

Crawling into the compartment, I tried to lie down in a tight, curled position. I was too big … I couldn't fit! I looked up at Bob as tears started to run down my face and my body began to shake from panic.

"It won't work!" I whined to Bob. "I can't do it! I can't fit. You go; you're smaller and you'll fit in here better than me." I started up from the cramped compartment.

Bob shook his head and pushed me back down into the compartment. "What do you want? For *me* to get killed?" Bob laughed nervously. "This is your plan; you've got to try. Don't worry. Everything is going to be all right. You're going to make it."

"But you just told me I was going to die. Now you're saying everything will be all right," I skittishly whispered back. "Make up your mind!"

"I'm going to miss you, pal," Bob said as he shoved me further into the compartment. Lying on my left side, my knees and legs were crammed into a twisted fetal position. My face and right shoulder were pressed up against the bottom of the hatch, my left arm crossed over my mouth so I could bite off the Mandrax. In my right hand I clutched the ice pick knife with its point pressed under my chin. I planned on jamming the ice pick in through my chin and into my brain if the Mexicans ever caught me. I didn't want to be taken alive.

Bob used all his weight to force the hatch down on me. It was so tight I couldn't move from my twisted position. I had Don Orelio's silver dollar in my left shirt pocket and the Milky Ways were stuck in the corner. As Bob began screwing back the wooden strips, I felt like I was being buried alive in an under-sized coffin. Claustrophobia and panic welled up from my guts. I bit off a Mandrax and waited to slip off into unconsciousness.

I woke to pain. My legs were burning inside. The blood wasn't circulating in my legs. I tried to shift them but my entire body was jammed tight. I was trapped. I felt like the walls of the compartment were closing in on me and had stopped just before they were to crush me into a bloody pulp.

I held back my groans. I didn't know how much time had passed, but I told myself to wait. Swallowing another Mandrax, I thought to myself, *Please God, let Billie hurry*, and drifted off again into pain releasing oblivion.

Each time I woke, I tried to stay awake and bear up against the growing pain in my legs. The rest of my body began to hurt, and I felt an aching pressure in my stomach as my bladder filled up. The pressure became too much for me to control. I disgusted myself as I pissed in my jeans. I ate another Mandrax.

A shaft of light grew in the compartment. I realized it was morning as sunlight beamed through an air hole the size of a nickel. The light gave me new hope and strength. I tried again to change my contorted position but my body was still immobile. Today Billie was to pick up the car from the prison, and my anticipation of being driven to freedom blocked out some of the pain. My mind floated to thoughts of the friends and family I would be seeing if my escape was successful.

I still feared I would be caught and tortured. I heard people moving around the outside of the car and thought they were getting ready to move it out of the prison, when I was startled by paint fumes coming through the air hole.

They were painting the car again! The Volvo had already been painted and it was supposed to leave the prison today. Something had gone wrong! The fumes were making me dizzy and nauseous. I knew I would have to stay awake should anything else go wrong. I feared I would suffocate from the acrid fumes. My claustrophobia returned as my mind tried to figure what had gone wrong with the plan. Blind panic almost overwhelmed me. I had no way out, no exit. I was a trapped animal dying a slow death.

The Mexican sun began to baste the car with its 120 degree heat. I was drenched with sweat as my metal compartment heated up. My skin began to burn and blister where I touched the heating metal. My compartment was turning into an oven. I started to believe the escape had been discovered and the Mexicans were getting revenge by slowly letting me suffocate and roast to death!

Blood oozed out of my nose and dribbled over my lips and chin. My muscles were cramping up, and I felt as if the searing metal of a raging stove was burning me. The heat overcame me and I blacked out.

My mind whirled between total unconsciousness and a nightmarish world created by a fevered delirium. In my delirious wanderings, I believed I was being tortured by fire. I didn't know where I was and I couldn't escape from the pain.

I thought I heard Kohout beat on my compartment and tell me to be quiet ... everything would be all right and I could forget about the bottle of cognac. I begged him to let me out, but Kohout told me it was too dangerous. It would be over soon. I had to hang on.

The car door slammed and the engine started. I clawed at the hatch, trying to pull it tighter. The plan was happening! The car was moving! I heard the gate to the work area open as the car continued to move. I heard the gate close behind the car. My blood was roaring in my ears. Soon, I'd either be free or dead!

Suddenly, the car stopped. The engine shut off and someone opened and shut the car door. Silence. I strained my hearing to tell me what was going on outside. I waited.

The car wasn't leaving the prison yet. It had only been driven to another area where neither Bob nor Kohout could reach me. It would be impossible for them to set me free.

As the compartment cooled down with the coming of the night, my metal-burned skin chilled, and I began to shake. My teeth chattered and my stomach and chest began to ache from the shivering that racked my entire body. My shivering kept me awake through the night and my mind partially cleared. The prison officials knew. They had to know. I began to cry. I clutched the point, musing over whether to drive it through my brain. My mind yelled, *No! I won't die! I won't let those bastards kill me! I'll live as long as I can. As long as I'm alive, I can fight back. Fuck them.*

I noticed I was lying in a sticky puddle. My thoughts told me it was blood. It was all over my jacket. I licked my sleeve. Chocolate and caramel! The Milky Ways had melted, and I was coated with them.

Being very careful to ration the Mandrax, I bit off another tab. I slid off into unconsciousness. Night evaporated into another searing day. I woke up to yet more pain, heat, and nausea. I was bleeding from my nose and ears. My stomach wanted to heave and I tried to turn my head but it was jammed tight. I puked on myself. I was about to go mad. Biting my sleeve I found another Mandrax.

My mind drifted in a fiery sea of delirious insanity. I heard Smith calling me from very far away, "Hey man, hey man, you've got to stop screaming or you're gonna get us all killed." I heard someone screaming in my mind and realized it was me. My screams told of my pain, helplessness, and futility of being trapped, unable to move. Putting my wrist in my mouth, I bit down to keep the screams from rising out of my throat. I tasted blood and bit harder. More blood to wash away the pain with a different pain, a pain I could control. I kept biting.

I was vomiting at irregular intervals; my stomach was convulsing with the dry heaves. I couldn't organize my thoughts; my mind was scattered. I was hallucinating. *The guards must know I'm inside. They're waiting for me to die.* I tried to clear my mind. *I must die now. Do it! Drive the point through my chin and into my brain!* I wept. I tried to remember all the good things that had happened in my life. I didn't want to die forgotten. I prayed I would be remembered. I had been so lonely. I thought of my parents and begged, *Please, please don't let them know I died like this.*

Weeping and shaking, I pushed the point of the ice pick under my chin. The tip broke the skin. Just then, the car door opened and slammed shut. The engine started. My sanity was slipping further away. I was going beyond the realm of reason. I pushed the point a little harder as the car began to move. "No!" I hissed, gritting my teeth. "No, they won't let me kill myself in peace. They'll drag me from the car and kill me! Well, I won't let them! I'll kill them! I'll kill them!"

The car stopped. I heard someone bang on the car and start to search it. I wanted to scream out to them and let them know I was inside. I would kill the guard if he dragged me out of the compartment. I clawed at the hatch to pull it down tighter. I also feared they would smell my rancid body odor.

The searchers started tearing the car apart: yanking out the seats, lifting the hood and trunk lid, crawling around inside and pounding on sections to find hollow sounds. I was so tightly stuffed inside, the compartment sounded solid. The hubcaps were pulled off, than beaten back on. I clutched the ice pick tightly. Did they know I was inside?

Please, please, please God … I heard another gate open then it was closed behind me. I was out of the prison!

I heard Billie's voice arguing with someone in Mexican—probably a guard giving her a hard time. I couldn't understand what was being said. Instead I choked back a hysterical laugh. I was insane with pain and anticipation. More arguing, and then the car door slammed, and the car started to move once again.

The plan was that I stay quiet till the car was clear of the prison, and then Billie would tell me when it was safe for me to be let out. The car seemed to drive for miles, weaving down bumpy roads. Why didn't Billie speak to me? My thoughts bolted around inside my head for an explanation for Billie's silence. *Oh, no … the guard! It has to be the guard. He is with Billie. The guard is driving me into the desert to be killed.* I was a madman, insane with pain and frustration. "No, not now, not after all this …" My voice got louder and louder but it was drowned by engine noise.

I'd been in here so long and now someone was going to pull me out and kill me? "Noooooooooooooo!" Insane anger gripped me. I expanded and rose up with such bursting force that the hatch screws ripped out of the wood and the hatch was torn loose.

Letting out an anguished scream, I broke from within the compartment. I felt like I was moving in slow motion, but my thoughts were racing. I would twist around and come from behind with my ice pick … stab the guard to death. I'd murder the bastard who was going to murder me. I would die fighting!

Rising part way out, my right hand twisted free, still clutching the ice pick. Shirt and skin tore on exposed screws as I turned to lunge forward at the driver. Swinging my arm around, I pushed up the hatch only to realize my legs would not work. I was numb from the waist down! My circulation had been cut off too long!

I lost momentum and energy and fell back into the compartment. The hatch fell back on me, still covering most of my body. I couldn't see the driver. I started to weep. I was almost there … so close. It was over; I had lost. I waited to die.

The car brakes slammed on and the hatch flipped up slightly and then fell back on me again, hitting me on my head, dazing me even more.

I dimly heard a girl's voice say, in Mexican, "My God! You're here; you're alive!" It was Billie's voice. Looking up, I saw Billie holding up the hatch. A fog hung over my mind. I wasn't sure if this was real or just another hallucination. I knew it was real when Billie tried to pull me out and complained of my awful stench. I managed a faint smile.

Billie was muttering sympathies at my pitiful condition as she dragged me from the compartment to the side of the road. She started sobbing.

We were still in Mexico and still in danger. The Federales could come at any time. I hung onto Billie as she arduously dragged me off the road to a small ravine. Billie wet her bandana in a small muddy stream that flowed next to the ravine and wiped the crud from my face and hands. I was weak and dehydrated. Billie let me sip slowly from a canteen of water while she hugged and cradled me. She began to massage my useless legs to restore the circulation. I stared up at the sky and felt a deep calm. I was finally free.

Billie didn't know I was in the car when she drove from the prison. She was stopped from picking up the car twice. On Thursday, my first day in the compartment, Billie came to get the freshly painted car, but Pluma Blanco had a meeting and was absent from the prison. The guards wouldn't let Billie pick up the car without the director's okay.

Friday, my second day, Bob followed through with our plan and reported me missing. The entire prison was closed off to the outside. Nothing and no one was allowed to enter or leave the prison. Pluma Blanco apparently believed Bob's story. Bob even helped search for me to put further distance between him and my escape. Pluma felt I was hiding somewhere in the prison, for he refused to believe anyone could escape from his maximum-security system.

My groans and screams must have revealed my hiding place to some prison workers. Many prisoners were interrogated, yet no one told. Billie was turned away from the main gate until the search was completed late Friday night. Pluma finally let Billie recover the Volvo, but only after it was thoroughly searched. Billie argued with a guard for postponing her fictitious trip to visit relatives and drove from the prison confused and worried about my fate. She didn't know if I was dead, captured, in solitary, or being tortured.

She drove about ten miles and then turned the car back toward the prison to find out what might have happened to me. It was then that I broke out of my compartment. If I had stayed in the compartment much longer, I would have broken out in front of the prison's main gate.

Billie told me the escape would bring army patrols, and she must leave and finish setting up the last part of my escape. She had to make arrangements for someone else to take me to the border. I still couldn't move my legs so Billie covered me with some sagebrush. While she was gone, I attempted to massage my legs and sadly savored my freedom. I was alive and free.

I looked up at the sky again and started to feel dizzy as my mind whirled with vertigo. The wide expanse of sky and desert confused my senses after being crushed in the dark compartment. Today was the Saturday before Christmas, 1974. I had been in the compartment for two and a half days.

Billie returned a few hours later with Kornie. Billie looked worried. While she helped me un-cramp my legs, I looked up towards the top of the ravine. Kornie's long hair was blowing in the dust-filled wind as she gazed down the road. The sun reflected off the black stock of an AR-15 rifle she cradled in her arms. She was waiting for the Federales, to protect me. I began to cry. A sixteen-year-old girl was willing to risk her life for me.

Eventually, Billie helped me stagger to the car. The sisters helped me into the back seat and handed me the AR-15. The girls got in the front seat and drove with their heads hanging out the car windows so they wouldn't have to smell me. We laughed and I felt better, much better.

For fifteen minutes, we drove along the Mexican frontier. I hadn't seen the outside world in so long. Animals, trees—everything was alive. The air was different. It was fresh, with the exception of my own self. I felt like I was breathing for the first time.

We pulled up to a small house. I asked Billie if this was her home, and she shook her head to affirm it was not. Billie and I walked through the front door as Kornie refueled the car, pouring gas from a plastic container.

Inside the house, sitting at a small table, was a woman in her mid-twenties. She had short brown hair and wore jeans, cowboy boots, and a T-shirt that had a Rolling Stones logo on it. Billie introduced her as Eileen. Eileen stood and put out her hand as to shake mine, until she got a good look at my appearance. She quickly withdrew her hand and stuck it in her back pocket. Billie and Kornie could not take me to the border. It was too dangerous. Eileen was an American, and she would take me to the border, where she could cross over without too much trouble.

Kornie walked in, holding the AR-15 by the end of the barrel and sat it in a corner. "You must hurry, Steve," Billie said, still looking worried. They did not bring me an extra set of clothes to change into. No one had expected me to be in so raunchy a condition. There was no time to clean up.

I moved toward Billie to give her a hug, but she looked horrified and took a step back. "Oh yeah," I said, looking down at my filthy condition.

Billie walked up to me and touched my cheek. "Go safely."

I turned to say good-bye to Kornie and she ran to me and gave me a big hard hug despite my odor and appearance.

Eileen would drive me to the border, where I would attempt to cross on foot. The compartment lid was broken and it would be obvious it was used to smuggle something. She was going to have difficulty on her own, crossing into the United States. I saw no evidence of any other vehicles, so the Volvo seemed to be our only option.

Eileen and I got into the car and waved good-bye to Billie and Kornie, who both stood in the doorway of the house. Eileen glanced over at me. "Please leave your window down." She started the car and we headed north.

Eileen drove the car within a few hundred yards of the Arizona-Mexico border station. She looked over at me and said, "Sorry, Steve, this is it. I've got to let you out now." She promised to meet me on the United States side of the border in an hour.

Trembling, I crawled out of the car. I looked like a manic who wandered down from the hills after being lost for years. I was dressed in rags, my hair was disheveled, and I was covered with blisters, burns, blood, puke, and piss. The only clean part of my body was where Billie had cleaned my face and hands. I had no means to prove I was an American citizen and would have to talk my way past customs.

Walking on wobbly legs towards the border station, I felt like I was floating. I was trying to stay calm and look normal, but I was ready to attack the customs official and run like hell if my bullshit didn't work.

Two uniformed customs officials, one man in his late thirties and a dark-haired girl in her mid-twenties stared at me as I neared their border station. The man looked stunned. "What are you supposed to be?" he asked. I didn't answer. I didn't know what to say; my mind was blank. The customs official asked me again disgustedly. "Are you an American?"

I took a deep breath, felt the weight of the ice pick inside my jacket, and my mind said, *Here goes!*

"Of course I'm an American. Don't you see the American in me?" I said with my best Southern drawl. "My name is Mike ... Mike Cooney. I'm from Washington, North Carolina."

The two officials watched me fidget on wobbly legs. "Are you bringing anything back from Mexico?" the man asked suspiciously.

"Look at me! Look at me!" I practically yelled. "Do I look like I'm bringing anything back? I've been in this damn country only three hours. I've been beaten up, robbed—I have no money, no ID, no anything! I was thrown into a cesspool."

They were staring at me open-mouthed. I looked down at myself and noticed I was still caked in melted chocolate, caramel, and remnants of Milky Way candy bar wrappers. "And then ... and then they rolled me in chocolate!"

The two customs officers continued to stare as if they didn't know what to say next. My story did fit my appearance. The woman customs officer moved her hand to her mouth and giggled.

The man, half to himself, half to her, asked incredulously, "Is that really chocolate?" He looked back at me. "Are you really an American?"

"Yes, I am. I'm from North Carolina, U.S. of A., and I'm visiting Wally Love at the K Bar Ranch in Nogales, Arizona," I insisted. "Do you want to search me?" I said as I lifted my arms in the air.

Both officials looked startled, then disgusted. "Search you? We don't even want to be near you! Now get the hell out of here!" the man said as he waved me through.

As I passed the border station, I heard the woman official exclaim, "Whew, that guy stinks!"

I was in the United States. I moved away from the border station and turned in circles. I didn't know which direction to take. I was *free!* I stared at the border fence.

I floated over toward the fence. *I'm on the U.S. side of the fence,* I thought, relieved. I put my fingers through some of the links and squeezed. "Yes! Yes!" I screamed toward the Mexican side of the border. "What are you gonna do now, *Pinchi Chingadas?*"

Some people stared in my direction. Most ignored the lunatic. I saw cars approaching. In a jolt of panic, I thought, *What if they're Federales? What if this really isn't the United States?* I let go of the fence and turned to run as fast as I could on my weak legs. I quickly became winded and stopped to catch my breath. I hadn't gone fifty yards. I asked a few people who were nearby, "Is this the United States?" They hurried away without answering. In my confused mind I began to think, *What if this is all a big lie? What if this is a trick to drive me crazy?*

I started to imagine that all the things around me were props. A fake border ... a fake fence. I wasn't in the United States after all. This was just another hoax the Mexicans invented to fuck with my mind.

Then I saw a Safeway Supermarket and my mind mad a bizarre association—Safeway ... safe ... I would be home, safe, at Safeway. I ran towards the store but ran out of breath about thirty yards from the store entrance.

Hunched over, breathing heavily, I asked another passerby, "Is this the United States?"

I looked up into a bewildered face. "Yes, this is the U.S.," the person said.

Still puffing, I trotted to the Safeway. I went through the electric doors, hoping that I could hide in the Safeway until Eileen arrived. The Safeway customers looked at me like I was a derelict.

I wandered around the store, gazing at items and trying to stay in isles where there were no people. I was blankly staring at canned soup when someone startled me. I whirled around to face what must have been the store manager.

"Here, take this and get out of my store!" the man said with some revulsion. He was handing me a bottle of Ripple. I took it from him, hung my head, and silently walked out of the store. I squatted down on a nearby curb and tasted a sip of the wine. It was awful! Maybe some things never do change.

The running tired me out and helped slow down the panic in my mind. I wasn't feeling as anxious and decided to wait on the curb for Eileen.

I looked straight down the street to the border station. It was about two hundred yards from me, but I could still spot the Volvo when it drove across. Suddenly, I remembered my parents! I found a phone booth and called them collect. My mother answered. She wouldn't believe it was me. She thought it was another cruel hoax and cried hysterically over the phone. I kept telling her over and over, "I'm in the United States. I'm free! I'm coming home, Mom." She hung up the phone before I could convince her it was actually me.

I went back to sitting on the curb with the cheap wine. Eventually, I saw the black station wagon drive up to the checkpoint. Eileen ran into difficulty at the border crossing. The border officials found my broken compartment and accused her of using it to smuggle drugs. Eileen told them the truth: "It was used only to smuggle Americans out of Mexico." After an intensive search and finding no contraband, they let her go.

Eileen drove up the street until she spotted me sitting on the side of the road. She stuck her head out the window. Shaking her head and laughing, she said, "Hey you, wino, get in the car!"

We drove to Wally Love's ranch in Nogales, Arizona, about ten minutes from the Safeway. Wally's wife let us in the front door while Wally was speaking to my parents on the phone. My Mom called him after she hung up on me. When he saw me he appeared to be in shock. Like my parents, he too thought my earlier phone call was a Mexican hoax. Wally gave the phone to me, and I assured my parents I was safe. They said they would arrange for my flight home.

I told Wally about the escape and then showered and changed into some of the clothes I'd given Wally weeks before in the prison. I also put on Jessie's gray cowboy hat. Too soon, I said good-bye to Wally and his wife. My gratitude was too deep to express in words what this rancher had done for me.

We then drove to Tucson, where Eileen lived. She drove me to the airport where I thanked her for helping save my life.

"Hell, it was kinda fun, except for the part where you stank." She punched me on the arm, and I planted a big kiss on her lips.

Trancelike in my plane seat, I watched the sprinkled lights of Christmas pass beneath the plane. Holding the silver coin in my hand and wearing Jessie's cowboy hat, my thoughts turned to Pati, Frank, Bob, and Daniel. I was a displaced person. I didn't feel like an American anymore; part of me was a Mexican and would always remain so.

On Christmas Eve, 1974, at 12:04 in the morning, exactly eighteen months after being incarcerated in Mexico, I landed at the Philadelphia airport to be met by my family.

I left the plane and went to the terminal concourse. I stood watching my parents, but they didn't recognize me. I heard my sister, Kathy, exclaiming, "Maybe that Mexican over there would know where Steve is," as she pointed to a very lonely man in a gray cowboy hat and a thick black moustache.

The nightmare was finally over.

Chapter Forty-One

Another morning broke over the sage-and-mesquite-splotched Sonora desert. The walls of the Nogales prison cast cold shadows across the lowest courtyard where a group of prisoners were lined up in loose ranks.

Tower guards pointed the muzzles of their rifles down at the half-awake prisoners, who grumbled and rustled with their morning sounds. It was time to call morning lista.

Don Orelio stroked his moustache and began to call out the Mexican and American names in a gruff voice.

"Miquel Averex?"

"Aqui!"

"Carlos Robles?"

"Si!"

There were hundreds of names to be called and answered to.

"Daniel Ruiz?"

"Aqui."

"Charlie Raney?"

"Here!"

"Roberto Smith?"

"Here!"

"Esteban Wilson?"

Pluma Blanco refused to believe anyone could escape from his maximum security prison. He believed I was hidden somewhere within the prison. He knew Esteban Wilson was missing, but escape was impossible. He had the guards search various sections of the prison daily. He would keep the name on the lista for weeks and not report to his superiors there had been an escape.

Silence blanketed the group of prisoners as Don Orelio repeated my name.

"Esteban Wilson??"

Muffled noises rippled through the prisoners as they shifted their feet and whispered to each other.

Don Orelio bellowed at the crowd. The prisoners looked at each other as the name echoed off the prison walls. Smiles and grins broke out on their faces as the prisoners from the upper level clattered cups against bars and mockingly answered the call. "Aqui, Aqui!"

Some of the prisoners in the group began to laugh loudly as a man yelled to Don Orelio that Wilson was in the toilet. The guards shifted uneasily as Don Orelio called the name one last time. There was no answer. Prisoners began to clap, hoot, and cheer. Don Orelio yelled orders for the group to be silent, but they ignored him. The guards awaited his orders. There were none. He turned his back on the prisoners, broke into a big grin, and pulled a candy bar from his shirt pocket. Don Orelio slowly walked away from the cheering prisoners.

Daniel cheered and hopped up and down, until he noticed Bob Smith, standing still, eyes glazed with tears. Bob looked at Daniel, gave him a thin smile, and then broke out laughing and crying.

With clenched fists in the air, Bob cheered triumphantly with the other prisoners.

Esteban Wilson was gone.

Epilogue

My job at the Tideland Mental Health Center was waiting for me when I returned.

I needed to do something for Bob and the other prisoners. I had no political connections, so I did the only thing I could. I told our story to anyone who would listen. There was an article in the New York Times and other newspapers. Playboy finally printed one of the letters I wrote from the prison. Penthouse did a feature on me. I was interviewed on several radio stations. Because of these articles and interviews I was asked to testify before the House Select Committee on Intelligence sub-committee and as a witness for the California Supreme Court.

These events helped to establish the United States/Mexican prisoner exchange. This was a program where Mexicans held in United States prisons were exchanged for Americans held in Mexican prisons. Nearly three years after my escape, many of the Americans, including Bob Smith, were released as a result of this program. Coincidently, Bob was released on my birthday.

I helped Bob with the finances he needed to complete his biology degree at East Carolina University. He became a biologist and conservationist in the Florida Keys and now designs monkey-friendly homes in Costa Rica. He still loves to surf.

The DEA agents, Anderson and Mailer, were ambushed in Mexico. Anderson was shot and wounded. Mailer was killed. Anderson was also called to testify before the House Select Committee on Intelligence. When searched, he was carrying a nickel-plated .357 magnum pistol with notches carved into the side.

Pluma Blanco was stabbed in the back by a prisoner and died from his wound.

Alejandro and Cochon, who played the war games, were reportedly killed in a ley de fuga.

Daniel Ruiz died from an overdose.

Billie, Pati's cousin, became a professional female boxer.

At age thirty-three, I married Cyndy, and we remain together. We met at a Rolling Stones Concert and she was by my side at The Committee hearings and the California Supreme Court. For our honeymoon, I took her to Cartagena, Columbia. We never had children, but lovingly raise shih-tzus.

Every day I wear Don Orelio's silver coin around my neck. Over the years, I have found duplicates of the coin, and I give them to friends to pass on my "magic." I still have Jessie's hat.

I retired as a mental health professional and certified substance abuse counselor after thirty years. During those years I specialized in anxiety disorders and post-traumatic stress. I was also a certified critical incident stress debriefer.

Every December since my escape, I have a celebration. My friends call it the "Escape from Mexico Party." If you ever see someone wearing an "Escape From Mexico" T-shirt, you'll know they have a connection to me. The celebration is a special time I have set aside to remember. In some ways, it is a celebration of the memories of fear and anguish. It is a celebration of all things that can go wrong. Yet, it is also a celebration of hope and life. It is a celebration of freedom. It is a celebration to remember the precious gift of friends and how easily they can pass. Yet, most of all, it is a celebration of the memory of dreams. Without dreams of freedom, of love, of friends, of happiness, there is nothing.

For more information on Lucio I would suggest the National Security Archive's "The Dawn of Mexico's Dirty War, Lucio Cabanas and the Party of the Poor", and the film documentary "The Guerrilla and the Hope: Lucio Cabanas".

For more information on the DEA and the United States drug policies of the time I would suggest "Agency of Fear: Opiates and Political Power in America" by Edward Jay Epstein.

978-0-595-44453-3
0-595-44453-9

Property of
Tom Pohlman
302 King Arthur Rd.
Greenville, NC 27858
252 - 355 - 5314

ECU - Environmental
    Health + Safety Office

802 King Arthur Rd.

EGN - Environmental

Printed in the United States
98618LV00003B/214-216/A